Bonds of Brotherhood
in *Sons of Anarchy*

# Bonds of Brotherhood in *Sons of Anarchy*

## Essays on Masculinity in the FX Series

Edited by Susan Fanetti

McFarland & Company, Inc., Publishers
*Jefferson, North Carolina*

LIBRARY OF CONGRESS CATALOGUING-IN-PUBLICATION DATA

Names: Fanetti, Susan, editor.
Title: Bonds of brotherhood in Sons of Anarchy : essays on masculinity in the FX series / edited by Susan Fanetti.
Description: Jefferson, North Carolina : McFarland & Company, Inc., Publishers, [2018] | Includes bibliographical references and index.
Identifiers: LCCN 2018001696 | ISBN 9781476671918 (softcover : acid free paper) ∞
Subjects: LCSH: Sons of Anarchy (Television program) | Masculinity on television.
Classification: LCC PN1992.77.S63944 B66 2018 | DDC 791.45/72—dc23
LC record available at https://lccn.loc.gov/2018001696

BRITISH LIBRARY CATALOGUING DATA ARE AVAILABLE

**ISBN (print) 978-1-4766-7191-8**
**ISBN (ebook) 978-1-4766-3235-3**

© 2018 Susan Fanetti. All rights reserved

*No part of this book may be reproduced or transmitted in any form or by any means, electronic or mechanical, including photocopying or recording, or by any information storage and retrieval system, without permission in writing from the publisher.*

Front cover images © 2018 CGinspiration/Lisa-Blue/iStock

Printed in the United States of America

*McFarland & Company, Inc., Publishers*
 *Box 611, Jefferson, North Carolina 28640*
 *www.mcfarlandpub.com*

# Table of Contents

*Introduction. The Hypermasculine World of* Sons of Anarchy     1
    SUSAN FANETTI

### Part 1. Institutions of Influence: Hegemony and Identity

"Bros Before Hoes": Violence Against Women in the Name     9
of "Bromosociality"
    SHAWNA MARKS

Leather Is Thicker Than Blood: Institutional and Hegemonic     24
Masculinity
    JAMIESON RYAN

Cynical Tolerance: Gender, Race and Fraternal Fears     39
    CHRISTIAN JIMENEZ

The Sins of the Father(s): Masculine Identity as Poisoned     50
Inheritance
    JAMIE L. BRUMMER

### Part 2. Shapes of Influence: Culture and Narrative

Incapable of His Own Distress: Genderbending Ophelia     65
    JESSICA WALKER

Motorcycle Monasticism: Masculine Religiosity in MC Culture     77
    JOSSALYN G. LARSON

Compilation Score and Trans-Diegetic Music: How Music Helps     93
Give Voice to the Voiceless
    JESSICA SHINE

## Part 3. No Seat at the Table: Outliers in SAMCRO's World

Lover, Killer, Father, Friend: The Complex Case of Nero Padilla    107
    ANDREW HOWE

Nero's Frontier: Western and Latino Masculinity, Fatherhood and Family    119
    MONICA MONTELONGO FLORES

The Performative Crisis of Otto Delaney: Destruction, Dematerialization and Masculine Identity    130
    SUSAN FANETTI

## Part 4. Transgressing Brotherhood: Tig and Venus

Attempting Redemption with Tig and Venus    145
    LAURIE NORRIS

Riding Crisscross: Venus Van Dam and the Politics of Transgender Representation    157
    PETER NAGY

*About the Contributors*    167

*Index*    169

# Introduction
## The Hypermasculine World of Sons of Anarchy

SUSAN FANETTI

*Sons of Anarchy* (*SOA*) debuted on FX on 3 September 2008. Its finale aired six years and seven seasons later, on 9 December 2014. Over the course of its run, it became the highest-rated show in the history of the FX network at that time (Andreeva) and a cultural phenomenon, shining a bright light on a dark world. Known for its over-the-top violence, *SOA* depicts a world defined by its extreme performances of conventional masculinity: the world and culture of outlaw bikers and the motorcycle clubs (MCs) to which they belong.

Though it's been well established that *SOA* is, in its frame, at least, a modern-day homage to *Hamlet*, Kurt Sutter, the show's creator and showrunner, describes MC culture itself as his prevailing fascination in developing the series. He was interested in "the first guy who said, 'Let's put on these vests and have a few beers and call ourselves the Hells Angels or the Nomads,'" and the "*Hamlet* archetype fell on top of it" (qtd. in Bennett 16). Coming from a gig in the writers' room on FX's *The Shield*, a show rife with antiheroes in the world of law and order, Sutter was interested in the other side of that gray world—the outlaw. Getting the material, physical details of MC culture right was critically important to him and preceded even his full concept of the story he meant to tell; it was the "vest" (known in the culture as a "kutte" or "cut"[1]) and the "few beers" he focused on getting right, understanding that such material authenticity would give him "the room to tell bigger stories" (qtd. in Bennett 17).

Sutter describes spending a lot of time with bikers in Northern California (this was primarily the Oakland charter of the Hells Angels [Carpenter]): "I'm really obsessive about all the details of the show in terms of the look:

the bikes, the kuttes, the patches, and that the world is very true and exact" (qtd. in Bennett 17). He did well in these details; while he's faced criticism from the MC community for the broadness of his "bigger stories," there is wide agreement that he got many material details, and important cultural details, right ("10 Things"). The *look* is the sign, the performance, of belonging; the look both represents and bounds the cultural ethos.

The physicality of the details creates the world of outlaw bikers in *SOA* and builds the character of the culture, as well as the personality of the characters themselves. This is more than simply realistic costuming; this is *identity*—not only for the show Sutter created but also for its place in the culture it has fictionalized. Authenticity was so important to Sutter that he not only hired an active member of the Hells Angels (HA)—David Labrava, of the Oakland HA chapter—as a technical advisor, he gave him a recurring role on the series, as *SOA* Nomad (and later Redwood) charter member Happy Lowman. Labrava appears in all seven seasons of the series and is a featured performer of the final season. Throughout the series run, Sutter hired several more active HA members in roles as Sons: Rusty Coones as Rane Quinn, Chuck Zito as Frankie Diamonds, and even Sonny Barger, founding member and first president of the Oakland HA chapter, as Lenny the Pimp (IMDb).

Barger, in his memoir *Hell's Angel: The Life and Times of Sonny Barger and the Hell's Angels Motorcycle Club*, describes his MC as a "very select brotherhood of men who will fight and die for each other, no matter the cause" (67). Membership in that tight, ride-or-die brotherhood is signified on their bodies: the leather and denim, the ink, the way members wear their hair and beards, even in their posture and their stride. This is more than simply affiliation, more even than identity.

Membership in—and unbreakable loyalty to—such a brotherhood is *agency* as well. It's no coincidence that the members of motorcycle clubs tend strongly to hail from disadvantaged, disenfranchised backgrounds (and to be racially and ethnically homogeneous). In *Angry White Men*, Michael Kimmel writes that the "lower middle class has always defined itself by its fierce economic independence and by its sense of community belonging of citizenship in a political community in which their voices would be heard" (22). Membership in an MC offers codified respect carved into a world stingy with respect, and it offers protection against that same world, whose movements would otherwise disregard the well-being of its members.

With a mission of respect and protection, the outlaw biker community is also surprisingly traditional and conformist, fringe though it may be. In its visible uniformity, MC culture is not merely masculinized but is an exemplar of hypermasculinity. The culture enshrines the most rigid heteronormative constructions of gender, not only for its male members but for the women attached to them. Marita Sturken suggests that this strict, and strictly gendered, ethos found greater acceptance in a post–9/11 world, as society itself, especially as reflected in media representation, turned back to more traditional constructions of gender: "After September 11, the images of gender shifted to an emphasis on traditional working-class masculinity and wives holding down the home front" (444). After 9/11, an American culture long insulated from the horrors of terror turned in stunned shock to tradition to find its comfort and safety—to the traditionally coded and comprehensible constructions of gender, where strong men do what they must to protect the weak.

A few short years later, the country and the world, still reeling from 9/11 and still fighting the wars that followed, was thrown into the economic maelstrom of the Great Recession, a crisis brought on by the willful exploitation of the working class by the structures of societal power. In a time of fear and uncertainty, in a world turned end over end by acts of terror and greed, where the weak and struggling could find no quarter, the culture of outlaw bikers, always hypermasculine and devoted to the protection of their own at any cost, suddenly found societal esteem. Enter *Sons of Anarchy*. Viewed through this retrograde lens, the Sons' performance of masculinity creates a sense of safety and comfort for the audience, in the same manner in which the members seek to protect what, and who, they love and value.

The protection and place of women is important in this culture because in a culture in which women can only be "Other," their place and their circumstance demarcate the center. Like any marginalized group, outlaw bikers are defined by boundaries; their performance of gender is a boundary that they control. Mimi Schippers, in "Recovering the Feminine Other: Masculinity, Femininity, and Gender Hegemony," notes that in "the on-going process of recurring patterns of social practice, the quality content of masculinity and femininity becomes not just the gender identities or gender displays of individuals, but also, and perhaps more importantly, a collective iteration in the form of culture, social structure, and social organization" (91). Women are important to the biker community because of what they represent for the members: they are damsels to be protected and trophies to be won. MC women are Woolfian mirrors, reflecting their men's virility and potency back to them, and those women to which they bond represent family, legacy, humanity—a version of the so-called "American Dream" in a culture isolated from culturally accepted performances of that dream.

In *Masculinities*, R.W. Connell points out that "[m]asculine gender is (among other things) a certain feel to the skin, certain muscular shapes and tensions, certain postures and ways of moving, certain possibilities in sex. Bodily experience is often central in memories of our own lives, and thus in our understanding of who and what we are" (52). She is speaking specifically about physical masculinity—the literal physical form and function of the male-sexed body—and suggesting that the experience of dwelling in a body with that form and function shapes one's understanding of self. Acknowledging both the logic of that argument and its limits, I would push the idea beyond actual physiology—the muscles, bones, and tissues that make a male-sexed body so-called "masculine" in the most widely culturally signified sense—and argue that, in a culture like MC culture, where visible, material signs of belonging can be literal matters of life or death, more than self-concept is on the line. In a culture of outliers and outlaws, a visibly unified, uniform presence is a shield against the pressures and dangers of the mainstream.

Connell notes that "[t]rue masculinity is almost always thought to proceed from men's bodies—to be inherent in a male body or to express something about a male body" (45). Nearly everything about MC culture is mediated through the bodies of the male members, and through the masculine expression of those bodies. This is one of the details that Sutter gets right in *SOA*: the leather or denim kuttes, the patches, the chained wallets, the jeans, the boots, the multitude and variety of carefully crafted tattoos, which the actors were able to choose for themselves, with Sutter's approval (Bennett 120)—even the carriage of their bodies—all of these elements serve as symbols reifying the masculine positioning of MC culture.

Another feature of MC culture, real and fictional, is its militarism—not only its violence but the way both the organizational structure of a club and its strategic and tactical operations mimic organized military structure. While clubs are generally democratic, they also maintain a top-down hierarchy that takes from executive structures, with a "president" and "vice president," but also military order, with a "sergeant at arms" (SAA), whose primary job is protecting the president and the club (IHaveANoseOnMFace). Kuttes and patches, jeans and boots—those are, in a very specific sense, members' uniforms. Their tattoos, even their beards and long hair, are coded in MC culture just as "high and tight" haircuts, medals, and platoon tattoos are coded in military culture.

This nod toward and respect for authority, even among rebels and nonconformists, is another marker of conventional masculinity. While they resist the government, "The Man," as it were (a not-coincidentally gendered concept)—in fact, rejection of the establishment is the foundational ideal of outlaw culture—they embrace a structural authority that is coded as masculine in its exertion and assertion of power and privilege and represents a purity of the patriarchal ideal. "All manhood acts," Douglas Schrock and Michael Schwalbe suggest, "imply a claim to membership in the privileged gender group" (284). Even more than power and privilege is the militaristic directive to *protect* that informs outlaw MC culture: to protect their family, their club, their ideals, themselves from the pressures of a society that does not comprehend them.

Schrock and Schwalbe note that elements of conventional masculinity such as "strength, courage, fierceness, and willingness to sacrifice" are valued by a patriarchal society that believes that such traits "suit males to being warriors, leaders, and benevolent fathers" (286)—that is, *protectors*. Members of biker culture distill their performative concept of masculinity to that ideal: protection. It is, at its core, a decidedly conventional and physical expression of masculinity. The violent world that they create and in which they exist gives them ample opportunity to draw their boundaries at the margins of society and define themselves as men willing to fight and die for the things they love.

Considering all these features of the real culture its fiction describes, there's little question that *Sons of Anarchy* is a hypermasculine text. The series Kurt Sutter created, with inspirations ranging from Shakespeare to the Hells Angels, virtually reeks of testosterone. *SOA* showcases—and celebrates—conventional, and often toxic, performances of masculinity, but it also complicates those performances and interrogates the efficacy of this hypermasculine culture for its own goals, especially its ability to protect.

Despite its popularity and cultural impact, *Sons of Anarchy* has yet to garner significant scholarly attention. This collection seeks to open the door of inquiry and take on one of the most compelling questions the show invites: what do we make of *SOA*'s expressions of gender and masculinity? The scholars here explore many of the influences on, inspirations for, performances of, and challenges to conventional masculinity in *Sons of Anarchy*.

These essays are organized into four parts, grouping scholarly lenses on the definition and performance of gender and masculinity in *Sons of Anarchy*. The essays that make up first two parts take various approaches to the question of influence—societal, institutional, and cultural—on the narrative and the world of *SOA*. The essays of the last two parts take more direct looks at the way particular characters exemplify and challenge traditional constructions of gender and masculinity.

In Part 1, "Institutions of Influence: Hegemony and Identity," four essays examine societal and institutional pressures on the performance of masculinity in *SOA*. Shawna Marks, in "'Bros Before Hoes': Violence Against Women in the Name of 'Bromosociality,'" interrogates the limits of gendered notions of protection in *SOA* and in MC culture, suggesting that the strong male-male bond of patched members creates a toxic and dangerous environment for the women in the culture. In "Leather Is Thicker Than Blood: Institutional and Hegemonic Masculinity," Jamieson Ryan also considers the strength of the club bond, especially the material trappings of that bond, and its pressures on traditional family bonds and hegemonic status. Christian Jimenez turns the lens on race as well as gender in "Cynical Tolerance: Gender, Race and Fraternal Fears." The final essay in Part 1, Jamie L. Brummer's "The Sins of the Father(s): Masculine Identity as Poisoned Inheritance," examines the significant and various fatherly influences in *Sons of Anarchy*.

The essays that make up Part 2, "Shapes of Influence: Culture and Narrative," consider different cultural influences on *SOA* as a story, and the way those influences shape the show's expressions and performances of gender and masculinity. Jessica Walker, in "Incapable of His Own Distress: Genderbending Ophelia," takes up Sutter's use of *Hamlet* as a narrative scaffold and considers the character of Opie Winston's (played by Ryan Hurst) positioning in the role of Ophelia. In "Motorcycle Monasticism: Masculine Religiosity in MC Culture," Jossalyn G. Larson explores the expression of religion—traditional and otherwise—in *SOA* and its implications for the performance of masculinity in the show. And Jessica Shine uses the lens of gender to analyze the strong influence of music on the narrative of *SOA* in "Compilation Score and Trans-Diegetic Music: How Music Helps Give Voice to the Voiceless."

Part 3, "No Seat at the Table: Outliers in SAMCRO's World," focuses on two characters whose presence is crucial to the main arc of the *SOA* story but who do not sit at the carved table in the Sons' chapel. Andrew Howe, in "Lover, Killer, Father, Friend: The Complex Case of Nero Padilla," and Monica Montelongo Flores, in "Nero's Frontier: Western and Latino Masculinity, Fatherhood and Family," dig deep into the character of Nero Padilla (Jimmy Smits), who is not a Son, and the way he shapes the club and the narrative from his seeming outsider position. On the other hand, Otto Delaney (played by Kurt Sutter himself) is a Son, doing hard time in prison, and his increasing distance from the club is as significant as Nero's presence near it. My own essay, "The Performative Crisis of Otto Delaney: Destruction, Dematerialization and Masculine Identity," explores Otto's narrative arc.

The final part focuses on what may well be the most interesting depiction of non-club bond in the series. Part 4, "Transgressing Brotherhood: Tig and Venus," consists of two essays that explore Venus Van Dam, a transgender character (portrayed by cisgendered male actor Walton Goggins), and her relationship with Tig Trager (Kim Coates), a longstanding member of the Sons of Anarchy, as well as the patch coded in the narrative as most "deviant." Laurie Norris, in "Attempting Redemption with Tig and Venus," and Peter Nagy, in "Riding Crisscross: Venus Van Dam and the Politics of Transgender Representation," take differing approaches to examine and problematize Venus and Tig's relationship and Venus's position as a one of the show's most prominent "damsels in distress."

Masculinity in *Sons of Anarchy*, as in MC culture itself, is synonymous with loyalty. Coded in leather and ink, expressed in steel and on flesh, the brotherhood wholly describes its members and their relationships in and to the world. Their bonds are tight and defining, and when they break, meaning and purpose is upheaved. That is, at its core, the story of *Sons of*

Anarchy. The essays herein explore the dimensions and limits of the Sons' brotherhood.

## Note

1. Either spelling of the term is correct. "Cut" seems to be more prevalent in the U.S., but Sutter uses "kutte" (Bennett). Both spellings appear in this collection, at the contributors' discretion.

## Works Cited

Andreeva, Nellie. "'Sons of Anarchy' Season 5 Premiere Hits Series High, to Become FX's No. 1 Telecast." *Deadline*, http://deadline.com/2012/09/sons-of-anarchy-season-5-premiere-hits-series-high-to-become-fxs-no-1-telecast-334734/. Accessed 25 July 2017.
Barger, Sonny, with Keith and Kent Zimmerman. *Hell's Angel: The Life and Times of Sonny Barger and the Hell's Angels Motorcycle Club*. Harper, 2001.
Bennett, Tara. *Sons of Anarchy: The Official Collector's Edition*. Time, 2014.
Carpenter, Susan. "Biker's 'Sons of Anarchy' Appearance Isn't an Act." *The Orange County Register*, http://www.ocregister.com/2012/12/07/bikers-sons-of-anarchy-appearance-isnt-an-act/. Accessed 30 April 2017.
Connell, R.W. *Masculinities*. 2nd ed. University of California Press, 2005.
IHaveANoseOnMyFace. "I am a member of one of the motorcycle clubs known as illegal in many countries, or '1% clubs.' AMAA." *Reddit*, https://www.reddit.com/r/IAmA/comments/1bunfc/i_am_a_member_of_one_of_the_motorcycle_clubs/. Accessed 8 May 2017.
Kimmel, Michael. *Angry White Men: American Masculinity at the End of an Era*. Nation, 2013.
Schippers, Mimi. "Recovering the Feminine Other: Masculinity, Femininity, and Gender Hegemony." *Theory and Society*, vol. 36, no. 1, 2007, pp. 85–102.
Schrock, Douglas, and Michael Schwalbe. "Men, Masculinity, and Manhood Acts." *Annual Review of Sociology*, vol. 35, 2009, pp. 277–95.
*Sons of Anarchy*. IMDb, http://www.imdb.com/title/tt1124373/?ref_=ttfc_fc_tt. Accessed 30 April 2017.
Sturken, Marita. "Masculinity, Courage, and Sacrifice." *Signs*, vol. 28, no. 1, 2002, pp. 444–45.
"10 Things Sons of Anarchy Gets Right About Bikers." *WhatCulture*, http://whatculture.com/tv/10-things-sons-anarchy-gets-right-bikers. Accessed 4 May 2017.

PART 1. INSTITUTIONS OF INFLUENCE:
HEGEMONY AND IDENTITY

# "Bros Before Hoes"
## Violence Against Women in the Name of "Bromosociality"

SHAWNA MARKS

This essay uses the idea of "bromosociality" as a lens to examine homosociality, hegemonic masculinity, and subsequent violence against women in the television show *Sons of Anarchy*. Sons of Anarchy Motorcycle Club, Redwood Original (SAMCRO), the motorcycle club that the show is centered around, is positioned as the most important aspect of its members' lives and is often referred to as a family or "brotherhood." This brotherly love is consistent with an increase in films and television shows that feature and celebrate "bromance" (Brook 253). However, in *Sons of Anarchy*, this "bromance" is more sinister in nature as these brotherly bonds can excuse and encourage violence against women. This is achieved through a heightened homosociality and its key principles. According to Sharon Bird (121), these key areas are emotional detachment, competitiveness, and the sexual objectification of women. This essay will explain the violent acts committed against women associated with SAMCRO and their rivals through Sharon Bird's interpretation of homosociality. Furthermore, consistent with her findings, I will argue that this violence occurs as an act of maintaining hegemonic masculinity and relate this explanation to similar instances of gendered violence in male-dominated institutions, sport and military (Flood 351). As disturbing as the acts of violence committed against women in *Sons of Anarchy* are, they are rooted in group norms that many men are expected to adhere to. The same concepts that can be applied to this television show, namely homosociality and hegemonic masculinity, can be used to explain real-life examples of violence committed by men who are members of similarly tight-knit male groups.

While violence against women in television and film is a common plot device, the prevalence of this phenomenon in this particular series can be understood in the context of male friendship bonds. I argue that the heightened bonds in the Sons of Anarchy motorcycle club are likened to a brotherhood and thus can male homosocial settings be referred to as "bromosociality." Bromosociality is similar to homosociality in that it applies to non-sexual same-sex relations, contributes to the maintenance of hegemonic masculinity, and is characterized by group norms in male friendship groups such as emotional detachment, competitiveness, and sexual objectification. However, it differs in its applicability and is useful only to examine male friendship groups that are likened to brotherhoods and thus positioned as more important than all other relationships, including family. This positioning is powerful and means that characteristics of hegemonic masculinity and homosociality become even harder to subvert and can have dire consequences for individual men.

I argue that these powerful unquestionable bonds are utilized in conjunction with hegemonic masculinity and encourage men to view themselves as distinct and superior to women and non-hegemonic men. This distinction occurs as part of the tenets of homosociality. This means that men in bromosocial groups are encouraged not to develop emotional connections with women, to view them as conquests, and participate in sexually objectifying them. This perpetuates the dehumanizing of women, which in turn allows men to rationalize the oppression of women and subsequently rationalize and justify violence against women.

Of course, regular men will have different lived experiences and therefore different interpretations and applications of homosociality to the men in *Sons of Anarchy*. The events discussed take place within the context of a television show and so are of course subject to dramatization. However I would argue that homosociality is further intensified in *Sons of Anarchy* as the bonds between SAMCRO club members are characterized as familial, rather than simply as friendship. In fact, John Teller's, Jax's deceased father and founding member of SAMCRO, initial vision for the club was as a brotherhood, a vision that Jax Teller intends to continue. This dynamic is further evident in the constant tension between the club as family and actual families, such as partners and children. The men involved often reconcile these conflicts in a wave of grand speeches about brotherhood and family in relation to the club, such as Clay's assertion that Jax's strength has the potential to inspire his "SAMCRO brothers" ("Albification," season two, episode one). Jax and Opie can be understood as having the strongest brotherly connection, and this bond frequently causes them to make decisions that have dire consequences and place the needs of the club above the wishes of their family members.

Bird (121) says that there are three key principles present in male heterosexual homosocial interactions that constitute a hegemonic masculinity script. These key principles ultimately reproduce and maintain the dominance of hegemonic masculinity and thus perpetuate the subordination of women and nonhegemonic masculinities. The three key areas Bird (121) specifies are emotional detachment, competitiveness, and the sexual objectification of women. These principles will be discussed in depth, drawing on examples from *Sons of Anarchy*, and explaining how the combination of each area and homosociality overall is used to justify violence against women.

Emotional detachment in the context of homosociality serves the function of discouraging intimacy and maintaining strict boundaries. This process characterizes emotional responses as individual weaknesses, evidence of vulnerability, and signal a lack of control. The participants in Bird's (125) study viewed emotional detachment as normal and natural and described it as imperative in male homosocial groups. The men in this study were reluctant to name "feelings," instead referring to them as "those things," "personal stuff," "those matters" and said that they preferred not to get into "that real intimate stuff" (Bird 125). It was expressed that male friends would become uncomfortable when attempts were made to talk about emotional issues. Men are discouraged from seeking emotional support from each other and would experience a lack of emotional connectedness as a result. These men believed that they were naturally more independent and less emotionally attached than women, while still recognizing social norms that characterize displays of emotion in male homosocial settings as inappropriate. However, the norms associated with homosociality are cited as imperative in building bonds, particularly in male-dominated settings like the military and team sports (Curry 120; Flood 341; Messner 51). This lack of emotional connectedness seems likely to be detrimental to forming lasting bonds, but the reverse is true in homosocial settings when combined with sexual objectification and competitiveness.

Homosociality functions to create meaningful bonds, then, not through emotional connectedness but by prioritizing non-sexual relationships with men over other relationships with the opposite sex. This extends to non-sexual relationships with women, as evidenced in Bird's (127) study, where the impact of emotional detachment on his relationship with his mother was recognized by a participant. Romantic relationships with women are also likely to be affected, a factor that was specifically explored by Michael Flood (344) in his work with Australian men attending a military education facility. Flood (349) found that men used sex with women to form bonds with each other and that this process ensures that homosocial relationships became prioritized over heterosocial relationships. The sexual objectification of women is then more impactful in creating and maintaining male friendship bonds than emotional connectedness.

Emotional detachment is particularly evident in *Sons of Anarchy* when analyzing emotional responses to tragedies. The men in this show only display emotion in the most extreme circumstances, often following the death of a loved one. However even in situations like these, displays of sadness are minimal and anger quickly becomes the primary emotion. Anger is characterized as the only appropriate response to traumas and perceived injustices, meaning that violence is the primary response to emotional trauma. There are many examples of this throughout the show including murderous retaliations for the deaths of key members of SAMCRO. However, violent responses do not alleviate the emotional pain characters feel, a factor which is likely to contribute to instances of attempted and completed suicide depicted in the show.

Suicide is depicted twice in the course of *Sons of Anarchy*, and in both cases is represented as the "only way out" for each respective character. For one character attempted suicide occurs because he feels that there is no alternative solution after he finds out, while being blackmailed by law enforcement, that his father was African American. As the club's bylaws prevent the membership of black men, he feels guilty for working with law enforcement and afraid that if he reveals his true heritage to the members of the club they will either exile or kill him, and thus attempts suicide. Although he is discovered after attempting suicide and confesses his reasoning for this to another SAMCRO member, the internal and emotional conflict that he feels is never addressed, despite this character clearly describing symptoms of mental illness. "I don't want to die. I just.... I don't like being alone. I'm not good on my own ... my head gets so loud and nothing syncs up. I start thinking about my thinking and getting lost in the details of nothing" ("Poor Little Lambs," season seven, episode four).

His emotional response is characterized as inappropriate in following episodes, as future episodes focus on his emotional conflicts in the context of loyalty to the club. This could have occurred because attempted suicide is considered feminized and "is viewed as reactive, manipulative and attention-seeking" (Jaworski 48). The character is depicted as more emotionally vulnerable and weak following his suicide, and his narrative becomes that of an antagonistic character whose disloyalty is a prime conflict throughout the show. This is consistent with Bird's (126) finding that emotional detachment serves the function of discouraging intimacy, thus maintaining strict emotional boundaries.

A second character completes suicide in the finale of the show in response to the murder of his wife. He initially responds to her death by embarking on a murderous rampage aimed at the rival club believed to have committed the initial murder. However, upon learning the identity of the true killer, someone close to him, he becomes so overwhelmed with sadness that he commits further multiple murders and eventually completes suicide.

This character is depicted as being so irreparably emotionally traumatized that suicide is the only appropriate response to his grief. This is despite the character never attempting to seek any professional or informal emotional support. It is never seen to be appropriate for him to seek any support and is never questioned, which is consistent with Bird's (121) finding that emotional detachment is assumed to be natural. The only response he takes is to respond to his trauma by committing violent acts, the usual method for solving grievances in *Sons of Anarchy*. However, when violence does not alleviate his grief, he is perceived to be left with no other option but to end his life, rather than seek emotional support from his peers.

Sharon Bird (126) argues that emotional responses are considered inappropriate and can lead to exclusion from homosocial groups. Men tend to distance themselves from other men who express emotional intimacy, regarding these responses as characteristic of individual weaknesses, vulnerability, and a lack of control (Bird 125). Additionally, completed suicide is considered an act of courage, pride, or resistance and thus is considered an active and willful response that asserts independence in times of crisis (Jaworski 48).

Competitiveness functions on an interpersonal level within homosocial groups but specifically concerns men's individual identities being in direct competition with the identities of other men (Bird 127). This then facilitates hierarchy and discourages cooperation with one another by encouraging men to view distinctions between each other, resulting in a constant assessment of one another's masculinity (Bird 130). Homosocial interactions also provide feedback that is useful for men to shape their performance of masculinity to suit the situation (Bird 128). Competition is used to establish and enforce ground rules about appropriate forms of masculinity and contributes to perpetuating male dominance, particularly through displays of hegemonic masculinity (Bird 127). These displays are constructed in opposition to femininity in order for masculinity to be positioned as superior to femininity and for displays of masculinity to be validated and gain symbolic significance (Bird 125). Competitiveness in homosocial interactions is so pervasive that men believe they are naturally competitive. A participant in Sharon Bird's research remarked that "guys don't know what it means not to be competitive," reiterating that competitiveness is viewed as an essential and natural part of homosocial interactions that men take for granted (128).

In *Sons of Anarchy*, men compete with each other within SAMCRO and with other rival outlaw groups using violence as a means of retaliation against others in order to confirm a dominant position. Violence is presented as a solution to emotional trauma throughout the show, but also to perceived wrongs committed by rival motorcycle clubs and other outlaw groups. Internal conflicts within SAMCRO, in particular issues between the club President and Vice President, are also often responded to through the use of violence.

There are countless examples of violent retaliations littered throughout *Sons of Anarchy*, particularly in response to club members who are hurt or killed by members of rival outlaw groups. Evidence of this can be found when analyzing retaliations to the deaths of each prominent club member, including Opie's death in prison and the abduction, torture and murder of Bobby. In both cases, Jax, the club Vice President, and the rest of SAMCRO decide to commit atrocities against the rivals they believe are responsible for the deaths of their friends. However, the most violent and horrific acts of retaliation are perpetuated against women who are personally attached to a SAMCRO or rival club member.

Much of the violence perpetrated against women in *Sons of Anarchy* occurs under the guise of protecting the "honor" of women associated with members of the club. This happens without the affected women driving retaliation efforts and in some cases occurs even when these women actively try to prevent any retaliation from taking place. It is logical to conclude, then, that the act of retaliation in response to violence against women does not occur for the affected women but rather to protect the reputation of the club.

There are many examples of this, including retaliation against L.O.A.N. for the gang rape of Gemma, the wife of club President Clay and mother of Vice President Jax, despite her efforts to cover up her assault in order to prevent the club retaliating even when L.O.A.N. continue to intimidate her following the rape. Similarly, the retaliation against rival Damon Pope for the brutal murder of club member Tig's daughter, Dawn, occurs as a response to the emotional pain Tig feels and the loss he has suffered. This retaliation continues despite the fact that Pope has retaliated against Tig for murdering his daughter, Veronica Pope. The retaliation against Pope is also used to frame Club President Clay for murder in an internal power play. It is fair to conclude that any retaliation against rival groups for the harm they have inflicted on women associated with SAMCRO is done, at least in part, to assert the dominance of SAMCRO in relation to competing groups and to rectify any damage to their reputation.

The use of violence against women to compete with rival clubs and outlaw groups is particularly evident in these case studies. Gemma and Dawn were both targeted in these scenarios because of their connection to club members. Gemma is the victim of sustained violence committed by rivals and club members throughout the show, with this being routinely trotted out as a plot device. Violence against these women can be considered a personal attack on the club and would be more impactful, thus better communicating the rivals' dominance and power through violent acts.

Women are also caught up in internal conflicts in SAMCRO and are used as objects in power struggles over leadership and to communicate dominance in a hierarchy. Sex with women is used as a means for competition in order to establish dominance over other women, particularly with the women who work in brothels owned by the club, or those who feature as groupies, referred to in the show as "sweet butts" or as "crow eaters," in reference to the crow that forms the club logo. The most notable example of this when Clay has sex with a rookie club member's love interest, Cherry, in order to assert his authority. However, violence against the women in *Sons of Anarchy* is even more poignant in its blatant display of competitiveness. This is never more apparent than in the constant rivalry between Jax and Clay over their differing visions for the club. This rivalry results in increasingly damaging retaliations, with Jax framing Clay for murder and Clay orchestrating the unsuccessful murder of Jax's wife after learning that she has information that could damage his claim to leadership. This rivalry epitomizes the competitive aspect of homosociality, particularly as the competition between Jax and Clay affects the remainder of the club and is effective in establishing the dominance of one leader over another.

The sexual objectification of women has several key components that ultimately excuse and encourage violence against women (Bird 128). These are the construction of women as conquests, as objects for sexual pleasure, and as distinctly different from men. These factors are essential in the maintenance of hegemonic masculinity and are consistent with Sharon Bird's (130) findings in her work on homosociality. Sexual objectification is perhaps the most important factor in homosocial relations between men and perpetuates emotional detachment and competition in its practice.

The sexual objectification of women allows men to construct masculinity as "not only different from female but as better than female," encouraging them to distance themselves from femininity and therefore from anything considered female (Bird 121). This sets clearly defined boundaries between femininity and masculinity and facilitates the constant surveillance of men in regards to their masculine performance. Men survey themselves and others, resulting in constant competition with each other. This often involves competing for the attention of women, particularly in regards to sex. Competition over women and the distinct separation of women from men also facilitates the objectification of women which in turn dehumanizes women. This allows men "to depersonalise the oppression of women," a likely factor in the constant violence against women in *Sons of Anarchy* (Bird 123).

Women and men have clearly defined roles in *Sons of Anarchy*, which is essential for maintaining distinctions between genders and for excusing violence against women. The men in SAMCRO do not express emotional vulnerability, are fiercely independent, solve problems with violence, are sexual aggressors, and demonstrate fearlessness. The masculinity expressed by men who deviate slightly from this stand out in stark comparison. In particular, Juice and Tig are often seen as sources of amusement or derision for the other men because they deviate from the traditional masculine traits listed above. Juice is emotionally vulnerable and is considered unstable and untrustworthy as a result. After an emotional breakdown, he is depicted as a burden on the other emotionally independent characters and is gradually excluded from the group.

Similarly, Tig is represented as someone who relies on emotion for decision making, which results in poor choices on several occasions, such as when he is so guilt ridden that he confesses to botching the assassination of another SAMCRO member which resulted in the accidental murder of that member's wife. While Tig is well-loved despite his emotional vulnerability, he is also depicted as particularly aggressive, seemingly to garner more credibility in his masculine identity. Tig is responsible for the security of the club as Sergeant at Arms and therefore commits more violence than other members. Overall, though, Tig is seen as the most deviant member of the group and is often the butt of jokes as a result. His eccentric sexual preferences include necrophilia and incest. These sexual practices are considered deviant by the club and are used for comedic value at different points in the show. Overall, there are very strict limitations on masculine identity available to the men in SAMCRO and deviance from these bounds is actively discouraged and used to exclude men who don't live up to the expected norms.

Women in the show have similarly limited gender roles, although they share some qualities with male characters, and are ultimately represented as distinct from men and do not occupy positions of power in the show. Gemma, Tara, and Wendy particularly are simultaneously emotionally vulnerable and tough and are all courageous and fiercely independent. However, their identities are marked by their position as mothers and lovers, and these identities are central to their function in the show. Although Gemma is highly involved in much of the dealings in the club she is considered valuable for the emotional work she does. She mediates relationships and offers emotional support to club members, taking on a mothering role for all SAMCRO members. She is very protective and can be vicious toward the groupie characters. However, she is represented as a prime antagonist and extremely manipulative, particularly toward Jax. She is shown not to wield any actual power and is stopped when she tries to intervene in club matters, most notably when her husband orders a hit on another member's wife. This intervention results in violence against her, likely as a means of communicating her lack of power. It is clear that the main female characters in this show are seen to exist in a narrow realm, the home and bedroom, and not given much room to exist outside of this, whereas the men in SAMCRO have limited options for their expression of masculinity but have more diverse roles and functions open to them.

The objectification of women often occurs in the context of referring to women as objects to be used for sexual pleasure or as conquests. Women in

*Sons of Anarchy* are often depicted as sexual objects and are sometimes dehumanized to the point that nameless women are gifted to one another for sex. This occurs when Devil's Tribe gifts Bobby an expensive sex worker without charge and again when Clay rewards Tig with three women for sex after he completes a difficult mission that caused him to miss a party. Sexual exploits are often shared in these group situations, particularly as a way to "one up" each other. This is evident in *Sons of Anarchy* when members "steal" women from lower ranking peers, such as Clay engaging in sex with a rookie member's girlfriend in a display of power. These situations represent women as property or objects to be stolen and view sex with women as a method for communicating authority while simultaneously entering into competition with each other.

Participants in Bird's study also said that women who enter an interaction where competitive sex talk is occurring become an "issue of conquest" and a hierarchy forms amongst the men as efforts to "conquer" the women take place (129). The mutual degradation and sexual objectification of women are the practice that men's bonds are built upon and is particularly present in *Sons of Anarchy*. This observation is supported by Michael Flood's (345) work on homosociality in the military, which found that men used sex with women as a bonding exercise and would engage in sexually objectifying competitive sex talk as a way to relate to other men. This practice is used to form hierarchies and is part of an ongoing assessment of one another that men in groups carry out (Bird 130). This assessment may happen for instance when a man in the group makes a degrading comment about a woman and the other men assess each other in order to see if they should follow his lead. The club President, Clay, often objectifies women, which would encourage the other SAMCRO men to follow his lead, according to Bird's (129) interpretation of homosociality.

The women in *Sons of Anarchy* are routinely sexually objectified, degraded, and depicted as objects for the sexual pleasure of men. Most women in the show are featured because they work in the brothel, Diosa, or porn studio, Cara Cara, that SAMCRO owns, or because they are groupies that hang around the clubhouse. This is not to say that sex workers are inherently objectified but rather that the way that women are represented in *Sons of Anarchy* is objectifying. This is true because all female characters in the show exist only because of their relationship to a male character. Minor female characters, with the exception of a few instances, are seen as sex objects or objects of competition between other women, and often as both, while main female characters are depicted similarly, present because of their romantic relationship with a primary male character and represented as being in conflict with each other usually for the affections of a man. The enduring conflict between Wendy and Tara is a particularly poignant example of this.

Wendy and Tara are depicted as being in constant competition for Jax's affections and likely contribute to his perceived alpha male status in SAMCRO. Jax is depicted having sex with women more often than any other character, including supposed sexual deviant Tig. Jax has numerous affairs with the women who work at Cara Cara and Diosa, as well as routinely using his ex-wife Wendy for sex when his relationship with Tara is enduring conflict. However, despite Jax's persistent infidelity, his actions are embodied in the conflict between Tara and Wendy and to a lesser extent between Tara and Ima (a sex worker at Cara Cara). Ima Tite is represented as a femme fatale of sorts, invoking the common Madonna/Whore dichotomy. She is characterized as promiscuous, selfish and appears to meddle in other's relationships by having sex with attached men. However, these men escape vilification, and Ima is often the victim of violence due to her affairs with SAMCRO men.

Similarly, the conflict between Tara and Wendy employs a dichotomy and pits the women against each other. Rather than both women being in conflict with Jax, they turn on each other and a dichotomy between the two women is present, which later develops into a conflict centered on motherhood. Wendy is persistently represented as reckless and selfish, while Tara is stable and pure. It seems that the conflict between the two characters exists to represent Jax's internal conflict over remaining a member of SAMCRO. Jax often muses about the effect of SAMCRO on the quality of his life and considers leaving the club for a normal life. Tara represents that possible future and happiness as she holds a reliable job as a doctor and is content in a mothering role. Wendy, however, is unstable, uncertain, and depicted as selfish through drug addiction and an overdose during her pregnancy with Jax's child. The conflict between Tara and Wendy then seemingly exists to implicitly represent Jax's internal monologue and thus further his character development, rather than those of the women.

Violence against women is a trope used to further the narratives of the men in the show in increasingly graphic and gratuitous ways. While violence is constantly enacted against male characters, it seemingly drives their character development further and is the catalyst for many important moments in the series. This is evidence of the routine degradation and dehumanization of women present throughout the series, and a key consequence of the sexual objectification, and tenets of homosociality, in *Sons of Anarchy* (Bird 121). This phenomenon is heightened as homosociality becomes "bromosociality" and subsequently strengthens. I argue that emotional detachment, competitiveness, the sexual objectification of women, and the heightened brotherly bonds between SAMCRO members contribute to the justification of using violence against women and the continual perpetuation of this behavior.

*Sons of Anarchy* uses violence against women as a plot device in a variety of ways but most often as a catalyst for enacting revenge on others. There are countless examples of violence against women including instances where this violence causes their deaths. This violence is not limited to any specific "type" of women, as club members' wives, lovers, and daughters, police officers, and sex workers alike are subject to extreme violence. The violence depicted is often graphic and gratuitous and does not further the narrative of these women. These moments are often critical to the narrative of the show and character development, constituting much of the conflict represented. For instance, the murders of two separate club members' wives in the first season become vital to the essence of those male characters, constitute much of these characters' internal and external conflict, and are key to understanding their actions later in the series. Similarly, the murder of a local policeman's wife becomes the catalyst for his affiliation with the club after previously refusing to work with them. This trope is also utilized in the murder of the daughter of a rival, which leads to the subsequent murder of a club member's daughter. This latter death is exceptionally graphic, as the daughter is burned alive in front of the club member, which is a factor in the extreme response that follows. These murders become the catalyst for the primary conflict of that season which claim the lives of key characters but eventually maintain the dominance of SAMCRO through extinguishing the rival.

There are many other examples of violence, particularly sexual violence, against women connected to the club that do not lead to their deaths, but occur to further narrative conflict. There are two substantial examples of this, both of which involve the Club President's wife. Early in the series, she is instrumental in finding a man who raped a young girl and holding him to account, which occurs as a favor to a local businessman who is connected to the club and means that he then owes them. A full season later the Club President's wife is gang-raped by rival club members. She is reluctant to tell anyone in the club about this because she knows that it will lead to conflict, but eventually does so because the rapists continue to intimidate her afterward. Fearing a further attack, she discloses the details of the rape to the club, which leads to major conflict that ultimately convinces her son, the Vice President, to remain at the club despite his desire to leave and live a "normal" life. This event is then crucial to the stability of the club and the development of key character narratives.

The death of a female federal agent also occurs to further character development and narrative conflict, and she is often subject to violence and explicit threats. This agent is implicated as a prime antagonist whose conniving ways led to the death of a club member's wife and are overall damaging to the club. She is the subject of much derision and endures more sexually explicit violence than male antagonists, as can be illustrated in the threat issued to her: "I promise you, I'm gonna shove a gun barrel up that bony ass of yours and I'm gonna blow your black heart out" ("SO," season three, episode one).

Her death is also explicit, she is shot at close range with a semi-automatic weapon, and is shown in its entirety. Her death is designed to be satisfying to audiences in that it mirrors the death of the club member's wife that she is considered to have caused and is carried out by the affected club member. The writers make these intentions clear in that the character informs the agent that he wants her to feel what his wife felt when she died. The details of this death allow us a rare glimpse into the agony that he has been feeling, as he is a particularly stoic character who rarely expresses any emotion besides anger. This is consistent with findings illustrated above that emotional detachment is considered necessary in homosocial groups, with anger being the only acceptable form of emotional expression.

The violence depicted against women usually occurs to serve a purpose in furthering the narrative in *Sons of Anarchy* but occasionally seems gratuitous and is particularly harmful as it relies on stereotypes about marginalized groups of women. These include the disposal of the body of a minor character, Amelia Dominquez, following her accidental death, and the sustained violence against adult film star, Ima Tite. Amelia dies after accidentally stabbing herself, and a professional "'cleaner" is then hired to dispose of her body. This disposal is shown in its entirety and consists of the male "cleaner" measuring her body parts, stroking her hair, and groping her breasts while other characters watch before eventually disposing of her body in a slop sink. The sexual humiliation of her dead body is made more disturbing as she has been previously sexualized, depicted engaging in sex acts with a SAMCRO member, which is significant as the character is Latina and described as an illegal immigrant. Her depiction can be considered both racist and sexist and consistent with the common overt sexualization of Latina women in popular media such as contemporary examples Jennifer Lopez, Sofia Vergara, and Eva Longoria, and the persistent idea that immigrant women's lives are worth less than native-born women (Chang 12; Guzmán and Valdivia 206; Merskin 134).

Ima Tite is also subject to violence without narrative gain, and this violence is significant due to the levels of violence real-life sex workers face (Lutnick and Cohan 41). Ima is represented as an antagonist who causes conflict in club members' personal relationships by having sex with romantically attached club members. In each of these cases, she is the source of derision and violence, rather than the men involved. She is subjected to violent threats from women and men associated with the club and is savagely beaten by the club Vice President. This occurs because he has decided to be more committed to his wife and wants to communicate this message to Ima. The fact that violence is used to "send a message" and invoke fear is never questioned and is an example of the dehumanization of women in *Sons of Anarchy*, consistent with homosociality (Bird 128). This violence is also significant because of the violence sex workers endure and that this is often excused as being an expected part of their profession, reminiscent of the common assertion when adult film star Christy Mack was savagely beaten and raped by ex-boyfriend War Machine, culminating in her being hospitalized with severe injuries (Ford).

This argument is a common reason sex work advocates call for the decriminalization of sex work (Baratosy and Wendt; Lutnick and Cohan 41). Ima Tite is vulnerable to violence because she works in an industry in which workers are subject to violence because of a lack of respect for sex work as "real work" and for sex workers subsequently, while also being denied access to legal repercussions for fear of being arrested themselves in areas where sex work is criminalized. The identities of Amelia and Ima, as an illegal immigrant and sex worker respectively, allow them to be dehumanized more than other female *Sons of Anarchy* characters. This is a likely factor in the sexualized and humiliating violence against them and is consistent with Sharon Bird's findings that homosociality facilitates the dehumanization of women through their sexual objectification.

However, the most poignant example of bromosociality as a justification for violence against women occurs when the club President enacts violence against his wife after she attempts to intervene in club matters, specifically his attempted murder and physical disablement of their daughter-in-law. This is the most pivotal act of the prioritization of club brotherhood over family and the justification of this for enacting violence against women. The intention of the prioritization of the club is transparent as the President viciously beats his wife, breaking her nose, after she threatens to inform other club members about his actions, knowing that this would cause major conflict for SAMCRO. The President's wife often intervenes in club matters through quiet intervention and is consequently able to wield some power, but this act of violence can be seen to communicate that she actually holds no power at all. This violent act is characterized as the turning point for this character, despite instigating the murder of another club member's wife, meaning that violence against women is again used as a plot device. Significantly, the President feels justified in enacting violence because he considered it to be necessary for the wellbeing of the club, a typical rationale in most cases of violence against female loved ones, of SAMCRO or rivals, in *Sons of Anarchy*.

These violent acts occur because they are rationalized as necessary for the good of the club's brotherly bonds, constituting 'bromosociality' in action. Bromosociality, like homosociality, refers to same-sex non-sexual groups but differs in its specificity to men and is characterized by a heightened bond, likened to familial bonds. This phenomenon could be also observed in real life in settings such as fraternities, team sports, and the military and has potential to be applied to the prevalence of violence against women in these areas. Similar to homosociality, the heightened connection present in bromosocial relations also contributes to the maintenance of hegemonic masculinity, which is performed by SAMCRO members (Bird).

Bromosociality differs significantly from homosociality, though, in that the characteristic familial-like bonds which emphasize the importance of the brotherhood relationship raise the stakes for individual men and thus make it harder for them to subvert hegemonic masculinity and the tenets of homosociality. The tenets of homosociality, specifically emotional detachment, sexual objectification of women, and competition, are thus adopted as essential parts of the brotherhood and result in suspicion and exclusion of members who fail to adhere to these norms, which in *Sons of Anarchy* can result in the deaths of these individuals. Furthermore, these tenets are detrimental to women's wellbeing as they encourage men to depersonalize the oppression of women, see women as distinct from themselves, and subsequently dehumanize women, leading to violence against these women. Bromosociality encourages the members of SAMCRO to see themselves as distinct to women and to prioritize the club over their female loved ones. This gendered distinction is key to understanding the motivation for violence against women and the continued rationalized perpetuation of it.

Violence against women in *Sons of Anarchy* often furthers the narrative in some way but also occurs as a response to protect the club, even if this means enacting violence against their own female family members and romantic partners. Similarly, rivals enact violence against the loved ones of SAMCRO in order to assert their own dominance, meaning that this justification is not specific to SAMCRO. Overall, bromosociality can be employed as a theoretical tool for analyzing instances of violence against women committed by men with male group membership similar to those found in *Sons of Anarchy*.

I have presented many examples of violence against women in *Sons of Anarchy* throughout this essay that illustrate the prevalence of these acts and the brutality enacted against women in the show. This violence is used to further the narrative of the male characters and introduce conflict but is sometimes simply gratuitous. Although these examples are exaggerated works of fiction, they are somewhat rooted in reality, with examples of rationalized oppression of women by groups of men presented in the literature on the military and sporting teams. It is vital that we continue to interrogate these examples even when they occur in fictional settings so that we might begin to understand the social construction of masculinity, sexuality, and gendered violence.

## Works Cited

Baratosy, R., and S. Wendt. "'Outdated Laws, Outspoken Whores': Exploring Sex Work in a Criminalised Setting." *Women's Studies International Forum*, vol. 62, no. 1, 2017, pp. 34–42.
Bird, S.R. "Welcome to the Men's Club: Homosociality and the Maintenance of Hegemonic Masculinity." *Gender and Society*, vol. 10, no. 2, 1996, pp. 120–32.
Brook, H. "Bros Before Ho(mo)s: Hollywood Bromance and the Limits of Heterodoxy." *Men and Masculinities*, vol. 18, no. 2, 2015, pp. 249–66.
Chang, G. *Disposable Domestics: Immigrant Women Workers in the Global Economy*. Haymarket Books, 2016.
Connell, R.W. *Gender and Power: Society, the Person, and Sexual Politics*. Stanford University Press, 1987.
Connell, R.W. *Masculinities*. University of California Press, 2005.
Curry, T.J. "Fraternal Bonding in the Locker Room: A Profeminist Analysis of Talk About Competition and Women." *Sociology of Sport Journal*, vol. 8, no. 1, 1991, pp. 119–35.
Flood, M. "Men, Sex, and Homosociality: How Bonds between Men Shape Their Sexual Relations with Women." *Men and Masculinities*, vol. 10, no. 3, 2008, pp. 339–59.
Ford, C. "What Christy Mack's assault teaches us about modern misogyny." *Daily Life*, 13 August 2014, http://www.dailylife.com.au/news-and-views/dl-opinion/what-christy-macks-assault-teaches-us-about-modern-misogyny-20140813-3dmi1.html.
Guzmán, I.M., and A.N. Valdivia. "Brain, Brow, and Booty: Latina Iconicity in U.S. Popular Culture." *The Communication Review*, vol. 7, no. 2, 2004, pp. 205–221.
Jaworski, K. "The Gender-ing of Suicide." *Australian Feminist Studies*, vol. 25, no. 63, 2010, pp. 47–61.
Lutnick, A., and D. Cohan. "Criminalization, Legalization or Decriminalization of Sex Work: What Female Sex Workers Say in San Francisco, USA." *Reproductive Health Matters*, vol. 17, no. 34, 2009, pp. 38–46.
Merskin, D. "Three Faces of Eva: Perpetuation of The Hot-Latina Stereotype in Desperate Housewives." *Howard Journal of Communications*, vol. 18, no. 2, 2007, pp. 133–51.
Messner, M. "Women in the Men's Locker Room." In *Sex, Violence & Power in Sports: Rethinking Masculinity*, edited by M. Messner and D. Sabo. The Crossing Press, 1994, pp. 42–52.
"Poor Little Lambs." Sons of Anarchy: Season 7, written by Kem Nunn and Kurt Sutter, directed by Guy Ferland, episode 4, FX, 2014.
"SO." Sons of Anarchy: Season 3, written by Kurt Sutter, directed by Stephen Kay, episode 1, FX, 2010.

# Leather Is Thicker Than Blood
## Institutional and Hegemonic Masculinity

JAMIESON RYAN

Institutional uniforms announce a person's job and act as a signifier of power. Scrubs and police officer uniforms demonstrate the social role and instill a set of expectations upon the wearer. In his seminal text, *Discipline and Punish*, Michael Foucault writes, "[i]s it surprising that prisons resemble factories, schools, barracks, hospitals, which all resemble prisons?" (228). Foucault is signaling how these institutions function, and are structured, in similar ways to prisons through their means of control, classification, and power. However, in FX's drama *Sons of Anarchy* (2008–2014), created by Kurt Sutter, institutional workers are arguably freer than the titular motorcycle gang of the show and are certainly freer in their gender performances; freedom is one of the core values and attractions of the Sons of Anarchy Motorcycle Club Redwood Original (SAMCRO), but their masculinity is a restrictive prison. *Sons of Anarchy* takes place in the fictitious town of Charming, California and the series follows the physically violent (and often deadly) conflicts between the Sons and rival gangs; however, the ideological conflict of masculinity (and power) that takes place between the Sons and institutional workers is more nuanced and arguably more interesting. Foucault illustrates that institutions, despite their intended purpose, are not as ideologically different as they appear, and the Sons resemble the very institutions they seek to divide themselves from. Doctors have their scrubs, cops have their badge, and the Sons have their leather vest, or "cut," but their cut does not truly represent the freedom they impose upon it; instead the Sons uniform acts as a two-fold signifier that both announces their difference to the outside world while also restricting the Sons' behavior to a rigid set of codes, or in other words a rigid ideal of masculinity.

Little scholarly work has been conducted on *Sons of Anarchy*, despite it being one of FX's longest running and highest rated dramas, and one of the shows that was largely responsible for turning FX into a respected scripted drama network. I will primarily use masculinity and gender theory to dissect the notions of manhood and performance in the show. I define masculinity as not something inherent or born into but rather a cultural construct that one enacts and performs, and follow Daniel Worden's conception that "masculinity does not reside in a male body but instead in a series of performative gestures and public presentations. Being 'like a man' has little to do with possession and everything to do with performance" (1). I use the term "institutional workers," but I will be specifically looking at law enforcement and hospital workers as these are the main institutional workers in the show.[1] Moreover, the notion of hegemonic masculinity, the dominant form of masculine performance that overtakes a culture or institution, is fundamental to my reading of *Sons of Anarchy*. SAMCRO embody hegemonic masculinity and exhibit numerous traits, as defined by Mike Donaldson: "exclusive, anxiety-provoking, internally and hierarchically differentiated, brutal, and violent. It is pseudonatural, tough, contradictory, crisis-prone, rich, and socially sustained" (645).

I will first highlight the similarities between the masculinity of the Sons of Anarchy and institutional workers, and how the very things the Sons pride themselves on (their differences from accepted institutions) are the same things that lead to their toxic hypermasculinity. I will then examine the role of villains in the show and how gender and race play an important role in outlaw and institutional antagonists. I will demonstrate how SAMCRO hinders progress within Charming not because of their self-described concern for and protection of the town, but because keeping Charming in the past allows the club to maintain their old beliefs and their outdated vision of masculinity. The final section of my essay will look at how Tara Knowles, a doctor and Jax Teller's partner, challenges the club's notion of masculinity and offers its largest ideological threat. I argue that in *Sons of Anarchy*, the motorcycle club creates a false myth of masculinity that is not only detrimental to others (especially Others), but also to the club and its members. The institutions in the show do not offer an ideal masculinity, but they do exhibit the growing social awareness and equality that is necessary for an institution to properly serve and survive in the 21st century; institutions rather than gangs offer the largest ideological threat to the Sons of Anarchy Motorcycle Club.

## Institutional and (Club) Sanctioned Masculinity

SAMCRO embody and enact hegemonic masculinity, and I would argue that legally recognized institutions (like law enforcement agencies and hospitals) in the series do offer a dominant masculinity and that their masculinity is not hegemonic. Michael Kimmel notes that hegemonic masculinity has the "common characteristics [of]—violence, aggression, extreme competitiveness, a gnawing insecurity—and these are also the defining features of compulsive masculinity, a masculinity that must always prove itself and that is always in doubt" (93). Laura Abrams, Ben Anderson-Nathe, and Jemel Aguilar, in their practical sociological study of masculinities in juvenile correctional facilities, further elucidate the features of hegemonic masculinity as groups concerned with "power, competition, stoicism, sexism, and homophobia" (38). The Sons fit and exhibit the traits described by Kimmel as well as Abrams, Anderson-Nathe and Aguilars; the Sons are violent, aggressive, often extremely competitive,[2] insecure (but only privately or with one member they feel closest to), stoic, concerned with power, and the club is a sexist, racist, and homophobic organization. The only extreme emotions that are seemingly allowed within the club are aggression or anger as they further the masculinity of the club. Abrams, Anderson-Nathe and Aguilar also note that, historically, "hegemonic masculine identities [have been] linked to crime" (24). Hegemonic masculinity is a toxic hypermasculinity that is more about exclusion than it is about inclusion, which is similarly echoed by SAMCRO as new members[3] are rarely admitted and the club continually attempts to differentiate themselves from other gangs as well as law enforcement throughout the series. The Sons fashion themselves as not simply different but also as better than others (especially Others, who for the Sons is anyone who is not white and to a lesser extent male). Masculinity is a performance and thus the clearest example of SAMCRO's masculinity is through their aggression (their performative violence and yelling) as these actions are hard to miss or misinterpret. The Sons similarly display this heightened masculinity while around law enforcement officers, but the club offers a more nuanced reading of their masculinity when in institutional hospital settings where such public displays are not allowed.

Institutional workers like police officers, doctors, and nurses do have a dominant masculinity, but I would argue that in the world of the show[4] this masculinity is not a hegemonic masculinity but rather a dominant role. The difference between dominant and hegemonic being that a dominant masculinity is the preferred attitude within the institution (but not mandatory and not toxic) while hegemonic masculinity is a negative and detrimental ideal of masculinity.[5] Police officers in the show offer the best examples of masculinity (rather than healthcare workers) because the Sons deal with law enforcement more often than they do healthcare workers, and when they do need medical help they usually seek Tara, as the rest of the hospital staff remain largely flat characters throughout the series. Police officers in the show do not offer an ideal masculinity, if there even is such a thing, but their masculinity is limited by workplace codes and the law. Police officers should not be racist or sexist or they can be reported and reprimanded, while the Sons are not bound by such rules and their identity is defined by their exclusionary nature.

Essentially, institutional masculinity in the show is more withdrawn because there are clear regulations and laws that workers must abide by while the Sons' outlaw nature, central to their masculinity—within and outside the law, is one of the main ideological splits between these brands of masculinity. SAMCRO often think of themselves as better versions of the cops, such as when they hunt down a child rapist rather than informing the police ("Fun Town"), but the gang will never have the legitimacy or rules of a sanctioned institution. The Sons become aggressive when they feel threatened, and nearly all their interactions with cops[6] are hostile confrontation. These confrontations are most overt because the cops are the enemies of SAMCRO and can arrest them, but the Sons aggression also comes from the legitimate power that the cops hold and that the Sons yearn for: sanctified control. Similarly, the Sons become mocking when they feel threatened, and most of their interactions with healthcare professionals involve the Sons taunting or deriding these workers, with most of their scorn being sexual in nature (as most nurses are female in the show).[7] Legitimacy is something the Sons strive for, even if they never admit it; they cannot have the legal and recognized power of institutional workers but they can have the power of fear and the recognition (and appreciation) of Charming.

However, there are a few similarities between the Sons and institutional workers in the show. Michael Kimmel notes that there are "certain patterns to these [masculine] actions: American men try to *control themselves*; they project their fears onto *others*" (6). Both SAMCRO and institutional workers try to "control themselves" as well as others, but where police or hospital workers tend to attempt this control for the good of the individual or community the Sons attempt to control for their own selfish gain; this is another distinguishing factor between these two institutions: police privilege the community, doctors the patient, and the Sons themselves. Similarly, the struggles between the Sons and legitimate institutions can be read as both a physical and ideological power struggle. The gang fights in the show "are often also messages of dominance and control being communicated to the community and the dominant hegemonic masculinity" (Moolman 113). The community of Charming, especially in the earlier seasons, is most often on the side of the Sons, and the fight between law enforcement and the Sons is not merely about legality but also about convincing the community that the Sons are not a necessary evil, but in fact merely evil. The Sons cannot physically own Charming but they can attempt to own the goodwill of the town (and its ideologies) and thus the battle between the institutions, which act as a buffer between normal Charming citizens and the club, and SAMCRO offer the only legal conflict that the club can engage in with the law: an ideological battle for legitimacy in the minds of Charming citizens.

The Sons gain their masculine bravado not only from their actions, uniform, and power but also from their motorcycles. Joshua Maynard notes that in motorcycle culture "the masculinity of the rider is also linked to the masculine character of the machine" (103). The motorcycle is an overt power symbol throughout the series, but it also has subtler associations. The motorcycle and the roar of the engine are repeatedly used as a motif in the show to drown out conversations the Sons do not want to hear—the audience sees the Sons rev their engines overtop of cops or politicians talking, but this same noise never drowns out the conversation of a club member. Moreover, the motorcycle similarly represents the model of the gang's masculine identity: it is at once a sign of freedom and a uniform among the club, but at the same time the motorcycle represents the rigidity of this masculine code. Members can customize and personalize their bikes however they see fit, but still all the bikes look the same (there are no flamboyant decorations or more seemingly "feminine" paint jobs)—the motorcycle is an illusion of freedom just like the club's masculine code. Sons are allowed their freedom, but only within their established and rigid code, and it is only fitting that the two characters who die on/because of motorcycle accidents[8] are the two characters who struggle most with the rigid and immoral masculinity of SAMCRO. Furthermore, cuts and motorcycles are black while lab coats and hospital walls are white—I do not mean to propose a simplistic reading that black is bad and white is good, but that black (in this case) is hidden and white is open. Black is meant to hide blood and be intimidating for the Sons while white is meant to purposely be bland and more welcoming as things are not as easily hidden and workers are more approachable.

Masculinity in the show ultimately comes down to control and power, and about subverting others' power in order to control them. Institutions offer one of the rare glimpses of vulnerability, which is a natural emotion that is rarely shown in the harsh masculinity of the club. The Sons are scared by each other, Others' gangs, and by law enforcement (when their arrest is imminent and guaranteed), but the Sons almost never outwardly show their fear because of their adherence to the club's masculinity as vulnerability undercuts their hegemonic power structure. However, the Sons are often scared when they are in the non-threatening hospital environment.[9] Hospitals inherently uncover vulnerability and often force patients to confront their own mortality, which SAMCRO rarely does, and thus Sons often posture their masculinity through taunts and jibes like Tig does and only rarely reveal their vulnerability like when Chibs does to Gemma in "Fa Guan." Chibs, as a patient, is stripped of his power (as well as his cut), and his masculinity within the SAMCRO ideology—he is not above his fellow patients and is dealing with an equality he is not accustomed to. Thus, the importance and ideological conflict between the more equal institutional gender identity and the Sons' hypermasculinity is one of the strongest and subtlest conflicts in the show.

Nicole Cox and Lauren J. Decarvalho write that "one of the greatest threats to hegemonic masculinity has been feminism" (822) and the Sons can largely avoid femininity in their isolated microcosm of a clubhouse but when they are in a hospital they come face to face with both strong feminine identity and feminism (most of the doctors, nurses, and other health care professionals that the Sons encounter in the hospitals are women). Similarly, a large percentage of the police officers are also females or minorities and some of the strongest characters in the show such as Agent Stahl, Lieutenant Roosevelt, and District Attorney Patterson are females or minorities or both. Feminism is not only the club's largest threat but it is also seemingly a death warrant for members and the "softer" members who do not conform to the club's extreme toxic masculinity.[10] SAMCRO's extreme masculinity, which allows them to bully others and procure power, is also what prevents them from fully achieving the level of power they desire. Cox and Decarvalho write that "*Sons of Anarchy* is much more than a show about men. It is a show about the pressures, expectations, contradictions, and crises that men face in performing their gender, and the repercussions that ensue when they fail to do so correctly" (836). Cox and Decarvalho accurately describe SAMCRO's masculinity as a job; masculinity becomes a stand-in for real work as the club members are rarely shown working in their auto shop. SAMCRO gain their pride from their façade and masculinity (along with their illegal endeavors but they cannot flaunt this), whereas institutional employees gain their sense of worth from their legitimate work and family. Family and work are more sustainable forms of gender identity than an illegal gun-running business, and this is largely why the Sons act so aggressively toward institutional workers: as a posturing for themselves, to intimidate the workers and belittle their self-worth so the Sons feel more powerful.

## The Villainous Other

The Sons are a racist and sexist organization, but as Michael L. Wayne notes, "Charming is racially homogeneous. Nonetheless, from the beginning of the series, the show makes significant efforts to distance SAMCRO, as a collective, from overt racism" (193). The show distances SAMCRO from overt racism (even though racism is an aspect of their masculinity) by juxtaposing the club to white supremacists like Ernest Darby, and most explicitly with Ethan Zobelle and AJ Weston of the League of American Nationalists (a white supremacist group and the antagonists of season two). It is a common trope for heroes to defeat villains who are like them so that the hero can clearly separate themselves from what they are not; physical conflicts are also ideological conflicts to separate "us from them" and these battles similarly occur in *Sons of Anarchy*. Even though the Sons are racist, their racism is lessened as they battle (and defeat) the series' more overt racists. The club's racism is shown throughout the show but is never truly a focus or even properly addressed; all the members of the club use racially derogatory terms to black and Hispanic characters despite the Sons relying on business with the black One-Niners and the Mexican Mayan gangs.[11] This racial divide is hinted at through throw-away lines like when Jax says, "White on white, what's that about?" ("Albification") after he sees two white men fighting in jail. Just like uniforms, or cuts, clearly mark a person/organization so too does a person's skin act as a uniform and mark them for a side in the series' outlaw culture; law-abiding institutional workers are not governed by such racist and restrictive ideologies and their uniforms are something that can be both taken off as well as discarded.[12]

SAMCRO's racism is largely ignored until the season four storyline involving Juice Ortiz. Wayne writes that "Ortiz's character becomes significantly darker when Assistant U.S. Attorney Lincoln Potter ... and Lieutenant Eli Roosevelt ... of the San Joaquin County Sheriff's Department use knowledge of Ortiz's family background as leverage" (194). SAMCRO is an all-white club, so Potter and Roosevelt blackmail Juice when they discover his father was black. Juice knows he will be expelled from the club if they find out, but he also fears for his life, and this shows both the racism of SAMCRO and Juice's internalized self-loathing because of his race and involvement with the Sons. Juice's storyline becomes much darker when it is revealed that he is darker. The police pressure Juice to betray the club and provide evidence of the Sons' involvement with the cartel, and after Juice steals a cocaine brick for evidence and murders a fellow club member to cover up his actions, Juice attempts to hang himself from a tree and end his life. His chosen method of suicide is extremely important in this instance both because Juice has easy access to guns (and any other time the audience is shown a character contemplating suicide it involves a gun) and because of the history of lynchings in America. Matt Zoller Seitz, a renowned film and television critic, described Juice's "attempted self-lynching, [as] one of the most spectacular acts of internalized racism and self-loathing that's ever been seen on American TV"

(n. pag.). Juice's storyline not only codifies SAMCRO's masculinity as hegemonic and white, but also exhibits how engrained the club's ideas of identity are. Juice attempts suicide rather than get expelled from the club and thereby reveals there is seemingly no life, not even an imaginable life, after SAMCRO whereas for institutional workers there is life both after they retire and after they end their shift; institutional identity is something workers can put on and remove and not something that defines them.

Over the show's seven seasons, the Sons face numerous antagonists, but their enemies are problematically racialized. The only white gang SAMCRO faces is the True IRA.[13] Marcus Alvarez, Hector Salazar, Romeo Parada, Damon Pope, Henry Lin, and August Marks are all major antagonists the Sons face and all of them are minorities. Charming is hegemonically white, but it seems that all the criminals (besides the Sons) are either a racial minority or extreme white supremacists—no villain is racially/ideologically comparable to the Sons.[14] Arguably the most interesting villain from the show and one of the few antagonists to be a major threat for multiple seasons is Agent June Stahl from the Bureau of Alcohol, Tobacco, Firearms and Explosives. Agent Stahl offers one of the biggest threats to the Sons not only because she successfully incarcerates them and nearly destroys the club on several occasions, but also because she does it as an institutional woman who has masculine tendencies and represents feminism. Stahl at once exerts her femininity but also is not afraid to flirt and banter with the Sons' snide remarks. Most of the shows villains are non-white males who challenge the Sons white hegemonic masculinity, but it is interesting that the biggest threat to the club is a white woman, further signaling Cox and Decarvalho's point that "one of the greatest threats to hegemonic masculinity has been feminism." Moreover, it is interesting to note that despite Tig killing Opie's wife, Donna, on Clay's orders, Stahl is still blamed for the act.[15] Tig repeatedly says, "Stahl's the one who really killed Donna" ("Service"), despite him shooting Donna and thereby illustrating his inability to claim responsibility, which is hugely important and representative of the group's masculinity: they must always be right or else their authority is challenged and others are to blame for their own mistakes.

The Sons are a racist organization and their greatest antagonists are not the culturally or racially different gangs that populate the series but rather similarly white enemies like Agent June Stahl. Institutional masculinity is varied from job to job and person to person and is not a blanket term or idea; there is room for movement, expression, and individual identity. Whereas, SAMCRO's masculinity is characterized as rigidly white and homogenous. Each antagonist represents an Other that challenges the group's severe gender identities and their (ideological) actions call for a recognition of feminism and equality. After all the fighting and all the bloodshed, it is not the gangs that pose the largest threat to the Sons but rather the law enforcement, the gang itself, and the ideological representation of a more egalitarian society.

## Tradition (and Old Ideas of Masculinity)

Charming is a fictional town meant to be a stand-in for any (or every) American small town; thus, the drama that unfolds without a regional vernacular and instead with a national framework means events in Charming could happen anywhere. This notion is furthered as Charming is more of a character itself than most of its inhabitants, as residents are almost entirely overlooked throughout the series. Garrett L. Castleberry in "Revising the Western: Connecting Genre Rituals and American Western Revisionism in TV's *Sons of Anarchy*" notes, "the Sons see themselves as protectors of Charming, keeping unwanted big businesses, urban developments, and increased law enforcement beyond its borders. In other words, SAMCRO works diligently to keep the progress of civilization at bay" (271). However, the Sons are doing more than just protecting Charming; they are protecting themselves. A more modern Charming would mean a more modern ideological Charming—more socially aware/conscious, and this would pose an ideological threat to the Sons, as they rely on antiquated ideas of gender and racial politics. Castleberry further says, "[SAMCRO's] sacred meetings are called 'church,' and at these meetings the men-only vote on key decisions that affect the future of the club. Thus, the Teller-Morrow compound forms a fortified border, a modern-day fort, protecting SC from threats outside its walls" (Castleberry 271). More modern sensibilities would mean more modern masculinities that challenge the Sons' brand.

Castleberry's article points to the similarities between the show and western movies, but one thing that Castleberry only touches upon but does not truly investigate is the similarity between the two in their shared notions of masculinity. Worden notes how "masculinity is a site for the production of new social possibilities" (16). However, there is no "site for the production of new social possibilities" in the Son's strict vision of masculinity—in fact there is nothing "new" and in their conception, there will never be anything "new" about their masculinity. There is only the past and tradition. Even after learning about Juice's suicide attempt, Chibs is unwilling to even consider looking at the antiquated rules, and he says to Juice, "Listen, the rules have been around since day one. Different time. I'm not saying I agree with them all. But you know, if I start picking and choosing which ones to follow, then the whole thing just falls apart" ("With an X"). Chibs is referring to how the club cannot change its whites-only rule. Losing a racist rule does not jeopardize the rest of the rules or even the foundation of the club, unless this racist tenet is fundamental to the group, which it is: there is no future masculinity for the Sons; there is only the past, no matter how much the outside world advances for the better. However, Chibs does go on to comfort Juice by telling him that if his father's race is not listed as "black" on his birth certificate then it does not matter and he will not be kicked out of SAMCRO—Chibs' actions show that members oppose some of the restrictive and racist ideologies of the gang's masculinity in secrecy, but they do not oppose the masculine code in a public or real way that would affect change for SAMCRO and those they interact with.

The Sons, themselves, never deconstruct their masculinity, and it echoes the idealized and hyper-macho myth/vision of men that Western films invented and perpetuated. Jacqueline Moore, in discussing late 19th-century masculinity, states that, "[i]n part, white workers retained a sense of masculinity by considering themselves superior to blacks, Hispanics, and certain immigrant groups" (45). However, Moore's observations still accurately depict the Sons, as the club gains their physical and ideological power by subverting and comparing themselves to the very groups that Moore notes: blacks (the One-Niners), Hispanics (the Mayans), and certain immigrant groups (visible minorities but also largely the Irish). The Sons look to the future for more power, but derive their power from historical myths. Michael Kimmel, writing on frontier times, notes that "[s]ome [men] sought to return to those earlier years ... by excluding women, blacks, and immigrants, or by globalizing the frontier through imperial expansion" (43). Kimmel's remarks on Western masculinity completely reflect the Sons organization. The institutions are portrayed as lesser because they are trying to modernize Charming and with it modernize the ideologies and morals of the small town and in turn small town America. The fight of institutional masculinities within the microcosm of Charming is meant to reflect the ideological country as a whole—often antiquated ideas of gender and race of small town America against the more socially aware (but greedier and less personal) politics of urbanization.

## Tara: The Greatest Threat to SAMCRO

One of the reasons the "old ladies" of the club are so important to SAMCRO is not because they support their men but because they give the Sons something to defend. Silke Wenk illustrates that "[t]he feminine is also designed as a complement and a supplement to the masculine: through the defence of the feminine, masculinity produces and demonstrates itself. Masculinity is measured by its ability to defend the feminine, which can also mean 'the nation'" (68–69). The "old ladies" are something to defend because they will help produce the future of the club (albeit an old-fashioned close-minded vision of the future). Throughout the show, the "old ladies" and their wants and suggestions are ignored simply because the Sons imagine themselves as greater and thereby women are conceived not so much as people but as the reductive idea of mother or receptacles for children and the club's future. Geoff Eley writes, "[i]n one recurring chain of associations, women were addressed as mothers of the nation, reproducing its biological future, nurturing the next generations, teaching the 'mother tongue'—reproducers rather than producers, prized and revered objects of protection, rather than agents in their own right" (32). This "biological future" is shown in how the Sons' sons become members of SAMCRO: Opie is the son of Piney Winston and Jax is the son of John Teller—Jax also dresses his newborn son, Abel, in Sons of Anarchy baby clothes as if his destiny is already chosen for him. Women's wants never truly matter to the club or to their SAMCRO husband because despite what their husbands say the club comes first. Stahl is portrayed as somewhat monstrous for being wedded to her job, but the Sons are just as, if not more so, wedded to the club, but their dedication is not monstrous because they are men and the club is a "brotherhood."

Coming back to Cox and Decarvalho's important quote, "one of the greatest threats to hegemonic masculinity has been feminism," in the television series who (either male or female) represents feminism and in turn "the greatest threats" to SAMCRO? This embodiment will not come from any of the men, as anything less than their hypermasculinity is impermissible; instead feminism must come from a woman character on the show. However, as Cox and Decarvalho note, "[t]hroughout *Sons of Anarchy*, there are two groups of women who dominate the script: the porn stars, 'sluts,' and 'whores'; and the female leads—Gemma and Tara. These groups are significant as they uphold hegemonic masculinity in their own right" (831). Gemma is not the embodiment of the "greatest threat" to the Sons because she largely instills the values of the club even though they subjugate her; thus, Tara should be and is the embodied feminism that poses the necessary "greatest threat" to the Sons of Anarchy. It is not a coincidence that Tara is an institutional worker. Tara is a talented doctor, and the inverse of the Sons and their ideology: Tara is a woman while the club is composed of men; she saves lives while the Sons take lives; and she is an individual who is fine on her own while the club relies on itself and each other. Gemma is threatened by Tara from the pilot episode of the series because she knows the power that Tara has and the power she has over her son, Jax. Tara's construction as a contrasting figure to Jax is most apparent and best illustrated in the first episode of *Sons of Anarchy*, when the pair are brilliantly characterized through a montage of the Sons shooting Mayans and blowing up the warehouse to the quietness of the hospital room while Tara and the doctors perform surgery on Abel. This contrast climaxes when Jax returns to the hospital to visit his newborn son

Abel and runs into Tara. Tara says, "Clean yourself up, Jax" referring to the blood Jax has on him ("Pilot")—the expectation would be for the doctor to have blood on her and not for a hospital visitor. "Clean yourself up, Jax" is a central tenet of Tara's character as she tries to better, or clean up the man she loves and in turn the gang he belongs to.

Tara is seemingly the only one who sees the danger of SAMCRO and continually tries to escape its grasp with Jax. Tara's ideology gives, or maintains, life while the Sons is a destructive life-killing ideology. However, it seems almost destined that Tara meets the end she does.[16] Tara offers the strongest vision of masculine identity in the show as she represents strength but also leniency. Tara is at once, as Eley says, "reproducing [the] biological future" of the club, but she is also the one that protects her children, who are the embodied "biological future," by removing them from SAMCRO's reach— thus, she is at once the traditional female "reproducer" and the traditional male "protector." Tara is the embodied feminism that is "the greatest threat to hegemonic masculinity" of SAMCRO—and furthers Worden's statement from "masculinity is a site for the production of new social possibilities" to feminism "is a site for the production of new social possibilities" as Tara's life is the only one that offers new possibilities for herself, and to those she loves.

## Conclusion

Ultimately, one of the shows more somber and beautiful moments comes in the episode "Hands," when a sheriff's deputy comes up to talk to Jax while he is out with Tara and their children. Jax, who is outside Charming and does not have his cut on, is at first wary and hesitant because he does not trust cops (and to a certain extent institutions) and has only ever had negative run-ins with law enforcement. However, the officer simply comes up to talk cars and bikes with Jax, and the conversation turns out to be pleasant for both men. Outside the ideological code of the club, Jax is free to engage in beneficial discussions with a law enforcement officer. They still talk about masculine topics, and their gender (and uniform) still signposts them as masculine men, but this masculinity is not toxic and is instead beneficial, as it builds the community and strengthens the relationship between an institution and those it is meant to serve. This quiet and quick moment shows Jax and Tara that the club's masculinity and identity need to change, but it unfortunately takes another three seasons for Jax to realize this necessity and make a change.

*Sons of Anarchy* ends with an acknowledgment of the masculinity it represents—the show does not deconstruct or critically critique the masculinity it presents, but it at least acknowledges the dangers and limitedness of such an identity. Legal institutions will live on in one form or another long after the Sons, and the masculinity and gender roles they embody. One of the main differences between the Sons and legitimate institutions is that institutional workers can take their uniform off. Police officers and hospital workers can and do clock out—they take off their uniform and go home where they can revert to a less extreme masculinity and show that their institutional role is performative. However, the Sons never truly come off the clock; they keep their cuts on and their masculine façade up at almost all times. Gemma tells Donna that the Sons are "the glue" that keeps everyone together ("Seeds"), but the gang is not the glue and instead family is. Jax says this to Donna three episodes later: "We're not the glue, you are" ("Giving Back").[17] Jax is likely only saying this to Donna so that she supports Opie despite her husband ignoring her wishes for her and their children. It takes Jax another six seasons to realize the truth of what he said to Donna, but he eventually does realize that family is the "glue" of his life and not the club. Relationships do not survive SAMCRO (all the members are bachelors, divorcees, widowers, or eventually split from their wives). In *Sons of Anarchy* family is ultimately the true teller of a man's worth, and although this still may be a somewhat antiquated idea, it is nevertheless a much better vision of masculinity than the toxic hegemonic masculinity of SAMCRO.

## Notes

1. Interestingly, the show does have numerous institutional settings such as prisons and warehouses, but the workers inside these institutions are largely ignored. Similarly, the Teller-Morrow autoshop is the headquarters of the Sons and the main setting of the show, but little to nothing is known (or shown) about the actual mechanics who work there.
2. Rather than a general competitiveness, the Sons are competitive with certain members who challenge their role in the club. For instance, Jax and Clay are extremely competitive as they vie for leadership of SAMCRO while Tig becomes competitive (as well as insecure and needs reassurance from Clay) when Opie takes on more of an enforcer role in the club.
3. Graduating from the prospect level to a full member.
4. In the real world, there is a problem with sexism, homophobia and particularly racism in police forces, but these issues are not addressed within *Sons of Anarchy*. In the show, cops can be (and some are) unethical, but they are rarely overtly sexist or racist and in fact most of the strongest police are characters of color, or women, or both.
5. Again, in the real world, certain law enforcement agencies and police precincts do foster hegemonic masculinity but this is not the case in the show.
6. Excluding the cops they have bought such as Chief Wayne Unser or Deputy Vic Trammel.
7. Such as when Tig begins to pull down his pants and tries to show a female doctor where "a Doberman pinscher took a chunk of my ass" ("Old Bones").
8. SPOILER: John Teller (before the series begins) and Jax Teller.
9. This is partially because SAMCRO cannot easily defend members in a public hospital.
10. SPOILER: Such as Half-Sack, Juice, Bobby, and Jax. Half-Sack is too comedic, too kind, and treats his girlfriend as too much of an equal to ever be a Son and dies at the stage of prospect; Juice is, for the first few seasons, only a source of comedy and is never as "hard" as other members like Tig; Bobby is noted for being one of the kinder members within the

club; and Jax struggles with his role and future within the club, and how to negotiate his relationship with Tara while also fulfilling the masculine code of the club.

11. Juice Ortiz is the only main Son who is a visible minority. Juice claims to be Puerto Rican, which is a territory of the United States thus he is more "American" than the Mayans who are composed mostly of Mexicans.

12. Again, racism and sexism are a problem in workforces, especially environments predominantly run by white men as well as typically masculine jobs (as masculine often means white men), but *Sons of Anarchy* does not really address these problems.

13. The League of American Nationalists, could arguably be included but I am hesitant to do so because the League has bureaucratic and political support from American politicians. SPOILER: Zobelle is also an FBI informant, which lessens the role of the League as a threatening gang since the FBI would not hire/work with a gang leader they knew to be too dangerous unless he could provide more important and powerful arrests. Rather than the League being a gang I would argue they represent the systematic racism in America, and how law enforcement is more willing to work with white criminals than other racial minorities and how white supremacy is not viewed as a truly toxic or terrible ideology in the world of the show.

14. Lee Toric is the only villain who is white and not part of the True IRA or a neo-Nazi, but Toric is also not originally a criminal or outlaw either and only becomes one to avenge the death of his sister who was killed by a member of the Sons.

15. Because she tried to convince the Sons that Opie was a "rat."

16. SPOILER: Tara must die because she represents institutions and their ideology which have no future in the club. It is important that Gemma is the one to kill Tara because Gemma represents and embodies the old order of the Sons. However, Tara's death also signals the end of the club because SAMCRO begins to dismantle after her death.

17. Jax does not hear Gemma say this to Donna outside a grocery store and this likely means that this is a phrase Gemma repeats so it becomes a sort of mantra or incantation to push the agenda of the club.

## Works Cited

Abrams, Laura S., et al. "Constructing Masculinities in Juvenile Corrections." *Men and Masculinities*, vol. 11, no. 1, 2008, pp. 22–41.
Blom, Ida, et al. *Gendered Nations: Nationalism and Gender Order in the Long Nineteenth Century*. Berg, 2000.
Castleberry, Garret L. "Revising the Western: Connecting Genre Rituals and American Western Revisionism in TV's Sons of Anarchy." *Cultural Studies, Critical Methodologies*, vol. 14, no. 3, 2014, pp. 269–78.
Cox, Nicole B., and Lauren J. Decarvalho. "'Ride Free or Die' Trying: Hypermasculinity on FX's Sons of Anarchy." *The Journal of Popular Culture*, vol. 49, no. 4, 2016, pp. 818–38.
Donaldson, Mike. "What Is Hegemonic Masculinity?" *Theory and Society*, vol. 22, no. 5, 1993, pp. 643–57.
Eley, Geoff. "Culture, Nation and Gender." Blom et al., pp. 27–40.
Foucault, Michael. *Discipline and Punish: The Birth of the Prison*. Translated by Alan Sheridan. Vintage Books, 1995.
Kimmel, Michael S. *The History of Men: Essays in the History of American and British Masculinities*. State University of New York Press, 2005.
\_\_\_\_\_. *Manhood in America: A Cultural History*. Oxford University Press, 2006.
Maynard, Joshua Robert Adam. *Between Man and Machine: A Socio-Historical Analysis of Masculinity in North American Motorcycling Culture*. Dissertation, Queen's University, 2008.
Moolman, Benita. "The Reproduction of an 'Ideal' Masculinity Through Gang Rape on the Cape Flats." *Agenda*, vol. 18, no. 60, 2004, pp. 109–24.
Moore, Jacqueline. "'Them's Fighting Words': Violence, Masculinity, and the Texas Cowboy in the Late Nineteenth Century." *The Journal of the Gilded Age and Progressive Era*, vol. 13, no. 1, 2014, pp. 28–55.

Sutter, Kurt, creator. *Sons of Anarchy*. Linson the Company, Sutter Ink, Fox 21, FX Productions, 2008–2014.
Wayne, Michael L. "Mitigating Colorblind Racism in the Postnetwork Era: Class-Inflected Masculinity in The Shield, Sons of Anarchy, and Justified." *The Communication Review*, vol. 17, 2014, pp. 183–201.
Wenk, Silke. "Gendered Representations of the Nation's Past and Future." Blom et al., pp. 27–40.
Worden, Daniel. *Masculine Style: The American West and Literary Modernism*. Palgrave, 2011.
Zoller Seitz, Matt. "'Sons of Anarchy' Has Its 'Sopranos' Moment." *Salon*, http://www.salon.com/2011/11/09/these_bikers_are_prisoners_for_life/. Accessed 1 May 2017.

# Cynical Tolerance
## Gender, Race and Fraternal Fears

CHRISTIAN JIMENEZ

While *Sons of Anarchy* has received some full-blown treatments by scholars, and much remains to be discussed (Dunn and Eberl; Lotz), the show's construction of masculinity has occasioned much commentary (Donahue; Kolb; Rosenberg). Trying to analyze its distinct features is all the more crucial given its massive popularity (O'Connell). Yet, interestingly, discussions of gender rarely if ever focus on race in a sustained manner.

Cox and DeCarvalho, for instance, simply assume that the series focuses solely on "how men—and white, hetero-sexist masculinity—are presented to the masses" (818). This analysis will differ slightly. There is no doubting the main focus of *Sons of Anarchy* is on how white men perform their manhood via the motorcycle club. However, *Sons of Anarchy* grants women and racial minorities agency but often with highly disturbing baggage attached.

The following analytic essay will make a two-fold argument. On the one hand, *Sons of Anarchy* can be said to authorize a form of racial tolerance. But this racial tolerance is often subsumed in a highly sexist framework. To be sure, there is obvious evidence of how the series usually depicts African American and Latino characters as highly flawed while humanizing white characters again and again. For the most part, then, whites do look down upon non-whites and the show implicitly endorses this; but sometimes non-whites are shown to be as tough and violent as the white men portrayed.

## From White Only to Biracial Tolerance

At first glance, *Sons of Anarchy* is concerned with how Jax Teller and Clarence "Clay" Morrow fight for control of SAMCRO, a biker gang that also sells guns illegally in California. There is little doubt that SAMCRO is a male-only institution that revels in its sexism. The scholarly question is what kind of sexism the club represents and why it has found such resonance with a mass audience. The consensus is that the show helps men to perform a certain form of hegemonic masculinity.

Citing Mike Donaldson, Cox and DeCarvalho argue that hegemonic masculinity is defined by being a "culturally idealized form" of masculinity. This form of masculinity "is exclusive, anxiety-provoking, internally and hierarchically differentiated, brutal, and violent. It is ... tough, contradictory, crisis-prone, rich, and socially sustained" (Cox and DeCarvalho 819). In contrast, Shimpach argues masculinity is not as exclusive and anxiety-prone as Cox and DeCarvalho assume. To him,

> masculinity ... [a]lthough it functions as a sign and source of power, agency, and sexuality, masculinity is not an inherent, objective trait, but rather a performative engagement by the subject with culturally and historically specific conditions.... Moreover, the performance of masculinity need not be delimited by the subject's racial [identity].... At any given moment, masculinity operates in both the contingent and the plural [Shimpach 38].

This analysis takes a middling position. Anxiety and racial exclusion do come up frequently in *Sons of Anarchy*. The masculinity is sufficiently loose as to allow non-whites into SAMCRO (such as Juice and Bobby) as well as give women (albeit a constrained) voice in the series.

*Sons of Anarchy* features a number powerful women both directly attached to the club, like Gemma, and those more distant from it, like Tara. Lotz, examining *The Sopranos, The Shield, Nip/Tuck, Rescue Me, Dexter, Sons of Anarchy, Breaking Bad, Hung,* and *Men of a Certain Age,* found that of all these serial programs, of all the women featured, "only Tara (Maggie Siff) in *Sons of Anarchy,* who begins the series as an ex-girlfriend, then becomes girlfriend, fiancée, and wife, explicitly pursues a career; and with the exception of Tara, all of the women [on these other programs] are the primary caretakers of their children" (Lotz 72). This is all the more interesting in light of the highly dominant theories of how gender is visualized. Mulvey has argued women in cinema are subordinated through cinematic devices to concentrate on their bodies. *Sons of Anarchy* assuredly has those elements.

Women's bodies are often displayed for pleasure. But in many instances Sutter also avoids leering on women's bodies. The focus is also on women exercising authority in their own space. A major qualification is that female toughness must not come at the expense of a male's masculinity.

Hence although Tara is portrayed as a pretty young wife, she doesn't have a supermodel physique. Similarly, although Gemma is portrayed as sexually attractive, she is far older than most alluring women presented on television. The focus is usually on women in their twenties and thirties, not forties and fifties. In fact, the show

> does a commendable job of avoiding the "virgin–whore" dichotomy that has shaped many of our ideas about femininity and motherhood. Gemma is a vivacious woman who desires sex.... Other mothers on the show are also depicted as sexual creatures. Opie's girlfriend and eventual second wife, Lyla, is one of the stars of a porn production company with which SAMCRO becomes affiliated. She has a son of her own and is compassionate in her role as stepmother to Opie's children [Kolb 180].

Yet this allowance for women with agency has to be qualified because Gemma and Tara are presented not simply as white but purely white. Although SAMCRO is not racist in and of itself, it does rely upon racist attitudes and norms. Racism is narrowly justified because a lack of toughness shows one is willing to betray SAMCRO.

## *Race and Gender as Performances*

Race is no less contested a term than gender. However, there is a consensus that race, like gender, is mainly ideology. Bonilla-Silva disagrees and insists race has an independent dynamic. But even Bonilla-Silva agrees that race has a component of gender and class attached.

Sorting through the particulars of both gender and race would require an essay unto itself. Complexities aside, a racial identity can be said to imply a "a series of constraints on the kinds of roles an individual is allowed to play [and] is similar to sex and rank, in that it constrains the incumbent in all his activities" (Bonilla-Silva 473). A racial identity as such is, however, neutral. An Italian man might by his identity consider himself culturally closer to Latin culture than, say, Greek culture. No racism is implied.

A racist identity, however, holds that a member of a given race must and should enact a certain role. On this understanding, *Sons of Anarchy* does indeed not merely document racist beliefs but sometimes justifies them. Over and over again, whites are shown to obey a certain minimal decency that non-whites violate repeatedly. They tend to honor their promises. They stay faithful to their wives and avoid seeking charity unless absolutely necessary. They rarely betray close friends and relatives.

In contrast, African Americans and Latinos in the show almost always violate these cultural codes and show themselves to be animalistic and inhumane. Their sexual desires tend to be more extreme and less structured. They are quicker to turn on one another and seek aid even when they can help themselves. Hence many classic racist tropes do appear repeatedly in the series as Bonvilla-Silva would predict.

At the risk of simplification, the show seems to deploy a three-tiered approach to race. Whites occupy the highest level, as one would expect. But surprisingly, though African Americans and Latinos are often depicted negatively, they occupy a middling position. In sharp contrast, Asians, using the term broadly and narrowly, seem to have no place in or out of Charming. As violent and angry as the black characters and Latin characters are, at least they have discernible sexual identities and sometimes families. Overwhelmingly, the only Asians shown are men, and these men seem to have no real identity at all.

This leads to a final and ironic way class mediates sex and race in the series. The Asian men in one pivotal episode have to pay porn stars to sexually entertain them. The implication is clear. White, black, and Latin men routinely pay for sex in the series. However, Asian men must do so. They have no choice because they are unable to sexually attract women through their own efforts.

In contrast, Jax has the problem of too many women vying for his attention. Thus while some non-white races can potentially seduce white women as well as women of other races through their masculinity, Asian men, in particular, exist only as criminals or sexual perverts in the world of SAMCRO.

As Cox and DeCarvalho note, that toughness is valorized in SAMCRO as a key value (825–26). As astute as this observation is, it risks missing a key component as to why the series has succeeded: mythology. The setting as well as characters are mythic constructs explicitly based on Shakespeare's *Hamlet* (Donahue). Lotz notes *Sons of Anarchy*

> is set in a rural California town named Charming—an ironic moniker given its occurrences of drug and weapon trade, molestation, and white supremacy. Here, location in a small town functions importantly in the narrative, as the more patriarchal masculinity hegemonic within the motorcycle club derives its power from being outside of urban and industrialized areas in which education is more likely to secure the greatest accumulation of capital [Lotz 78].

In short, white capitalists, far from having the most racial and/or economic power, turn out to have only relative power in the series. The men of SAMCRO are proud of being "white trash." This is hard to explain using Bonilla-Silva's structural theory. Instead, the show repeatedly shows men who are tough if poor in a positive light (Cox and DeCarvalho). Even if Asian men or rich white men possess more wealth, this is often considered irrelevant and has no affect on the morale of the men in SAMCRO.

If men in SAMCRO are racist, they maintain such racism for reasons that aren't primarily economic. Only Clay uses racism habitually to enrich himself. Yet even with Clay, racism is used tactically. He has no systemic views about race positively or negatively. Moreover, the series features a black biker gang called the Grim Bastards, making it problematic to label the series as racist without qualification.

For instance, Robert "Bobby" Munson is identified through symbols large ("a prominent Chai necklace") and small (his perennial big beard). When SAMCRO takes over a porn business, Cara Cara, he is made an accountant. This would play into stereotypes regarding Jews and money, but Bobby's attitude is ironic (Abrams). Although we learn that Bobby's father was an accountant for the mob in Reno, Nevada, he admits to not being very good with numbers.

It would appear that sexism is more important a value to the men of SAMCRO than racism. But as we shall see toughness is crucial to mediating how a standard of masculinity is defined by whiteness. A man must be both tough but also be culturally "white" to be sympathetic.

The only non-racial norm the various gangs agree on is anti-homosexuality. It is striking how there are virtually no homosexuals on the series. Only in very rare instances are homosexuals ever depicted. "Although probably already assumed, it is worth explicitly noting that none of the characters is gay.... [I]n the male-centered serials, gay identity is 'too much' for this already overwrought negotiation of patriarchal masculinity to acknowledge.... [T]here is seemingly no room for homosexuality to enter into these men's negotiation of self" (Lotz 76). Lotz's statements in general are correct. But, again, *Sons of Anarchy* is unique even here. There is one exception to this non-gay rule.

The series for many episodes depicts a female lesbian, Agent Stahl, who is hunting the Sons down. Given the sympathy given to other tough women, this framing of Stahl as habitually evil and untrustworthy is hard to understand except with regard to her gender. But, again, she can't be demonized simply for being a woman—after all, Stahl freely victimizes women, too.

It seems we are left with the conclusion that lesbianism is a mortal sin on the series. But the level of sexism goes further because Sutter often portrays lesbianism in sex scenes occurring at Cara Cara. But this is not condemned at all. Hence lesbianism is permissible but insofar as men can safely control female desire. Female desire that is unregulated is looked down upon. In fact, the pornographic actresses depicted do sometimes suffer greatly for their link to pornography but not to engaging in lesbian sex. Presumably, lesbian sexuality, as long as it serves male needs and aims, is fine. Essentially, female desire, overall, must serve male needs.

This is made explicit in one episode, when Jax forces Gemma to have sex with Clay in order to gain access to his secrets. "I want you to be with him [Clay]. Sleep with him.... The dirty secrets will start to flow" ("Andare Pescare") if she gives into Clay's sexual desires. This is all the more astonishing given that Jax is Gemma's son. But having betrayed his trust, Gemma can no longer count on being considered a reliable person. Ergo, although racial identity gives whites in Charming, overall, many privileges, violating certain gender norms means those privileges can be lost.

## Jax versus Juice

To substantiate the thesis, let us look at how two non-white characters are depicted and contrast them to Jax. Of all the non-white characters, Juice and Alvarez, both Hispanic, are the most atypical in the series. While Alvarez is defined by his Latin background, Juice's commitment to his identity is much less intense. Asked if he knows Spanish, Juice replies mockingly: "I'm a Puerto Rican from Queens! I speak better Yiddish!" ("A Mother's Work"). The line is comical but has a deeper meaning when noted in connection with Bobby's Jewishness.

Although the show alludes to non-white characters having families and relatives, only a handful of non-white are actually visualized with their sons and daughters, and notably this only occurs with the Hispanic characters. The only time that non-whites interact with SAMCRO is solely for business purposes. Socially, they seemingly have no common ground.

Describing Jax, Sutter confessed that to him: "He's more a Christopher ... than he is a Tony," referencing *The Sopranos* (Lotz 108). The assumption being that like Christopher, Jax is only weakly committed to life as an outlaw. Jax only reluctantly uses violence, but as he tells the audience in voiceover. "If you're a man with convictions, violence is inevitable."

In contrast, African American gangsters like Leroy, or Alvarez as head of the Mayans, seem born to be criminals. They are also more emotive and childish than Jax. Whereas Jax tries to balance his need to revenge in dealing with the Mayans, Alvarez is much quicker to hold a grudge. The blacks and Latinos also engage in behavior that would seem out-of-bounds for Jax. In one episode, Alvarez reluctantly allows a family member to die to bring about a truce. Jax of course would never allow such a thing and would sacrifice himself before crossing such a line.

Ironically, this racial hierarchy is reflected not in the whites' racism of blacks (though this does periodically flare up) but how racist blacks and Latinos are. SAMCRO allows no black members but it has Juice, a Puerto Rican. In contrast, Laroy and the One-Niners have no white members. The Mayans similarly follow a strong policy of racial exclusion. No doubt Sutter loads the dice of how we are to see SAMCRO.

Nevertheless, Sutter is not entirely trying to avoid the issue of how racism does enter SAMCRO. A lengthy subplot involves Juice hiding his racial identity. Being Puerto Rican, Juice can be in the club. But federal agents discover his father is actually black, and this is a violation of club policy. More interesting, however, is Juice's reaction and how this is judged in light of SAMCRO's commitment to masculinity.

Juice fears his biracial identity will have him kicked out of the club. Juice, initially, cooperates with the authorities to hide his identity and engages in a series of increasingly erratic moves—taking excessive drugs, killing a fellow member, stealing coke, and so on. More interesting is Juice's emotive reaction. He cries—and quite often—seeing no solution to this dilemma.

What makes this interesting is that Jax is also shown crying as well. However, there is a vital difference. When Jax cries it is because he usually confronts a life-and-death crisis. He also cries for his children—tellingly, Juice has no sons or daughters, but Alvarez does.

Moreover, Jax usually survives the crisis and is stronger for it. Juice, however, is unable to mentally cope with the pressures he is under and tries to kill himself. Such an act makes him unacceptably womanly to SAMCRO. As Jax tells Chibs: "Sons don't kill themselves. Club's gonna vote him out. No one is going to trust him."

The controversial Juice storyline has occasioned much comment. Ironically, one African American writer congratulated Sutter for being so honest about the racism in biker culture. After all, one unambiguous lesson from this story is precisely that "racism ... isn't just hooded white supremacists." Chibs in not challenging the club's racist exclusion hurts Juice.

> In his moment of need, Juice doesn't hear support. But neither Chibs does actively defend racism.... For some people, Chibs' position may have been unclear—how can he allow racism to continue, but still care about Juice?... Chibs is careful with the language. After Juice's confession, he assures him things will be alright—not because that rule was wrong and it was racist ... but because Juice's birth certificate says "Latino" [Peterson].

Peterson's criticism is sharp. Yet she may be ignoring the obvious generic pulp atmosphere of the series. Nevertheless, Sutter is touching upon a real issue. As Sutter wrote in his own blog post, though seemingly fantastic, the no-black rule

> is a racial reality in outlaw motorcycle clubs. We've touched on the issue lightly over the first three seasons of SOA. The fact is that most of the bigger MC's do not have African American members. There are black clubs and there are white (Caucasian, Latino, Asian) clubs. Most live in harmony. HA and the East Bay Dragons have been friends for decades. That relationship inspired the Grim Bastards in season 3. We delve into the delicate why's and how's of this racial bi-law later in the season, but it was one of those odd, historical barriers that I've wanted to explore. It's a throwback to a different era that is still in practice today. I can honestly say that none of the guys I know in the life are racist, yet they function within a structure that is built upon a form of segregation. To me, that's fascinating and fertile story turf. The depth and weight of this rule varies from club to club and this season we see how it's handled by the *Sons of Anarchy* [Sutter].

Sutter's defense is odd. To him, the racism of the clubs is a minor issue. He himself never experiences it. But it does exist and is legitimate grounds for aesthetic investigation.

As stated, generally, Sutter rarely lets the viewer into the internal worlds of the Mayans or One-Niners. The only time this silence is breached is with Alvarez. Simply on content alone, Alvarez is one of the few villainous characters appearing almost as much as the main characters. This distinction might be a case of narrative convenience, but looking at the text carefully one can see a clear set of marks distinguishing Alvarez.

When Piney enters a One-Niner club he is immediately questioned and stopped. His white skin means he is unwelcome. The racial barrier between the world of Oakland and Charming is sharp. And Leroy, despite his name, is not given kingly qualities. His motivation is singular.

However in the case of Alvarez, he shows many different qualities. Not all of these are positive qualities. He is willing to deal with Nazis. He is sometimes excessive in his revenge. He is also quick to anger as Leroy, a black gangster, is and often impulsive. But many episodes also show Alvarez has many sides to him and is willing to show mercy and sympathy. In one critical episode, the Sons, desperate because Tara has been kidnapped, track Alvarez to his home.

As with many scenes, Sutter is engaging the audience at various levels. It is an unwritten rule that families (in normal cases) aren't to be touched and lie outside the scope of male violence. Alvarez, simply upon seeing the Sons in his domestic home, assumes the worst and thinks they mean to kill him. The scene is played for laughs as much as thrills because one of the kidnapper's demands is that SAMCRO kill Alvarez. Given the bloody past history between SAMCRO and the Mayans this seems like a request that might be honored.

The Sons, however, only ask that Alvarez play dead. Not surprisingly, Alvarez responds that (for him) as head of the Mayans playing dead is almost as bad as being dead. Either status challenges his masculinity. The Sons' presence alone in his back yard is considered by him to be intolerable. But once the Sons explain themselves, Alvarez reluctantly agrees. He will play dead for, at least, a day since Tara, who is an outsider to the Mayan-SAMCRO war, is in danger.

Following the gendered logic, Alvarez is never shown being radically humiliated. Juice, however, because he has been judged unmanly by Jax, opens himself to be degraded. In one particular graphic sequence, he is raped. The rapists are, tellingly, Asian. The implication is fairly obvious. Whatever their deep differences, Jax, like Alvarez, is a man's man and would never try and take his own life. On this basis, Alvarez is closer to SAMCRO than Juice is, whatever his official status.

No doubt Sutter intends that the viewer be torn by Jax's actions. Part of the audience, irrespective of race, will see this as merely (albeit excessive) heroism on Jax's part when he kills and hurts others. But, structurally, a contradiction appears. When other members of SAMCRO act in such a revenge-filled manner, they pay a heavy price for this rashness. This includes Alvarez. He is physically hurt and suffers emotionally and economically, as does Clay. But unlike Clay, who loses the complete respect and loyalty of his brothers, Alvarez keeps his status as head of the Mayans. But, once more, the show is careful to make Alvarez's actions understandable but not commendable in the same way Jax's actions are.

The racism is even more obvious in that while white women (though rarely) are given opportunities for heroism, Latin and African American women (almost always) are consigned to either being maids, prostitutes, or hapless victims. Indeed the racism is so extreme that Asian women almost never appear in the show—even as sexual objects. Only a handful of Asian women ever appear at all on *Sons of Anarchy*.

In contrast, Asian men exist to be contrasted extremely with the white men of SAMCRO. When two Iranians pornographers run afoul SAMCRO it is noteworthy that the "Persians," as they are called, aren't just making porn but torture porn. Even at the level of pornography, then, Jax and his crew are simply on another plane of existence. In contrast, those steeped in a foreign (non–American) culture are capable of any perversity.

Once more, a scene involving Alvarez proves this in a bloody manner. Linked to the Juice story, some coke goes missing. Alvarez promises that whoever stole the coke, the "bitch" is dead. Who also adds, tellingly, whoever the thief is—a member of SAMCRO or a Mayan—is irrelevant. What is interesting is what doesn't happen. Earlier episodes set up Alvarez as a hothead. His usual tactic is simply attack. But he is oddly calm during this episode.

It would appear that Hispanic characters, though confined to a narrow space of being violent, are nevertheless allowed to be more thoughtful and trusting. Their sexuality is also viewed more positively because it is family-oriented and less perverse than Asian sexuality or rapacious than black sexuality.

While Charming is essentially a white town, Latinos are allowed marginally more agency than black characters. Sutter makes major exceptions both with friendly Latinos like Juice as well as even enemies like Alvarez. No doubt this is an accurate reflection of white American attitudes. All else equal, they would avoid both blacks and Latinos. But forced to choose between the two, the Latino is considered a lesser evil, and the show follows this attitude consistently.

## Conclusion

Several conclusions can, hopefully, be reached. Although the argument about hegemonic masculinity by Cox and DeCarvalho is strong, it needs qualification. Cox and DeCarvalho are correct insofar as violence and toughness are key ingredients in the way masculinity is framed in *Sons of Anarchy*. But the masculine sexism isn't as exclusive as they portray.

One reason Jax is unable to leave SAMCRO is precisely due to the lack of a formal education. As Lotz notes:

> Tara could support them if Jax left the club.... [But as] Jax explains, "I don't have any skills Tara. I'm an okay mechanic with a GED. The only thing I ever did well was outlaw. I just need to make some bank; set myself up with something." Though she replies, "I can go anywhere, I make good money," Jax shakes his head, dismissing this idea with ... "I'm not going to live off my wife. I can't" [Lotz 109].

Like race and class, hierarchies place women in different spheres. Jax assumes he should be able to take care of Tara. Doing this is what helps define him not just as a man but, specifically, a white man. He is unwilling to accept help from Tara because it might give her control.

But added to this is a certain cynical (and romantic) attitude toward femininity. A man should provide for his woman because this is his (honorable) duty as a father and husband. But underneath this surface is the obvious need for a man to remain in control and not have his masculinity threatened.

Hence within certain boundaries, other non-white races and even non-heterosexual sexual orientations are permissible. A major exception are Asian males, they are unable to ever be on par with whites or Hispanics. Similarly, lesbians can appear and socialize with the club members as long as they act a certain way. As Donaldson rightly notes: "A fundamental element of hegemonic masculinity ... is that women exist as potential sexual objects for men while men are negated as sexual objects for men" (Cox and DeCarvalho 832). Sexual freedom like emotional freedom is available only to certain men who have earned it.

Hence Jews and Latinos may enter SAMCRO but only as long as they are able to uphold a certain set of norms regarding toughness. Hispanics are allowed to be more human and decent because they are seen as culturally closer to the standard of white male manhood. White women can also approach this standard of masculinity but only within a certain set of rigid guidelines. In sharp contrast, only a handful of African American males are allowed to be "white" and tough. But Hispanics are given slightly more leeway and as a rule their entry into SAMCRO arouses little suspicion.

In conclusion, *Sons of Anarchy* does seek to try to uphold a certain kind of hegemonic masculinity. But this masculinity allows for a certain amount of flexibility. Depending on one's perspective, this can be read positively or negatively. On the positive side, the hegemonic masculinity of the past is not as racist as it once was. Latino males, and to a lesser extent African American men, can enter this patriarchy.

But certain minorities such as gay men or Asian men continue to be denied access. This racial tolerance is allowed only due to a fundamental and unyielding commitment to sexism and those capable of being tough in a manly, violent way. This sexism may be relatively less anxious and crisis-ridden than its previous incarnations, but it remains highly sexist nonetheless and willing to guard itself in the drapery of a highly tough and violent form of manhood.

## Works Cited

Abrams, Nathan. "Outlaw Jews," *Jewish Quarterly*, 12 Feb. 2014. http://jewishquarterly.org/2014/12/surprising-jews-sons-anarchy/. Web. 12 May 2017.
Bonilla-Silva, Eduardo. "Rethinking Racism: Toward a Structural Interpretation." *American Sociological Review* 62.3 (1997): 465–80. Print.
Cox, Nicole B., and Lauren J. DeCarvalho. "'Ride Free or Die' Trying: Hypermasculinity on FX's *Sons of Anarchy*." *The Journal of Popular Culture* 49.4 (2016): 818–38. Print.
Dunn, George A., and Jason Eberl eds. *Sons of Anarchy and Philosophy: Brains Before Bullets*. New York: Wiley-Blackwell, 2013. Print.
Donahue, Anne. "*Sons of Anarchy*: Shakespeare on Motorcycle Wheels." *The Guardian*, 11 Dec. 2014. https://www.theguardian.com/tv-and-radio/tvandradioblog/2014/dec/10/sons-of-anarchy-shakespeare-on-wheels. Web. 9 July 2017.
Gabbard, Krin. *Black Magic: White Hollywood and African American Culture*. New Brunswick: Rutgers University Press, 2004. Print.
Kolb, Leigh. "Mothers of Anarchy: Power, Control, and Care in the Feminine Sphere." In *Sons of Anarchy and Philosophy: Brains Before Bullets*. Eds. George A. Dunn and Jason T. Eberl. Malden, MA: Wiley-Blackwell, 2013. 175–86. Print.
Lotz, Amanda D. *Cable Guys: Television and Masculinities in the 21st Century*. New York: New York University Press, 2014. Print.
Mulvey, Laura. *Visual and Other Pleasures*. Bloomington: Indiana University Press, 1989. Print.
O'Connell, Michael. "TV Ratings: More Records for 'Sons of Anarchy' in Season 6 Premiere." *Hollywood Reporter*, 11 Sept. 2013. http://www.hollywoodreporter.com/live-feed/tv-ratings-more-records-sons-627448. Web. 9 July 2017.
Peterson, Letoya. "How *Sons of Anarchy* Got Racism Right." Facebookwww, 11 Nov. 2011. https://www.facebook.com/notes/racialicious-race-identity-and-pop-culture-in-a-colorstruck-world/how-sons-of-anarchy-got-racism-right/10150407649087287/. Web. 12 May 2017.
Rosenberg, Alyssa. "*Sons of Anarchy* Is a Show About Biker Dudes. And Feminism." *Slate*, 20 Sept. 2012. http://www.slate.com/blogs/xx_factor/2012/09/20/sons_of_anarchy_the_show_about_biker_dudes_is_also_about_feminism_.html. Web. 12 May 2017.
Serra, Bruno de Brito. "Chaos and Order. Anarchy in the MC." In *Sons of Anarchy and Philosophy: Brains Before Bullets*. Eds. George A. Dunn and Jason T. Eberl. Malden, MA: Wiley-Blackwell, 2013. 73–84. Print.
Shimpach, Shawn. *Television in Transition: The Life and Afterlife of the Narrative Action Hero*. New York: John Wiley & Sons, 2010. Print.
Sutter, Kurt. "Black and White of the MCs." 24 Sept. 2011. http://sutterink.blogspot.com/2011/09/black-and-white-of-mcs.html. Web. 12 May 2017.

# The Sins of the Father(s)
## *Masculine Identity as Poisoned Inheritance*

### JAMIE L. BRUMMER

> We are in a "liminal" moment in our cultural history. We are in the process of giving up a myth/ideology that no longer helps us see our way through the modern world, but lack a comparably authoritative system of beliefs to replace what we have lost.... Our choice is not between myth and a world without myth, but between productive revisions of myth—which open the system and permit it to adjust its beliefs (and the fictions that carry them) to changing realities—and the rigid defense of existing systems, the refusal to change, which binds us to dead or destructive patterns of action and belief that are out of phase with social and environmental reality.
> —Richard Slotkin, *Gunfighter Nation*, 654–55

When the smoke clears, the engines quiet, and the screams fade to silence, it becomes apparent that Kurt Sutter's televised drama *Sons of Anarchy* has more up its grease- (and blood-) stained sleeves than meets the eye. Masquerading as an adrenaline-fueled saga of outlaw bikers, drug and gun running gangs, crooked police officers, and shady businessmen and politicians, the series in fact offers a scathing critique of many of America's most iconic constructions of masculinity through the traumatic evolution of its broken hero, Jackson Teller. Paying homage to source material ranging from Shakespeare's *Hamlet* to America's mythic frontier figures, *Sons of Anarchy* forces its characters and its viewers alike to confront cultural assumptions related to masculine identity that seem increasingly at odds with contemporary experience.

The peril and promise of American masculinity pervades the series even as Sutter expertly distills these tensions into the fraught relationships between the show's protagonist Jackson (Jax) Teller and the father figures in his life: the ghost of John Teller, Jax's biological father and one of the founders (the First Nine) of the Sons of Anarchy Motorcycle Club, Redwood Original (SAMCRO); the machinations of Clay Morrow, Jax's stepfather, who has usurped his authority and who models a type of masculinity Jax inherently mistrusts; and the problematic mentorship offered by Nero Padilla who embodies a more complex gendered identity which could still either liberate Jax or destroy him. In the shadow of each of these powerful men is Jax (himself a young father when, in the series pilot, his son Abel is born prematurely) desperately trying to construct his own masculine identity from the personal and cultural shards and trappings he has inherited. Among these powerful men and many others *Sons of Anarchy* remains Jax's story—the story of a man struggling to define himself as a son, a father, a husband, a leader. It is the story of a man struggling to come to grips with a nearly addictive construction of mythic masculinity that empowers him even as it threatens to destroy him and all that he loves. And it is in this sense that Jax's hyperbolically bloody story transcends the town of Charming and becomes a parable of sorts for countless men in 21st-century America who share his looming suspicion that their masculine identity may have already rendered them extinct.

Drawing on the work of scholars within the field of Masculinity Studies such as Michael Kimmel and E. Anthony Rotundo as well as prominent voices from Second-Wave Feminism such as Judith Butler (with a dash of Freud for good measure), this essay will explore Jax's tragic struggle to stake claim to his own identity as he confronts past, present, and future father-figures who, each in his own way, represent the cultural inertia of increasingly archaic conceptions of masculinity which is Jax's true inheritance. Jax Teller, his "brothers" in SAMCRO, all the "old ladies," all the young children, their myriad enemies and meager friends pivot from conflict to conflict with each new episode. The amplified crises these sons (and daughters) confront are the magnified manifestations of a less obvious but equally explosive "crisis" in masculinity that lurks beneath the surface of 21st-century America. As Slotkin presciently noted nearly a quarter century ago, America and American men in particular have inherited a series of overtly masculine narratives which are increasingly "out of phase" with contemporary cultural and economic realities. The structuralist language Slotkin used which relied so heavily on myth and archetype has certainly evolved in the intervening years, but his core insight regarding the constitutive power of narrative is perhaps more relevant than ever. Stories define us, and Jackson Teller knows he should distrust the narratives which seek to define him; he instinctively senses the siren song hidden beneath their surface allure. *Sons of Anarchy* dramatizes his struggle to find or create a new narrative, a new story of manhood that might allow him to find a place in 21st-century America.

## *A Voice from Beyond the Grave*

> I realized that in my downward spiral of hopelessness I was actually falling into a huge hole created by my absence of basic human graces. The most obvious was forgiveness. If I was wronged by anyone, in or out of the club, I had to be compensated by money or blood. There was no turning the other cheek. When relationships become a ledger of profit and loss, you have no friends, no loved ones, just pluses and minuses. You are absolutely alone.
> —*The Life and Death of Sam Crow: How the Sons of Anarchy Lost Their Way*

When *Sons of Anarchy* opens, Jax Teller's world is crumbling around him: his club's financial solvency has taken a direct hit when a warehouse they use to store guns is destroyed by a rival gang; Jax's pregnant ex-wife is battling an addiction to methamphetamine and nearly dies giving birth to their severely premature son Abel; Clay Morrow, Jax's stepfather and leader of SAMCRO, views his stepson's rise within the club as a clear-and-present danger. And Jax is haunted by a ghost.

In the series pilot Jax discovers a manuscript written by his deceased father, John Teller (J.T.), a manuscript which does more to threaten Jax's masculine identity than any of the physical violence and trauma he experiences during the entire series. From beyond the grave, J.T.'s words set in motion a narrative which he is powerless to stop and which his son cannot ignore. With each turn of the page, J.T's words slowly become Jax's bible. The child is father of the man.

John Teller's ghost gives voice to a construction of masculinity that both fascinates and terrifies Jackson: a masculinity that can be verbal, learned, emotionally expressive, introspective, and relational (if only in death). These traits are in many ways polar opposite to the model of masculinity Jax has grown up with in his father's absence. Members of SAMCRO are the contemporary embodiments of the laconic, emotionally repressed, and intellectually stunted frontier heroes which have dominated the American cultural and literary landscape almost since its inception. Without too much hyperbole, American literature can be said to be founded on stories of men running away from the feminizing effects of artifice and civilization toward a more natural, manly (and brutal) wilderness.[1] From Cooper's Leatherstocking, to

Filson's Nathaniel Boone, to Davy Crockett, to Melville's Ahab and Starbuck, to Twain's Huckleberry Finn—America's literary boys and men "ran away to the frontier, to the West, to start over, to make their fortunes and thus to remake themselves, to escape the civilizing constraints of domestic life represented by the Victorian woman" (Kimmel 32). In *Sons of Anarchy*, simply replace the cowboy with the biker, the horse with the motorcycle, Indians with Mexicans or African Americans or whichever marginalized group currently represents the Other and the substitution is nearly seamless. The leather chaps may have given way to leather cuts, but the manhood they adorn has remained essentially unchanged since the country's founding.

For years Jax was content to wear the traditional costume of American masculinity and dutifully play his part. Patching into SAMCRO was his life's goal. His father's manuscript changed everything. The manuscript forced Jax to contend with a construction of masculinity that challenged not only his, but America's preconceptions of what it means to be a real man. Etymologically, the word teller suggests not only one who keeps accounts as gestured toward in the epigraph above, but also one who narrates or announces. J.T.'s manuscript initiates Jax into a new story, a new narrative of masculinity, a narrative from the grave that carries with it the ultimate paternal authority. As a 21st-century mythic hero, Jax can outwit and outfight almost any living man. Indeed the series is littered with examples of larger-than-life foes brought down by Jax's brain and brawn: Ethan Zobelle and the League of American Nationalists, Agent Stahl and the ATF, Damon Pope and the corporatization of west-coast drug trafficking to name a few. Jax proves himself capable of slaying all these dragons, but the voice of his father whispering in his ear is a force which he can neither defeat nor escape. In *The Life and Death of Sam Crow: How the Sons of Anarchy Lost Their Way* J.T. wrote, "The true outlaw finds the balance between the passion in his heart and the reason in his mind. His solution is always an equal mix of might and right." Jax soon comes to realize that achieving a perfect, "equal mix of might and right" is virtually impossible, an alchemical illusion that alternatively fuels his decision making and frustrates him to the point of self-destruction. Like the ghost of King Hamlet, J.T. imprints upon his son's psyche an idealized and idolized version of manhood and fatherhood which both inspires Jax and threatens to consume him. When the going gets tough, the conventional frontier hero can simply run away, head west, ride into the sunset, or in the parlance of SAMCRO, go nomad. At various points, Jax tries to do all these. The one thing he can never do, however, is escape his father's voice and his father's complex and conflicted sense of masculinity. It is easy to cave under the weight of mythic masculinity (how many times, for example, does Jax flee from the perils and promise of a conventional, domestic life with Tara) or abuse its momentum (the countless episodes of extreme violence, the casual sexual encounters, the ownership nearly every man in the series assumes over his "old lady"). Finding and sustaining a sense of balance, a sense of harmony between traditionally masculine traits (strength, action, judgment) and those considered feminine (forgiveness, emotion, reflection) requires a set of emotional, intellectual, and physical resources beyond Jax's inheritance—perhaps beyond the cultural inheritance of nearly all American men.

J.T.'s struggle to find some semblance of balance emerges in his letters. In a voice-over in season five, episode two, for example, we hear J.T. confess that "Gemma's always been stronger than me, I loved her for that. But as I lost my way she found hers. She's moved closer to Clay, grown deeply committed to the club. She's become more the woman I married and I've become less the man. The death of our love is my failing, not hers." J.T., like generations of American men before him, has been conditioned to view masculinity as a zero-sum game. Either become more manly, or become the opposite, the unthinkable ... more womanly. Though J.T.'s sense of masculinity may be more evolved than Jax's other models, it ultimately distills into the notion of the "true outlaw," a loner, a rebel, a human being whose gendered identity renders him essentially alienated: from women, from children, and even from his "brothers" in the club. This was J.T.'s experience and it is largely Jax's as well. It is *Sons of Anarchy*'s ability to explore this inheritance that renders the show and its characters so complex and allows it to speak with nuance and eloquence (even as the show's surface is dominated by ostentatious violence and profanity) on the present state of American manhood.[2]

## *Is It Good to Be King?*

If John Teller represents a more complicated, evolved, and introspective model of masculinity capable of pointing Jax toward the future, Jax's stepfather, Clay Morrow (played brilliantly by Ron Perlman), represents ideals of masculinity which can only pull him backward. His surname may evoke a new dawn, but his given name reveals his true nature. Clay is elemental, he is physical, he is old—he is the living embodiment of the past. His name (also suggestive of a claymore mine ... explosive and very lethal), his age, his arthritic hands as well as his insistence on running guns primarily because it is what SAMCRO has always done all are representative of a masculinity so firmly rooted in the past that to transplant it into new soil would be to destroy it. Both Clay and Jax understand this, of course, and it is the tension between two competing definitions of manhood that fuels their relationship.

Clay's masculinity literally stands in Jax's way. He has usurped J.T.'s place as father figure just as he has usurped Jax's place at the head of the table as club president. Clay's very existence emasculates Jax (in Clay's shadow, he remains the little prince) and places him in a classic Oedipal dynamic: Jax must either destroy Clay as part of his own emergence as a man, or be molded into yet another version of Clay. Jax's very existence, on the other hand, threatens to emasculate Clay. Jax's desire to move the club away from running guns would rob the aging Clay of his most obvious phallic avatar, an anxiety only amplified by Jax's alternative business model, which is grounded largely on the female-owned and operated porn studio, Cara Cara. This foray into more feminine territory (the porn industry being the closest thing to feminine economic empowerment the series allows) threatens Clay's masculine identity more than his inevitable stepping down as club president. Even as Clay rages against old age (one of his more humanizing moments shows him impotently trying to administer cortisone shots into his own arthritic hands), at some level he knows his days as president are numbered. To cede the club's economic engine to a female-owned and operated business, however, presents an existential crisis from which he simply cannot back down.

Both Clay and J.T. were formed in (or deformed by) the crucible of the Vietnam war.[3] But where the anti-establishment ethos of the Vietnam conflict catalyzed J.T. to create an alternative route toward manhood through which SAMCRO might be used as proving ground, the same conflict calcified antiquated notions of masculinity in Clay. R.W. Connell speaks to this in her book *Masculinities* when she writes, "defeat in Vietnam ... stirred new cults of true masculinity in the United States, from violent 'adventure' movies such as the Rambo series [or *Sons of Anarchy*], to the expansion of the gun cult and what William Gibson in a frightening recent study has called 'paramilitary culture'" (84). Clay came of age in combat, his sense of manhood is militaristic, weaponized, aggressive, and action-oriented. In season five, episode one, we see Clay, now but a shadow of his former self, stooped and nearly broken, admit to Gemma that "I'm not a complicated guy, Gem. I'm not like J.T.; I sink my teeth into a goal, I see it through. It's the ... it's the soldier in me. All I could see was the end game. All that money. The shit with Tara. Me lying to you—just part of the mission." Though his military service ended decades earlier, Clay exists in a perpetual paramilitary state. His identity requires a combatant, and his approach to running SAMCRO guarantees an endless stream of enemies: the Mayans, the white supremacist League of American Nationalists, the Niners, the Nords, the A.T.F., the Russians, the Irish. Jax, on the other hand, has never served in the military, has never fought in a conventional war, and has never desired to wear any uniform other than the colors of his MC. Where Clay's manhood needs to prove itself in constant physical combat, Jax often seeks intellectual compromise and reasoned, long-term solutions. Clay is a hammer and every conflict he faces is a nail. Jax would seek another path.

Clay's anachronistic sense of masculinity is on perfect display in his compulsion to freeze the town of Charming in time. The bulk of Clay's relationship with male non-club members (Chief Unser, Elliott Oswald, Jacob Hale, Jr.) revolves around his desire to hold progress and development at bay in Charming, thus ensuring that the town remain a safe haven, a land-out-of-time for a construction of masculinity that has long-since become extinct in modern America. Clay's often desperate machinations reveal a profound anxiety over cultural changes which have granted women and minorities increased social and economic power, advancements which accelerated in the aftermath of the Vietnam war. Clay may profess a desire to keep Charming safe, but his true agenda is to safeguard an outmoded sense of manhood from cultural changes that threaten his entire identity. As Kimmel notes:

> Since the country's founding, American men have felt a need to prove their manhood. For well over a century, it's been in the public sphere, and especially the workplace, that American men have been tested. A man may be physically strong, or not. He may be intellectually or athletically gifted, or not. But the one thing that has been non-negotiable has been that a real man provides for his family. He is a breadwinner [*Misframing* 16–17].

Clay's gendered identity, like generations of American men before him, is inescapably bound with his ability to earn, and his ability to earn rests almost entirely on running guns. Jax too struggles with the constant need to prove himself as a man, and like his stepfather associates his masculinity with his ability to provide economic security for his family. His marriage to Tara represents both a challenge and opportunity for Jax. Tara is a board-certified surgeon, a thoroughly modern woman more than capable of charting her own professional and economic destiny. Jax recognizes and respects Tara's professional accomplishments; in fact, he and the MC come to depend more and more on her skills as the series unfolds. At the same time, however, Jax's conventional notions of masculinity and gender roles are threatened by Tara's expertise and economic autonomy. In the opening episode of season four, Jax confesses to Tara that, besides outlawing, his earning potential is little more than that of an okay mechanic with a GED. As long as Jax's masculine identity is, like Clay's, defined by what he does (a set of external actions dominated by his ability to earn), what Tara can accomplish as a professional is a constant reminder of his inadequacy. The times in the series when he pushes Tara away and clumsily attempts to sabotage their relationship are motivated as much by the threat she poses to his masculinity as his ostensible desire to remove her from the culture of the MC and protect her physical safety. As long as Jax defines himself as a man according to Clay's terms, his personal relationships all suffer, not only his romantic relationship with Tara, but also the homosocial "brotherhood" he has cultivated within the MC, which in many ways is more foundational. Sally Robinson addresses the tensions American men (white men in particular) have in balancing iconic individuality with a desire for collective identity when she writes: "For white men ... the appeals of collectivism have always appeared thin: white men do not willingly fold their individual identities into a group identity except around perceived losses of power, articulated as impingements of rights. Anxiety over loss of privilege competes with a desire to forge a collective male identity around claims of victimization" (7).

Herein lie the horns of Jax's dilemma—to be a fully-fledged member of a brotherhood he has known and loved since birth he must assume a masculine identity that prohibits him from entering into a mature and truly meaningful relationship with Tara. To evolve his own understanding of masculinity and acknowledge Tara as a true equal, however (not merely his old lady), means he must challenge elemental assumptions he and his brothers hold regarding masculine and feminine roles and alienate himself from their embrace. It is this essential tension, more than feuding clubs, or beefs with law enforcement, or the constant struggle to earn that fuels Jax's tragic situation and provides the series with its most central narrative arc.

## *Sanctuary*

> That part of a man's inner self that sought expression through intimacy was that part—tender, dependent, vulnerable, warm—which suited him poorly for success at his worldly tasks in a competitive marketplace. Since rough virtues like assertive drive and contentious ambition were more fully accepted as official standards of manhood, the softer, more feminine virtues became increasingly suspect.
> —E. Anthony Rotundo, *American Manhood*, 282

Through the first four seasons of *Sons of Anarchy*, J.T. and Clay, the dominant masculine role models in Jax's life, have him completely spun around, fruitlessly mining the past for a set of outdated and broken artifacts from which he might construct his own identity. With season five Jax finally has a chance to look forward. The season's first episode introduces a new character, Nero Padilla (played by Jimmy Smits) who will become a model and mentor of masculinity that is more fully developed, more introspective, and though far from perfect, more aligned with 21st-century notions of manhood than any Jax has encountered before. Their budding relationship, fraught with its own tensions and opportunities, provides Jax his last, best hope at breaking free from the anachronistic constructions of masculinity he has inherited and the chance to evolve into the kind of man he has always dreamed of becoming, a man who can be a husband, a father, a provider, and an example to his own sons.

While it is true that Nero possesses more developed and mature masculine traits than either J.T. or Clay, it is important to note that he is not the embodiment of any progressive or feminist ideal of contemporary manhood. We first see his character in the season five opener having sex with Gemma in the same room where the bodies of two naked women lay passed out. Nero runs an "escort service" called Diosa (the goddess) and though he treats "his girls" with more respect and allows them more autonomy than someone like Georgie Caruso (a porn director played by Tom Arnold) and though he prefers the term "companionator" to pimp, ultimately he still traffics in women's bodies. Nero has a violent history with a gang he formed called the Byz Lats, he has served an extended prison sentence, and he retains the ability to act with extreme violence (including committing at least four murders during the three seasons that he appears in the series). Nero's masculinity represents a big step forward when compared to J.T. and Clay, but that is as much a function of their regressive state as any extreme progressivity on Nero's part. Like his Roman namesake, Nero is a fascinating combination of character traits, some laudable, some profoundly disturbing.

Still, Nero is different. Calm, even humble, he approaches conflicts and opportunities with a circumspection and spirit of compromise that immediately distinguishes him from the other strong men in Jax's life. Even his manner of dress and transportation differentiates him from his predecessors. Where J.T. and Clay would have seemed naked without the leather-and-chains costume of their club or apart from their Harleys, Nero wears cardigan sweaters (cardigans!). He wears pleated trousers and loafers. He drives a car instead of a motorcycle. Despite his checkered past and complicated present, Nero is trying to adjust to a new set of rules governing business and gender and the way he carries himself is an outward sign of his desire for something new.

Without ascending too high into the rarified air of gender theory and the heady abstractions of third-wave feminism, to better position Nero's approach to masculinity we might nevertheless benefit from a quick glance at Judith Butler's influential 1990 book *Gender Trouble: Feminism and the Subversion of Identity*. Building upon and interrogating the work of continental scholars such as Irigaray, Beauvoir, and Foucault, Butler paints a picture of gender as far more fluid, improvisational, and performative than previously acknowledged. She writes:

> In this sense, gender is not a noun, but neither is it a set of free-floating attributes, for we have seen that the substantive effect of gender is performatively produced and compelled by the regulatory practices of gender coherence. Hence, within the inherited discourse of the metaphysics of substance, gender proves to be performative— that is, constituting the identity it is purported to be. In this sense, gender is always a doing, though not a doing by a subject who might be said to preexist the deed [34].

While J.T. and Clay "do" gender largely in an essentialist and normative manner rooted in the mythic frontier heroes of America's earliest cultural awareness, Nero more openly experiments with masculinity in ways more aligned with Butler's definition. As Nero (and Jax) attempt to navigate a set of inherited and "regulatory practices of gender coherence," they find themselves in a fraught terrain where their actions both reflect pre-existing cultural norms and have the potential to constitute a new identity. Their choice, unfortunately, all-too-easily reduces to an untenable binary: either observe a set of behaviors which cohere and calcify into dated assumptions regarding masculinity (like Clay), or strike out to claim new territory for what it means to be a man (like J.T., like Nero, like Jax) and risk ostracization or even destruction.

Jax quickly intuits that Nero represents a construction of masculinity capable of sustaining itself, and perhaps a family as well, not merely from one conflict to the next, but for the long run. J.T.'s masculine vision was so clouded by self-doubt and so endangered by both men and women who considered even the faintest hint of transgressive masculinity a threat that it was incapable of saving him. Clay's masculinity, too, was doomed to fail. Like an alpha lion constantly fighting to stay in power, it was inevitable that Clay's hold on the club would, like his anachronistic sense of manhood, crumble around him. Nero's gendered identity is different—far from perfect, but closer to what Kimmel call

> a democratic manhood ... a manhood of responsibility, tested, and finally proved, in the daily acts that give our lives meaning. It is an expansive manhood, capable of embracing different groups of men, whether by race, class, ethnicity, or sexuality.... It is an egalitarian manhood, accepting and even embracing the equality of women in our lives, and preparing our children for the lives they will surely live of greater gender and sexual equality [*Manhood* 297].

The last sentence may be a bit of a stretch in Nero's case, but much of Kimmel's ideal fits Nero as comfortably as one of his sweaters. More than anything else—more than money, more than sex, more than power—Nero wants some measure of domestic peace and happiness. In their own way, J.T., Clay, and Jax want precisely the same thing. But their conception of masculinity (a conception not so different from that which America's frontier heroes mythologized in the 17th and 18th centuries) creates in them a profound anxiety regarding what domesticity might cost them. Nero, on the other hand, sees the possibility of a conventional domestic existence as more than worth any price it might cost him in terms of how the culture views his manhood.

It is precisely this potential Nero possesses, to define his masculinity in a way that includes domestic relationships, even depends upon them, that proves such a powerful lure for Jax. Jax, in his own inchoate fashion, desires a meaningful domestic life, but every masculine role model he has ever known has been terrified that domesticity required emasculation. Nero may be navigating a different course, and Nero's mentorship of Jax has far more to do with gender identity in the uncharted waters of the 21st century than it does with running an MC, or staying one step ahead of the law, or maintaining street cred. In their first real conversation, Nero tells Jax that while doing time in Chino he "gave up the needle, picked up some books. Saw the bigger picture." This bigger picture is then perfectly framed in a scene where Nero goes to visit his son Lucius, who suffers from spina bifida. The composition of this scene is critical: Jax goes to buy a newspaper (to gain information about what is real, what is true) and instead witnesses Nero with his son. The sanctuary Nero provides Jax is ultimately far more than a haven from the police; it is the chance to witness first-hand a man trying to extricate himself from the outdated masculine models of the past and create an identity where strength, humility, tenderness, toughness, passion and compassion are not mutually exclusive. Both Jax and Nero understand the "pecados del padre," the sins of the father, and both are intent on carving out a future for their boys that allows them the chance to be a different kind of man. J.T. died before he could pass on his own hard-earned lessons to Jax, all he can do is whisper from the grave. Clay is childless and defined by his own self-interest more than a desire to protect others. But Nero has seen more than just a world of hypermasculinity, of gangs, of incarceration; he also knows a world of paternal tenderness and a world where women can be partners (his half-sister Carla runs Diosa with him). As stated earlier, Nero is by no means the embodiment of feminist ideals when it comes to 21st-century manhood. He is scarred in more ways than one. But he's light years ahead of any other man who has influenced Jax. Jax senses this, which is why he entrusts Wendy and his sons to Nero. American manhood, at least as Jax has come to know it, is the quintessential dead end. Nero offers an alternative masculinity and a chance for Jax's sons to grow up with a different story of what it means to be a man.

## *The Bad Guys Lose*

In the closing episode of *Sons of Anarchy*, when Jax sets out on his final ride, it is J.T.'s restored bike that carries him away from his club, away from his family, away from Charming and westward toward the setting sun where America's masculine heroes always end up.[4] After everything he has been through, all he has gained and more importantly all he has lost, Jax has made his choice. Climbing atop J.T.'s classic Harley, Jax both literally and figuratively assumes his place within a lineage of tragic figures who would rather face certain death than deal with the existential threat to their masculine identity represented by civilization, by fatherhood, by domesticity. Contrast Jax's exit with Nero's. When we last see Nero he is not alone but in the company of a woman, Jax's ex-wife Wendy, and the two boys Abel and Thomas. They are in a Volvo SUV (the closest equivalent to a minivan *Sons of Anarchy* will allow) filled with infant car seats, with coloring books, with snacks for the trip. It's not Ozzie and Harriet, but it is a family and Nero, Wendy, and the boys are on their way to Norco to join his son Lucius and more kin.

Jax, on the other hand, has severed all ties: to the District Attorney,[5] to his club, to his sons, to his mother, to Tara at her grave, and finally to the ghost of J.T. himself when he visits the site of his death along the highway. His final words to his father are also his ultimate statement on himself as a man: "A good father and a good outlaw can't saddle inside the same man. I'm sorry, J.T. It was too late for me. I was already inside it.... It's not too late for my boys.... I know who you are now.... I love you, Dad." None of the men Jax took for role models could sustain their masculine identity and sustain a family as well. J.T.'s marriage crumbled before he abandoned his family and fled to Ireland. Clay's marriage was childless and ended in blood. The rest of the MC—Bobby, Opie, Chibs, Juice, Tig,[6] Happy—none of them could achieve what they most wanted, because what they most wanted was also their greatest fear. Here is the crux of the American man's dilemma, and here just below the hypermasculine surface of *Sons of Anarchy* is the series' most scathing critique: the stories American men love the most—stories of frontier heroes, of cowboys, of renegade loners and biker outlaws—are the same stories that doom this construction of masculinity. *Sons of Anarchy* shattered ratings records for the cable channel FX (just as *Breaking Bad*, another saga of the hypermasculine did for AMC). We may live in an ever more urbanized, technological, and egalitarian century, but the stories (the myths, as Slotkin would say) that continue to speak most forcefully to American men remain those from our past. The costumes have changed, the language is more charged, and the bloodshed is more graphic, but the story remains the same. American men are stuck in that liminal moment Slotkin spoke of, they always have been. Caught between the narrative inertia of the past and a present that doesn't know what to make of an outlaw when he tries to make a life not on the page, or on the screen but in the world, we see a generation of men who are angry, alienated, confused, and conflicted. In recent months this demographic has confounded the political pundits and helped propel books like *Hillbilly Elegy* to the top of the bestseller lists. Jackson Teller is their prophet— dashing and destructive, he is undoubtedly one of the most fascinating male characters American popular culture has produced in recent memory. As a man, however, he is a disaster. As long as American men understand themselves primarily as characters within the influential, enduring, yet anachronistic narrative of masculinity which has become their birthright, their collective story may be compelling (Jax's certainly is) but it will always end the same—filled with men who are confused, afraid, and alone.

There's the rub.

## Notes

1. "Ever since [Rip Van Winkle], the typical male protagonist of our fiction has been a man on the run, harried into the forest and out to sea, down the river or into combat—anywhere to avoid 'civilization,' which is to say the confrontation of a man and a woman which leads to the fall to sex, marriage, and responsibility" (Fiedler 26).

2. "*Sons of Anarchy* presents a contemporary form of white, hegemonic masculinity that is dependent on dominance, violence, and the oppression of Others. But beyond the axiomatic, there are also nuanced moments when the pressures of living out (and living up to) the expectations of hegemonic masculinity are laid bare as inherently flawed. As viewers are presented with an onslaught of white, heterosexist characters, they are simultaneously presented with characters and events that call into question the value (and cost) of enacting hegemonic masculinity—both for men and the women around them. The men on *Sons of Anarchy* live in a constant state of crisis as the norm, and the implications of such are both contradictory and complementary to upholding traditional masculinity" (Cox 821-22).

3. As Susan Faludi notes in her 1999 book, *Stiffed: The Betrayal of the American Man*, "The traditional primary infantry combat units—the company, the platoon, the squad—are all essentially all-male families, each ideally a circle of brothers melded together by a commanding father figure who cares about their welfare and shares the risks and sacrifices of battle. As much affection as the brothers hold for each other, it's the father-officer who binds them together" (321-22).

4. A quarter of a century ago Jane Tompkins wrote, "To go west, as far west as you can go, west of everything, is to die. Death is everywhere in this genre. Not just the shoot-outs, or in the scores of bodies that pile up toward the narrative's close but, even more compellingly, in the desert landscape with which the bodies of the gunned-down eventually merge" (24). She was speaking of the classic American Western, but her insights presciently capture key undercurrents in Sutter's *Sons of Anarchy*.

5. In the series finale when District Attorney Patterson asks Jax, "What happens at the end of the day?" he replies, "The bad guys lose." There is a sense in which all American men are bad guys. Or perhaps more precisely they are good at being guys, but bad at being men. In either case, as long as their ideals are embodied in men like Jax, they will always be tragic figures. They will always lose.

6. Tig comes closest to a meaningful relationship with the transsexual prostitute Venus Van Dam. Perhaps this is the series acknowledging greater fluidity in gender identity. Or perhaps the masculinity Tig represents can only display intimacy or weakness outside the normative boundaries of America's masculinized cultural narrative.

## Works Cited

Butler, Judith. *Gender Trouble: Feminism and the Subversion of Identity*. New York: Routledge, Taylor & Francis Group, 2015. Print.
Connell, Raewyn. *Masculinities*. Berkeley: University of California Press, 2008. Print.
Cox, Nicole B., and Lauren J. DeCarvalho. "'Ride Free or Die' Trying: Hypermasculinity on FX's *Sons of Anarchy*." *Journal of Popular Culture* 49.4 Aug. 2016. 818-38. Print.
Faludi, Susan. *Stiffed: The Betrayal of the American Man*. New York: Perennial, 2000. Print.
Fiedler, Leslie A. *Love and Death in the American Novel*. Normal, IL: Dalkey Archive, 2003. Print.
Kimmel, Michael. *Manhood in America: A Cultural History*. New York: Oxford University Press, 2012. Print.
_____. *Misframing Men: The Politics of Contemporary Masculinities*. New Brunswick: Rutgers University Press, 2010. Print.

Robinson, Sally. *Marked Men: White Masculinity in Crisis*. New York: Columbia University Press, 2000. Print.
Rotundo, E. Anthony. *American Manhood: Transformations in Masculinity from the Revolution to the Modern Era*. New York: Basic, 2001. Print.
Slotkin, Richard. *Gunfighter Nation: The Myth of the Frontier in Twentieth-century America*. Norman: University of Oklahoma Press, 2008. Print.
Sutter, Kurt, creator. *Sons of Anarchy*. Sutter Ink and Linson Entertainment in association with FX Productions and Fox 21 Television Studios. 2008–2014.
Tompkins, Jane. *West of Everything: The Inner Life of Westerns*. New York: Oxford University Press, 1993. Print.

PART 2. SHAPES OF INFLUENCE:
CULTURE AND NARRATIVE

# Incapable of His Own Distress
## *Genderbending Ophelia*

JESSICA WALKER

That *Sons of Anarchy* adapts William Shakespeare's *Hamlet* is well-documented; from its earliest days, the series was characterized as "*Hamlet* on Harleys," and the narrative parallels between King Claudius's crimes and Clay Morrow's are clear (Carpenter). Creator Kurt Sutter asserts, however, that the show is "not really a modern retelling of *Hamlet*, meaning that that arc does not inform the show as a whole.... But, you know, there are definitely Shakespearean overtones throughout the piece" (Sutter qtd. in Sloboda 91). Though to consider the full extent of the series' use of "Shakespearean overtones" is beyond the scope of this essay, a consideration of the elements fundamental to Shakespearean tragedy (the genre to which *Sons of Anarchy* bears the closest ties) can illuminate how Sutter's approach to adaptation and gender addresses one of tragedy's chief concerns: the characters' ability to shape their own destinies in the face of seemingly insurmountable internal and external elements such as fate, society, and personal shortcomings. That is: what choices are available to characters in a play such as *Hamlet*, and what do Sutter's alterations tell us about the choices available to his characters?

Cultural assumptions about gender at the time in which Shakespeare wrote greatly shape the choices available to his tragic characters. A greater variety of roles are available to men in his tragedies, and more autonomy and nuance within those roles: noble, doomed protagonists (Hamlet, Othello, Lear); irredeemable villains (Aaron, Iago); sympathetic antagonists (Tybalt, Aufidius); helpless victims of circumstance (Quintus and Mutius; Duncan and Banquo) or flawed figures whose actions contribute to their fates (Polonius, Mercutio); supporting heroes who survive the play (Lucius, Macduff,

Edgar). Shakespeare's female tragic figures are far more limited in their range; while "[o]ften the women in the comedies are more brilliant than the men, more aware of themselves and their world, saner, livelier," the tragedies are filled with "nightmare female figures" whose "evil is inseparable from their failures as women" (Bamber 2). Tragic protagonists Cleopatra and Juliet must share the limelight with male partners, while no real female equivalent to the active, heroic male survivor appears in Shakespeare's tragedies. His female victims tend to lack autonomy; women such as Lavinia, Ophelia, and Desdemona are relatively helpless, caught up in male violence rather than doomed by their own errors. Female antagonists like Regan and Goneril, Tamora, Volumnia, or Lady Macbeth, however complex, tend to share the same motive: to access, or vicariously experience, political power through men. Since blatant pursuit of political power is, to the early modern viewer, perhaps the worst crime possible for a woman, they come across as more villainous, taken as a whole, than Shakespeare's male antagonists. Above all, Shakespeare's women are denied the ability to make meaningful choices: while "the tragic hero is privileged ... with the capacity to change," Shakespearean tragic women "do not respond to the events of the play, to the suffering, with new capabilities" (Bamber 8). Sutter's adaptation explores the lack of autonomy available to such figures in a surprising way: by giving the powerless, passive female victim's role to a hypermasculine male figure, thereby underscoring the tragic toll that the constraints of gender take on their victims.

Though the series' storylines expand far beyond *Hamlet*, its main plot runs throughout *Sons of Anarchy*. In Shakespeare's play, Claudius murders his brother, King Hamlet, then claims his brother's crown and marries his widow, Gertrude. The murdered king's ghost appears to his son, the play's eponymous protagonist, revealing the crime and tasking him with revenge. Torn over whether, and how, to follow his father's instructions, Hamlet finally takes his revenge before his own death. In Sutter's series, Clay Morrow kills his friend John Teller (J.T.), the founder of the Sons of Anarchy Motorcycle Club, Redwood Original (SAMCRO). He then marries Teller's widow, Gemma, and takes his place as club president. After discovering his father's old journals, J.T.'s son, Jax, begins to question SAMCRO's activities, eventually discovering his stepfather's crime and taking revenge before he, too, dies at the series' end.

For the most part, the parallels between the two works are broad strokes rather than exact correspondences. J.T.'s "ghost" urges Jax toward questioning, reforming, and ultimately leaving the club, to escape violence rather than perpetuating it through vengeance; Jax's discovery of his father's murder and eventual revenge, while a significant plotline, is only one of the many challenges he faces over the course of seven seasons. Gemma bears far more resemblance to Shakespeare's manipulative, antagonistic wives and mothers such as Lady Macbeth or Volumnia than she does to Gertrude; Jax's wife, Tara, whose passion for her husband wars with her misgivings about his crimes, may be a closer equivalent. But the series retains one key subplot from Shakespeare in the form of Jax's best friend, Opie Winston, whose story echoes Ophelia's descent into madness and eventual suicide. Retaining Ophelia's plotline allows the series to underscore its central theme: the contradictory, inescapable, and utterly destructive nature of SAMCRO's toxic masculinity.

In Shakespeare's play, Ophelia finds herself trapped by the rigid expectations that circumscribe women's lives and choices in early modern literature. She is torn between her desire for Hamlet and her need to please her father, Polonius, and brother, Laertes, who have forbidden the relationship; her distress grows as Hamlet (himself torn apart by his father's murder and mother's remarriage) accuses her of being unfaithful. When Hamlet mistakenly kills Polonius, Ophelia descends into madness and dies under circumstances that may be accidental, deliberate, or somewhere in between. In Sutter's adaptation, these events play out twice as Opie copes with competing loyalties and the loss of a loved one to club violence in the first season and then again in the second through fourth seasons. Like Ophelia, he struggles against the inflexible and contradictory requirements of a culture which lauds family life yet demands criminal behavior that constantly threatens the family unit. He is unjustly accused of betraying his club, and his wife, Donna, is mistakenly executed in his place. Jax, occupied with his own concerns, withdraws from Opie, leaving him increasingly isolated and torn apart by the competing pressures of devotion to his wife, children, club, father, and best friend. Following the discovery that Clay has killed his father, Piney, in an attempt to hide his involvement in J.T.'s death, Opie ultimately sacrifices himself for the very club that caused his misery.

Ophelia's image is so strongly associated with femininity—the girl with flowers and flowing hair, incapable of speech or action, vacant-eyed, sinking passively beneath the water—that it seems counterintuitive to liken her to Opie, a stoic, 6'4", muscled, tattooed, impressively bearded member of an outlaw motorcycle club, arguably the most stereotypically masculine among a host of very masculine characters. His hypermasculinity, however, serves the same narrative purpose as Ophelia's hyperfemininity: to demonstrate the constrictive and destructive nature of gender roles, exposing SAMCRO's expectations as every bit as elusive and dangerous as those placed on early modern women. Ophelia "has been shaped to conform to external demands, to reflect others' desires"; trapped between the competing duties demanded of early modern women, she is expected to behave as a submissive daughter, obedient future wife, and innocent virgin all at once, when in reality she is a young woman approaching sexual maturity, with desires and opinions of her own (Dane 406).[1] In terms of his physical and legal power, Opie, as a modern American man, has more options available to him than Ophelia, who has no skills with which to support herself and no legal identity outside her family. Psychologically, however, he is no less trapped than she is. By placing Opie in the helpless, feminized position of a female tragic victim, *Sons of Anarchy* demonstrates the full power of SAMCRO's toxic masculinity as an inescapable force.

By opening with the birth of Jax's son and Opie's return to his family after his time in jail, the series immediately introduces the viewer to the fundamental conflict that will gradually destroy Opie and ultimately demand Jax's self-sacrifice: that "a good father and a good outlaw can't settle inside the same man" ("Papa's Goods"). However the club touts the ideals of "anarchy" and "freedom," in practice its complex social structure and marked emphasis on the group's needs over the individual's bear more resemblance to Hamlet's medieval Denmark or Shakespeare's early modern England.[2] SAMCRO requires its members to embody a rigid and ultimately self-contradictory definition of manhood, characterized by complete allegiance to the club (even when its individual members oppose one another) and deference to the president's will; ruthless violence to enemies, while remaining a loving (if not necessarily faithful) husband and father; disregard for others' property and disdain for conventional jobs, while still providing financial security for one's family; maintaining a tight family unit, without betraying any confidence that could harm the club. Of SAMCRO's members, Jax and Opie feel these contradictions the most sharply because they have both more extensive responsibilities to their families and stronger ties to the club. The only members of the Sons of Anarchy who are actually *sons* of club members, they were raised revering SAMCRO: "since I was five," Jax says, "all I ever wanted was a Harley and a cut" ("Potlatch").[3] Despite the dangers of criminal life, they cannot imagine a life beyond a club. "It's all we know," Jax tells Donna. "It's in our DNA" ("Giving Back"). Disgraced former member Kyle, no longer accorded the automatic respect he was given in a Sons of Anarchy cut, is now "just like every other shithead"; Opie would "rather be dead than be that guy" ("Giving Back"). Most of the club's members are either single and childless, or divorced from their wives and detached from their children. Jax and Opie are the only members raising their own families, a responsibility that does not always mesh well with club life: Opie strives to start afresh with his wife, Donna, and two young children after spending five years in prison, while Jax finds his son Abel's birth and his developing relationship with Tara fill him with concern for their safety if he continues his life of crime. The discovery of his father's writing leads him to question his faith in the club's vision, while Opie's father, Piney, has become similarly disillusioned and often clashes with Clay.

Like Ophelia, Opie struggles to conform to the contradictory ways in which his culture requires him to perform gender. His attempt to readjust to life after prison puts the competing demands of SAMCRO masculinity into sharp relief: he must find a way to reestablish his relationship with his wife; forge a connection to children he barely knows; uncover means to support them financially; reclaim his place in the club; and prove his commitment in the face of suspicions that he may not be ready to return to criminal life. Donna urges him to find legal work and tries to minimize SAMCRO's influence over him, protesting that "I married Opie, I didn't marry the club" ("Seeds"). Here she plays the Polonius role, reinforcing toxic masculinity rather than helping free him from it, accusing Opie of being "too weak to stand up to [the club]" ("Pilot"). Piney employs the same language, telling him to "[q]uit whining, grow a dick, take care of your business" ("Seeds"). Opie's mother, Mary, warns Donna of the cyclical nature of this culture: "This shit never ends.... He's a criminal, just like his father.... Take these kids and move to another planet before their father poisons them"[4] ("Capybara"). Unable to escape the previous generation's patterns, Opie is too devoted to the club to acknowledge the role it has played in his distress: "[Kyle]'s got nothing, right? No club, no family. Do me good to see that. Appreciate what I got"; "I'm having a hard time, man.... [T]his club means everything to me... . But everything else—Donna, the kids, work—are all heading in the opposite direction. I just can't hook shit up. I feel like I'm missing on every front" ("Giving Back").

Opie goes out of his way to "prove I'm SAMCRO" as he adjusts to postprison life, only to find, like his Shakespearean counterpart, that his devotion has been rewarded with undeserved suspicion ("Hell Followed"). Ophelia's difficulties stem from her culture's strict ideas about chastity: seeking to preserve the patriarchal order by providing men with legitimate heirs, the medieval and early modern world demanded a woman's complete sexual fidelity to her husband long before she even met him, by remaining virginal until marriage and faithful afterward. In order to preserve her value on the marriage market, Ophelia must take care to avoid any inappropriate behavior. "The chariest maid is prodigal enough / If she unmask her beauty to the moon: / Virtue itself 'scapes not calumnious strokes," her brother warns (1.3.36–37). Maintaining this image greatly restricted women's freedoms, since talking too much or being seen too often outside the home were thought to be indicators of, or contributors to, unchastity (Worsley 529). Though Ophelia embodies "the very essence of the honest woman," she cannot avoid falling under the suspicion of first her father and then Hamlet (Dane 410).

The early modern period's preoccupation with "honesty," a word meaning "chastity" when applied to women, manifests in SAMCRO as an obsession with loyalty to the club. However the club's members profess their love for one another, a constant undercurrent of suspicion pervades their culture; since sharing information with enemies or the authorities could lead to the club's destruction at any time, they protect themselves much as Renaissance patriarchy did, by indoctrinating their members with messages about the importance of loyalty. Just as the worst thing an early modern woman can be accused of is "dishonesty," the worst thing a Son can be is a "rat," and speech[5] and mobility—being seen in the wrong place or talking to the wrong people—are likewise grounds for suspicion. Both Ophelia and Opie are manipulated into appearing disloyal by those who use them to further their own agendas, reducing them to pawns caught between contending forces. Polonius compels his daughter to return Hamlet's gifts while he and Claudius, hidden, watch them interact for signs of Hamlet's madness; this is where Hamlet calls Ophelia's constancy into question, as if she were complicit in the ruse (3.1). Opie, similarly, is made to appear disloyal when Stahl creates a convincing fiction of his betrayal so she can build her case against the club. Just as Ophelia's obedience to her father brings her under Hamlet's suspicion, Opie's willingness to serve time to protect SAMCRO makes him suspect to those who worry that he may resent imprisonment ("Capybara").

Shakespeare's culture only demands such sexual fidelity from women. The mad Ophelia sings of a girl whose lover promises to marry her but then rejects her cruelly after she sleeps with him (perhaps implying a similar situation between herself and Hamlet); this "sexual double standard leaves him with impunity, unfazed, but ruins her" (Smith 99). Occupying the same feminized position, Opie is subject to a similar double standard: those with superior status in the MC, such as Jax and Clay, continually withhold information from the club, but the completely undeserved appearance of infidelity on Opie's part ends up costing him everything. Donna finally permits the integration of club and family life, which tragically leads to her demise when she encourages Opie to take their family to Abel's homecoming. Traveling not in the domestic family sedan but in her husband's masculine-coded truck, on her way to spend money earned with SAMCRO on powder for Gemma's washing machine, she is mistaken for Opie and killed ("The Sleep of Babies").

If *Sons of Anarchy* were restricted to "two hours' traffic of our stage," Donna's death would lead to Opie's swift decline, as Polonius's does for Ophelia (*Romeo and Juliet* Prologue 12). Instead, the series builds Opie's "madness" over the next three seasons, tensions between Donna and the club becoming replaced by those between Jax and Clay. Grief-stricken and unprepared for the challenges of single fatherhood, Opie seeks to lose himself in the club by increasingly deferring to Clay, backing him in his goals and even reconciling with him when he learns of his role in Donna's murder ("Service"). He tells Jax to "get over his dead daddy shit" ("Eureka") and "back down, get in line" ("Falx Cerebri") behind their president, but Jax's conflict with Clay continues to strain their relationship.[6] Hamlet's internal torment over his father's murder causes his behavior toward Ophelia to cycle rapidly: in the space of one scene, he declares his love for her, immediately retracts it, and then accuses her of sexual misconduct (3.1); the very next time they meet, he flirts graphically with her (3.2). Ophelia, not being privy to "the information that would help explain if not palliate Hamlet's bizarre behavior ... experiences an unsustainable amount of anxiety" that contributes to her eventual breakdown (Smith 97). Jax, likewise, withholds information from Opie and frequently changes his stance on the club. He tells Opie that his support of Clay makes Jax "feel like I'm losing all my friends" ("Potlatch"), but praises his involvement in the club, only to later reveal, when Opie is particularly fragile after the dissolution of his second marriage, that he wishes to leave SAMCRO: "You were right, man. I should have let you get out. Donna would probably still be alive" ("Hands"). Just as Ophelia comes to find Hamlet unrecognizable, "[t]hat unmatch'd form and feature of blown youth / Blasted with ecstasy" (3.1.159–60), Opie tells Jax he's "not quite sure who I'm talking to anymore" ("Booster").

In her madness, Ophelia, who has been treated simultaneously as a sex object and obedient virgin, becomes both, alternating tragic songs with shockingly sexual ones, handing out flowers and speaking nonsense. Opie likewise throws himself into the contradictions of hypermasculinity after Donna's death, becoming more reckless in his performance of both club violence and domestic fatherhood. When Jax comments that Opie has gone "a little cowboy" as of late, he replies, "I don't have a deathwish, man.... I got the club. Just throwing myself into it" ("Fix"). He initially takes "mercy" on Stahl for her role in Donna's death, but eventually becomes so hardened that his vengeance, when it finally happens, is driven by the club's code of retaliation rather than his own personal grief: "I want you to feel what I feel" ("Service") becomes "This is what she felt" ("NS"). His time in prison and emotional shutdown after Donna's death prevent Opie from connecting with his children; he avoids seeing them ("Albification") and eventually becomes too focused on club business to attend to their needs ("Gilead"). He marries Lyla and hopes to have children with her in an attempt to recreate the domestic space he shared with Donna, but is now so entrenched in SAMCRO that he cannot form the healthy relationships outside it that could restore needed balance to his life. Lyla, an actress in the adult films produced by the MC's porn studio, shares many of Opie's flaws: she is self-destructive, apprehensive about parenthood, and unable to consider a life beyond the dangerous work she has always known.

Shattered, as Ophelia is, by his father's murder, Opie cannot reconcile his devotion to the club with the need for vengeance that the club's culture has engendered in him. As his story approaches its end, he rejects both family and club. Though he had previously expressed a fear of returning to jail because he felt Lyla would be unable to adequately care for their children ("Booster"), now he asks her to take them, offering no explanation, before willingly going to jail ("Authority Vested"). He declares the club and its goals meaningless, that "it just ain't fun anymore—chasing cash we don't need and spending every dime trying to stay alive" and that Jax's choice to "kill Clay or save the club" was "the wrong choice" ("Laying Pipe").

Both Ophelia and Opie's deaths symbolically re-enact the constrictive, deadly nature of gender roles.[7] The circumstances surrounding their deaths are ambiguous, demonstrating how *Hamlet*'s most fundamental choice—to be or not to be—has been taken from them. Too mentally compromised to realize that she is in danger, Ophelia may have drowned accidentally; paralyzed by despair, she may have committed suicide by inaction, recognizing the risk but taking no measure to stop it; or her death may have been deliberate self-murder. Always quiet and docile, she loses, in her madness, all apparent ability to speak rationally or take action on her own behalf. When the branch upon which she sits breaks, she simply floats down the brook as her "clothes spread wide, / And mermaid-like awhile they bore her up" (4.7.175–56). She is described as "incapable of her own distress," that is, unaware that she is in danger (4.7.178), a "vulnerable young woman" who, occupied with the "innocent, child-like activities of crafting and draping garlands ... drowns, a guiltless victim of her own mad oblivion" (Smith 108). The femininity that has psychologically trapped her throughout the play manifests physically as water fills her skirts; unable or unwilling to fight anymore, she is dragged under.

While manliness is typically associated with action, Opie's death demonstrates how strict gender roles, whether masculine or feminine, render their victims powerless. The series adapts Ophelia's quintessentially feminine death into a violently masculine but equally passive demise: Opie, volunteering to settle SAMCRO's blood debt with Pope, is dragged into a prison cell and beaten to death. Taking on the club's sins will not redeem them; his action changes nothing, and only perpetuates the club's violence by creating another debt of revenge that must be repaid. The autonomy implicit in his final words, "I got this" ("Laying Pipe"), is undercut by a possible second meaning suggested by similar phrases he used to express his unwavering commitment to the club: "Do me good to see [Kyle without family or club]. Appreciate what I got" ("Giving Back"), "I got the club" ("Fix"). The phrase "I got this," therefore, can be read as "This is what I have"—*all* he has, a meaningless, violent gesture of loyalty to SAMCRO. One critic's description of Ophelia, the most blamelessly, pathetically tragic figure in *Hamlet*, and perhaps all of Shakespeare, could apply just as well to him: "used, abused, confused—utterly manipulated by the men in her life.... Scoffed at, ignored, suspected, disbelieved, commanded to distrust her own feelings, thoughts and desires, Ophelia is fragmented by contradictory messages" (Dane 406). With the possible exception of Otto, Opie is the member of the club most wronged by it, less a victim of his own error than of Stahl's ruthlessness, Pope's vindictiveness, Clay's self-preservation, Tig's recklessness, and Jax's internal conflict.

Ultimately, the two characters fulfill the same narrative purpose in their respective texts, as doubles and foils to the tragic protagonist. Hamlet, like Ophelia, is trapped between forces at odds with one another (his mother and his mother's husband, allegiance to his king and the duty to revenge his father's murder, his love for his father and his fear for his immortal soul). Both he and Ophelia, in response to being "given edicts by their fathers that rankle and invite suspicion" and "fail[ing] to understand fully how they are being worked upon by court forces," become increasingly isolated and unstable (Fisher 2). Denied recourse, Ophelia turns her grief inward, collapsing mentally under the strain. Hamlet has other options, such as the opposite courses of action demonstrated by Laertes, who reacts to his father's murder with impulsive violence, and Fortinbras, who responds with a slow but ultimately successful military campaign against Denmark to avenge his father's death. Hamlet can let his internal discord destroy him, as it does Ophelia, or he can use his comparably privileged state to make better choices. Ophelia acts as a foreshadowing device throughout the play; more vulnerable than Hamlet, the grief and distress affecting them both consume her first. Likewise, as *Sons of Anarchy* gradually establishes the "war of the mind" that will ultimately doom Jax, the same circumstances play out for Opie beforehand ("Papa's Goods"). Both men's wives depend on the club (Donna for income, Tara for safety) and yet urge them to leave it; police involvement leads to both women being killed in acts of misdirected club violence; both men are thrown into crisis upon discovering that Clay murdered their fathers; ultimately unable to reconcile family and club, both sacrifice themselves in hopes of protecting their loved ones.[8]

Returning to its roots as a *Hamlet* adaptation in its final episodes,[9] *Sons of Anarchy* contrasts Opie and Jax's deaths just as Shakespeare contrasts Ophelia and Hamlet's. Though Hamlet does not commit suicide, he willfully puts himself in a potentially deadly situation, relinquishing control over his future: "If it be now, 'tis not to come; if it be not to come, it will be now; if it be not now, yet it will come—the readiness is all. Since no man, of aught he leaves, knows what is't to leave betimes, let be" (5.2.222–24). Unlike Ophelia, however, Hamlet has choices, and sets his house in order before he dies by begging Laertes' forgiveness, exacting revenge for his father, and endorsing Fortinbras' rule in hope that Denmark may start anew (5.2). Likewise, while Jax echoes Opie in his moment of self-sacrifice—"I got this"—his death does not perpetuate the cycle of revenge; rather, he carefully orchestrates events in his final days to finally resolve the discord between family and club, sending his sons away with Wendy and Nero, who he knows will raise them outside SAM-CRO's violent atmosphere, and putting changes into place that will minimize the club's future involvement in illegal activities.

Television's greatest strength, as a medium, is perhaps its narrative length: a series such as *Sons of Anarchy*, permitted nearly a hundred hours in which to tell its story, can develop character to an extent unlikely for even the greatest five-act play, two-hour film or 500-page book. Such a format allows Sutter room to explore his Shakespearean inspirations well beyond the particulars of *Hamlet*, freely appropriating from the text, and from Shakespeare as a whole, to serve his vision. The series' adaptation of Ophelia to Opie pushes beyond the constrictive binary of helpless female victims and heartless female villains, driving home the tragic weight of the choices with which *Sons of Anarchy*'s characters must contend.

## NOTES

1. Ophelia's passivity is easily overstated. She is not without a mind of her own: she talks back to Laertes by teasing him about his own sexual misconduct (1.3.45–51), protests when her father dismisses Hamlet's romantic gestures (1.3.110–14), and tries to defend herself against Hamlet's accusations (3.1.108–09). Yet her efforts to assert herself have no effect; "[i]t does not matter that various clues are contradictory because each clue falls into silence" (Bamber 78). Any attempt to forge her own path against her culture's desires is doomed, as with Opie, who is first introduced with Jax's assertion that "Opie's leaning right these days." "Opie's gonna lean any way we need him to," Clay responds ("Pilot").

2. During the medieval period in which *Hamlet* takes place and the early modern period in which it was written, an individual's identity largely depended on his or her social group and position within that group's hierarchy—hence Ophelia's intense need to please both her father and potential future husband, as well as Hamlet's internal conflict as the stepson and subject of the man on whom he wishes to take revenge. Modern American culture tends to place greater emphasis on individual liberties than on group identity. Therefore, updated adaptations of Shakespeare's work often employ settings that echo the strict social codes and loyalty-supported hierarchies of the medieval and early modern periods—such as gangs (*West Side Story*, Baz Luhrmann's *Romeo + Juliet*), high schools (*O, Ten Things I Hate About You, She's the Man*), and corporations (*Scotland PA*, Michael Almereyda's *Hamlet*).

3. Mothers are relatively absent from this strongly patriarchal culture; like Ophelia, Opie "has clearly been bereft of maternal fostering" (Dane 406). His mother (ironically named Mary) resents having to care for her grandchildren and admits "I didn't raise [Opie]; we got no history" ("Falx Cerebri"). The "missing mother" trope, common in Shakespeare, often serves to highlight the dangers of patriarchy (since the errors of fathers such as Prospero, Shylock, Lear, or Polonius may have been curtailed by the presence of sensible wives). *Sons of Anarchy*'s use of the trope is more pointed: maternal influence must be integrated into the club's dangerous vision or rejected outright, as Opie does by leaving his mother and running back to Piney and SAMCRO at the age of sixteen ("Capybara"). This isolation from the maternal likens him to Shakespeare's Macduff, who also struggles between grief for his dead wife and manly revenge; Opie, too, could be described as not "of woman born" (*Macbeth* 5.8.13).

4. Gemma similarly refers to JT's writing as the "ghost of John Teller poisoning [Jax]," a metaphor that echoes the poison-in-the-ear image of *Hamlet*, whose protagonist is similarly "poisoned" by his father's demand for revenge ("Pilot").

5. Ophelia is a fundamentally silent character whose quiet acquiescence contrasts with Hamlet's "deafening vocal posturing" (Fischer 2); Opie, likewise, is "not much of a talker" in comparison to his frequently monologuing best friend ("Authority Vested"). He particularly

shuts down in times of stress, such as when breaking up with Lyla ("Call of Duty") or after Piney's death ("Burnt and Purged Away").

6. By making Opie Jax's best friend rather than his romantic partner, *Sons of Anarchy* deepens, rather than diminishes, the bond between them and the severity of the consequences when that bond is tested. Shakespeare's play is ambiguous about the true depth of Hamlet and Ophelia's feelings for one another. A relative lack of intimacy between them is in keeping with the play's context; women were not considered men's intellectual or spiritual equals in the early modern period, and men were more likely to seek close emotional bonds with other men than with their wives. Furthermore, Ophelia likely would be permitted little time alone with Hamlet, given that her virginity is a valuable commodity that must be closely guarded. While our culture is more likely to consider romantic partnership more significant than friendship, this is not the case in an intensely homosocial culture like SAMCRO.

7. These gendered symbols follow them into the grave; Ophelia is buried with "her virgin crants, / Her maiden strewments" (5.1.232–33, the flowers and garlands permitted to buried virgins) while Opie is buried in his cut, surrounded by SAMCRO relics such as cigarettes, tequila, and a photograph of himself and Jax as young boys on bicycles ("Stolen Huffy"). The competing demands that led to his demise now adorn his tombstone: "Beloved Father, Devoted Son, Fearless Brother, Loyal Friend" ("Papa's Goods").

8. Montages framing the episode in which Donna dies show that Jax's family storyline will echo Opie's. The episode opens with Opie in bed with Donna and their children, watching them sleep (the only family unit among the club's members); Jax shares a bed with Tara, Gemma turns her attention to her bird rather than Clay, and the other Sons appear with nameless groupies. The scene concludes with the announcement that Abel is going home to "join your family" ("The Sleep of Babies"). At the end of the episode, the now-widowed Opie sits on the bed, now facing away from his sleeping children, while Jax and Wendy watch Abel sleep.

9. Three episode titles in the seventh season are taken from *Hamlet*: "Some Strange Eruption," "What a Piece of Work Is Man," and "Suits of Woe." The final episode closes with a title card quoting Hamlet's letter to Ophelia:
>Doubt thou the stars are fire,
>Doubt that the sun doth move,
>Doubt truth to be a liar,
>But never doubt I love [2.2.116–19].

## Works Cited

"Albification." *Sons of Anarchy*, written by Kurt Sutter, directed by Guy Ferland, 20th Century Fox, 2009.
"Authority Vested." *Sons of Anarchy*, written by Regina Corrado, directed by Peter Weller, 20th Century Fox, 2012.
Bamber, Linda. *Comic Women, Tragic Men: A Study of Gender and Genre in Shakespeare*. Stanford University Press, 1982.
"Booster." *Sons of Anarchy*, written by Dave Erickson and Chris Collins, directed by Guy Ferland, 20th Century Fox, 2011.
"Burnt and Purged Away." *Sons of Anarchy*, written by Kurt Sutter and Dave Erickson, directed by Paris Barclay, 20th Century Fox, 2011.
"Call of Duty." *Sons of Anarchy*, written by Liz Sagal and Gladys Rodriguez, directed by Gwyneth Horder-Payton, 20th Century Fox, 2011.
"Capybara." *Sons of Anarchy*, written by Kurt Sutter and Dave Erickson, directed by Stephen Kay, 20th Century Fox, 2008.
Carpenter, Susan. "Think *Hamlet* on Harleys." *Los Angeles Times*, 26 October 2008, http://articles.latimes.com/2008/oct/26/entertainment/ca-sonsofanarchy26.
Dane, Gabrielle. "Reading Ophelia's Madness." *Exemplaria*, vol. 10, no. 2, 1998, pp. 405–23.
"Eureka." *Sons of Anarchy*, written by Kurt Sutter and Brett Conrad, directed by Guy Ferland, 20th Century Fox, 2009.

"Falx Cerebri." *Sons of Anarchy*, written by Regina Corrado, directed by Billy Gierhart, 20th Century Fox, 2009.
Fischer, Sandra K. "Hearing Ophelia: Gender and Tragic Discourse in *Hamlet*." *Renaissance and Reformation / Renaissance et Réforme*, vol. 14, no. 1, 1990, pp. 1–10.
"Fix." *Sons of Anarchy*, written by Dave Erickson, directed by Gwyneth Horder-Payton, 20th Century Fox, 2009.
"Gilead." *Sons of Anarchy*, written by Kurt Sutter and Chris Collins, directed by Gwyneth Horder-Payton, 20th Century Fox, 2009.
"Giving Back." *Sons of Anarchy*, written by Jack LoGiudice, directed by Tim Hunter, 20th Century Fox, 2008.
"Hands." *Sons of Anarchy*, written by Chris Collins, David LaBrava, and Kurt Sutter, directed by Peter Weller, 20th Century Fox, 2011.
"Hell Followed." *Sons of Anarchy*, written by Brett Conrad, directed by Billy Gierhart, 20th Century Fox, 2008.
"Laying Pipe." *Sons of Anarchy*, written by Kem Nunn, Liz Sagal, and Kurt Sutter, directed by Adam Arkin, 20th Century Fox, 2012.
"NS." *Sons of Anarchy*, written by Kurt Sutter and Dave Erickson, directed by Kurt Sutter, 20th Century Fox, 2010.
"Papa's Goods." *Sons of Anarchy*, written and directed by Kurt Sutter, 20th Century Fox, 2014.
"Pilot." *Sons of Anarchy*, written by Kurt Sutter, directed by Allen Coulter and Michael Dinner, 20th Century Fox, 2008.
"Potlatch." *Sons of Anarchy*, written by Kurt Sutter and Misha Green, directed by Paul Maibaum, 20th Century Fox, 2009.
"Seeds." *Sons of Anarchy*, written by Kurt Sutter, directed by Charles Haid, 20th Century Fox, 2008.
"Service." *Sons of Anarchy*, written by Brady Dahl and Cori Uchida, directed by Phil Abraham, 20th Century Fox, 2009.
Shakespeare, William. *The Tragedy of Hamlet, Prince of Denmark*. *The Riverside Shakespeare*, edited by G. Blakemore Evans, Houghton Mifflin Company, 1997, 1189–1234.
_____. *The Tragedy of Macbeth*. *The Riverside Shakespeare*, edited by G. Blakemore Evans. Houghton Mifflin Company, 1997, 1360–1387.
_____. *The Tragedy of Romeo and Juliet*. *The Riverside Shakespeare*, edited by G. Blakemore Evans. Houghton Mifflin Company, 1997, 1104–1139.
"The Sleep of Babies." *Sons of Anarchy*, written by Kurt Sutter, directed by Terrence O'Hara, 20th Century Fox, 2008.
Sloboda, Noel. "Hamlet in (and Off) Stages: Television, Serialization, and Shakespeare in *Sons of Anarchy*." *Journal of the Wooden O*, vol. 12, 2012, 85–99.
Smith, Barbara. "Neither Accident nor Intent: Contextualizing the Suicide of Ophelia." *South Atlantic Review*, vol. 73, no. 2, 2008, pp. 96–112.
Worsley, Amelia. "Ophelia's Loneliness." *ELH*, vol. 82, no. 2, 2015, pp. 521–51.

# Motorcycle Monasticism
## Masculine Religiosity in MC Culture

### Jossalyn G. Larson

The fifth season of Kurt Sutter's landmark motorcycle drama, *Sons of Anarchy*, provided a scene that was so blasphemous that it could have caused outrage amongst FX's audience. Tara, the well-vetted "old lady" of President Jax Teller and (secondarily) a medical doctor, visits former SAMCRO member Otto "Big Otto" Delaney in the Stockton State Prison infirmary. Still fuming over perceived offenses made against him by the club, Otto has threatened to rat on the Sons in an upcoming RICO case; Tara has arrived to dissuade him. Per Otto's request, Tara brings a silver and gold crucifix, which had been given to Otto's deceased wife, Luann, by his mother. Otto asks Tara to put the crucifix around his neck and to slip it under his shirt, and then to leave him alone to pray.

Otto does not pray, of course. Instead, he waits a few moments before buzzing for the nurse and demanding to be brought back to his cell. The nurse and orderly remove Otto's restraints, and Tara returns to the scene in time to see Otto knock the orderly unconscious, and bash the nurse's face into the wall. Tara begs Otto to stop, to no avail. Then, uttering a phrase that would have *SOA* fans all a-flutter—"Sons live, Redwood bleeds"—Otto plunges the crucifix into the nurse's jugular again and again, leaving her a bloody mess on the infirmary floor.

This scene, in the aptly-named episode "Crucifixed," is one of the most shocking, and one of the most pivotal, of the show's seven seasons. Otto's actions at once liberate the Sons from indictment by his testimony in the RICO case, but also condemn Tara to a conspicuous criminality, which she had previously managed to skirt. Otto's utterance—"Sons live, Redwood bleeds"—gestures toward a struggle that is not uncommon in motorcycle club narratives: Otto's reverence for the fundamental essence of the club pushes against his disdain for the actions of the SAMCRO chapter. Tara, whose ambivalence toward the club had previously allowed her to maintain a safe distance from its corruption, has become the scapegoat for the sins of SAMCRO.

Sutter's decision to take a sacred object and recast it as a murder weapon is neither accidental nor unanticipated. Each episode of *Sons of Anarchy* alludes to religion in some fashion, and those allusions often conflate the sacred and the profane. In the show's first season, Jax's ex-wife, Wendy, overdoses on a syringe that had been pressed between the pages of a Bible; in the second season, Jax's mother, Gemma, mocks a priest's rosary by suggesting that she would prefer to use the beads in a certain sexual act. Examples of Sutter's sacred/profane conflation abound throughout the series, and so it would seem that FX's more conservative viewers would take these conflations as assaults to their religious sensibilities. Yet a 2014 survey conducted by Facebook found that *Sons of Anarchy* received as much praise from conservatives as it did liberals (Gilman). This was a surprise to Christian Toto of the far-right newsmagazine *Breitbart,* who wrote that *SOA* displayed material "that hardly appeals to social conservatives, like serial slayings, the adult film business and gang-style warfare" (Toto). Indeed, the series' violent and sexual content should have appealed more to a left-wing audience, which tends toward "morally murky antiheroes," and should have repelled right-wing viewers who prefer reality shows and scripted serials that center on work and competition (Hibberd). But instead, *SOA* has retained a liberal antihero-loving audience while also engaging an audience whose conservatism is rooted less in moral approbation than in emotional control, militant hierarchy, and fundamentalism.

*Sons of Anarchy's* appeal reaches beyond traditional biases by tapping into aspects of masculine religiosity which have been eluding even established religious institutions. Within the last half-century, research into the characteristics of the religiously-affiliated has found that women tend to exhibit a greater commitment to religious practice than do their male counterparts (Baston, Schoenrade and Ventis). Though some research methods have rendered wide disparities between the religiosity of the genders while others have found only a minimal disparity, the general trend is that women tend to find religion more salient to their daily activities, and their commitment to personal faith, religious rituals, and orthodoxy is consistently stronger than men's (Sullins). Yet the modern male-dominated motorcycle club (MC) is steeped in religious symbology, as symbols borrowed mostly from a Judeo-Christian tradition are central to the induction of members and the practice of club business. MCs are founded on sacred objects (the bike and the patch), assimilate members through ceremonial rites, observe a hierarchical order that is more doctrinal than democratic, and even refer to club meetings as "church." Sutter made much use of the religiosity ingrained in MC culture by embedding religious symbols in pivotal scenes, and by emphasizing the MC's reverential proximity to the Church, as in the third season's introduction of Father Kellan Ashby and the setting of important scenes in Ashby's sanctuary.

In this study, I use Sutter's drama to examine why a masculine demographic that has been abandoning traditional religious practice would be so fervently attracted to religious symbolism in the motorcycle club. I suggest that the MC borrows much of its structure and tradition from medieval Catholic monasteries, which could be characterized as organized groups of men affiliated with (not necessarily branches of) the Church. I compare monastic gender structures to gender structures in the MC, and find that such a comparison reveals fascinating insights into the characteristics of masculinity in relation to a higher power (God or the club), as well as in relation to associated women, and to the secular world with which the group interacts.

Though MC patch holders are by no means celibate, I argue that the MC governs expressions of gender and sexuality in various contexts; a reading of the MC through the influences theology of Saint Bernard of Clairvaux, for example, imagines the patch holder as in a marital relationship with the club in which he is at once "bridegroom" when representing the MC to the outside world, and "bride" when affirming his loyalty to the club through ceremonial rites. Issues of violence and sexuality are important points of inquiry in this project, as they would at first seem to differentiate the MC from the monastery, but instead point to important traits of masculine religiosity and, by extension, the appeal of the MC.

## Multidimensional Masculinity and the Clergy of Chrome

In their investigation into "hypermasculinity" in *Sons of Anarchy*, Nicole B. Cox and Lauren J. Decarvalho observe that the series "perpetuates the idea that masculinity is enacted both through the connection to violence and the absence of emotion" (Cox and DeCarvalho 835). Cox and Decarvalho suggest that depictions of violence in *SOA* simultaneously reinforce physical aggression as preferable to emotional release in times of conflict, but also display the challenges that the characters face when they are held to such expectations. When SAMCRO's intelligence officer, Juice, is caught stealing a brick of cocaine in the fourth season, for example, Juice's response is to murder the member who catches him. Laden with the guilt of his deception and the violence that had ensued from it, Juice returns to the scene of the murder.

The episode, titled "Fruit for the Crows," opens with Juice curled up against a tree, staring at the ground, and reciting the Act of Contrition, a prayer most frequently used by Catholics at the conclusion of the rite of confession: "Oh my god I am heartily sorry for having offended you, and I detest all my sins not because of your just punishments, but most of all because I have offended you, my God, who are all good and deserving of all my love; I firmly resolve with the help of your grace to sin no more and to avoid near occasions of sin." Juice's recitation of this prayer demonstrates his desire to commit to a moral code, yet the realities of club life make it impossible for him to confess his sins to another member without forfeiting his life and, worse, his honor. Expression of remorse in the presence of another living person is at once essential to the rite of confession and scorned by the "hypermasculine" MC, so in spite of Juice's attempt to find reconciliation without violence, the episode concludes with Juice's attempt at suicide by hanging. Juice's impulse to resort to self-violence rather than face his guilt displays his complicity with the "violence-first" ideals of club life. The turmoil he experiences as a result of his conflicted morality leads to his attempt at self-harm.

If Cox and Decarvalho are right, then the preference for violence over emotional expression is central to the "hypermasculine" construct of the motorcycle club. Curiously, studies have found that emotional control and violence also bear heavily on men's religiosity, particularly when that religiosity is characterized by reverence for fundamentalism, but a difficulty committing to religious practice. Since the trend was observed in the early Eighties, researchers have tried to understand why women are more likely to commit to religious practice than men are (Baston, Schoenrade and Ventis) (Sullins). Some have argued that gender socialization has led to the disparity—that men are taught to avoid stereotypically feminine behaviors, and it is possible that religiousness is viewed as feminine (Thompson). Religion promotes subservience (Long and Heggen), communality through religious gatherings (De Vaus and McAllister), risk aversion (Miller and Hoffman) and emotional expression through public prayer and confession, all of which can conflict with men's socialization to be dominant, independent, competitive, risk-takers, and avoidant of emotions (Long and Heggen). Yet the most promising explanations for the disparity in the religiosity of the genders comes from studies that observe men's relationship to religion not holistically, but rather parse the traits of both masculinity and religiosity in order to find when and how religion can correlate with masculine drives and influences.

A 2011 study by psychologists A. Zachary Ward and Stephen W. Cook, for example, measured the religiosity of 154 male undergraduate students of a primarily western Judeo-Christian tradition according to 11 masculine norms and five aspects of religiousness: religious commitment; intrinsic, extrinsic, and quest religious motivations; and religious fundamentalism.

The study found that "emotional control among men was negatively associated with religious commitment and intrinsic religiousness but positively associated with extrinsic religiousness" (Ward and Cook 54). In other words, men who exhibited more emotional control and less emotional expressiveness were less likely to maintain a consistent commitment to their religion's beliefs and values, but were more likely to subscribe to and boast about religious fundamentalism. The study found a similar correlation in tendencies toward violence: fewer tendencies toward violence correlated with religious commitment, while greater tendencies toward violence correlated with religious fundamentalism (Ward and Cook 53). The researchers concluded that "a commitment to the values and beliefs of one's religion is associated with more emotional expressiveness and fewer tendencies toward violence, whereas believing in the fundamental truths of one's religion is not" (Ward and Cook 54). Ward and Cook hypothesized that conformity to the masculine norm of power over women would be positively associated with religious commitment and religious fundamentalism, but instead found that only the correlation with fundamentalism existed (Ward and Cook 43). The researchers concluded that "fundamentalism contributes to traditional, patriarchal views of gender roles, whereas religious commitment does not" (Ward and Cook 43).

The conflict between fundamentalism and commitment could explain why men have been turning away from religious institutions, but toward the MC. Men who exhibit greater tendencies toward violence, more emotional control, and who are more likely to subscribe to patriarchal norms are attracted to a fundamentalism that religious institutions eventually fail to uphold. Most religious institutions expect their members to move beyond fundamentalism and into commitment, whereby those members would be expected to avail themselves to emotional expressiveness and submissiveness, and to give up their tendencies toward violence (Ward and Cook). Generally, the motorcycle club does not expect this kind of conformity from its members. Patch holders are free and, indeed, encouraged to express themselves through violence and to repress emotion. Sutter's drama, however, plays on the conflict between fundamentalism and commitment by depicting the internal struggle of men who subscribe wholly to the fundamentalism of the club, but who also wrestle with the requirements of commitment.

## "Sons live": Fundamentalism and Commitment

In the fourth episode of *Sons of Anarchy*'s first season, Sutter provides a kind of sacred, foundational scripture, as a means of defining the mission and morality of the Sons. Jax is led to an old bridge and walks past a small white cross decorated with American flags. He steps beneath the bridge and the camera pans down revealing old, spent beer bottles and sandy footprints—possibly remnants of Jax's father, John Teller. As Jax sets foot where his father once stood, John Teller's voice guides Jax to the words on the wall: *"Anarchism stands for liberation of the human mind from the dominion of religion; the liberation of the human body from the dominion of property; liberation from shackles and restraint of government. It stands for social order based on the free grouping of individuals"* (Emma Goldman). John Teller's discovery of the text, described to Jax in a disembodied monologue, and his experience of having the words "ripped" from inside of his head recalls Christian narratives of God's call to his prophets—including Moses, Gideon, Samuel, Isaiah, Jeremiah, and Ezekiel—which depict God's voice as at once external to the prophet but also within him, and in which that call comes during a time of distress or crisis, often accompanied by pain or confusion. Teller's experience also recalls Islam's prophet Muhammad, and his receipt of the Quran in the cave of Hira. Islamic tradition says that the angel Gabriel embraced Muhammad twice before he was able to receive the scripture; Salman Rushdie's impious retelling of Muhammad's revelations in his *Satanic Verses* sees this experience as desperately painful—an ethereal wrestling match—in which the pain is ultimately so great the prophet vomits and the scripture is revealed. John Teller is similarly invoked as a prophet; the foundational scriptures of his club are manifested to him through pain and enlightenment, and the concept of anarchism is presented as divine truth.

## Fundamentalism of the Sons

If fundamentalism is characterized by a strict, literal interpretation of scripture, then this Emma Goldman quote is about as close as one can get to the guiding principles of the Sons. The quote upholds "liberty" as its foremost virtue. According to Moral Foundations Theory, "liberty" is characterized by a group's rejection of an oppressive group or institution, but it is tempered by the foundation of "authority/subversion," which guides us to institute new hierarchies where none yet exist (Haidt). "Liberty" is at once the rejection of authority and the opportunity to establish a new authority in the void. Ironically, the text on the cave begins by railing against religion: anarchism is said to stand for the "liberation of the human mind from the dominion of religion." The irony, of course, is that the Sons will borrow language, symbols, and ceremonial rites from religion in the scaffolding of the club (Corn 118). The implication, then, is that the ideal of anarchism guides the Sons to reject a commitment to social constructs of established institutions, and to supply their own constructs instead.

The remaining liberties in Goldman's quote—liberation from property and government—point to some of the most significant conflicts within the series. The Sons do, in fact, own property and they fight to protect it, occasionally quarreling amongst themselves over how that property should be acquired and secured. Additionally, the Sons are deeply entangled with government officials, though they strive to maintain their distance. Yet the relativism embedded in Goldman's final line, in which she defines anarchism as "social order based on the free grouping of individuals," essentially gives the club the ability to re-establish social constructs according to the desires of the group. John Teller calls the concept of anarchism "pure, simple, true," but as is often the case with fundamentalism, the pillars by which the ideal is upheld become far less stable as the group's members bring conflicting interpretations and intentions to the table.

If the study conducted by Ward and Cook accurately represents the correlation between masculine drives and religious traits, then strict adherence to the foundational text is linked to increased violence and decreased emotional expressiveness. When Otto declares that the "Sons live" before plunging his crucifix into the neck of the prison infirmary nurse, he is uplifting the foundational concepts of the club's anarchism by rejecting the profits of his confession and the government's rule of law, and he has taken a sacred religious object into the symbology of his club, recasting it as an instrument for the club's promotion and implying the endorsement of a higher power.

John Teller's assertion that the concept of anarchism as described by Emma Goldman is "pure, simple, true" is possibly the most tragic fallacy in the narrative. Each of the show's seasons struggles to interpret and re-interpret the pillars of the club's anarchism, and it is this struggle which leads to the miscommunications, business failures, and the plethora of deaths which drive the show's plot. In order to mitigate the disputes which could arise over various interpretations of the foundational text, the Sons need guidance for working within the structure of the club. The Sons have, of course, bylaws which govern the members and their interactions. But in all seven seasons, those bylaws are only mentioned three times—and each time, they are mentioned within the context of changing a bylaw that the club no longer deems appropriate. In "Crucifixed," for example, Juice confesses that his father is black, and the Sons' bylaws refuse membership to non-whites. Without hesitation, Jax suggests that the Sons "need to change a few bylaws." Additionally, in the series' penultimate episode, Jax asks Les Packer, President of the SAMDINO chapter, to revoke an "unwritten bylaw" that has been around since the 70s; presumably, he is referring to a restriction against suicide, which would vindicate John Teller and which, we later discover, foreshadows Jax's own suicide at the series' finale.

Sutter has kept the Sons' bylaws to largely himself, but it seems clear that those bylaws have established rules for how members of the club interact with one another, as well as how members interact with the world beyond the club. This is the "social order" described in the Emma Goldman quote—it is the Sons' sovereign commitment to self-government, and it is the document which articulates how the rites, practices, and symbols of the club translate to social interaction. But "commitment" does not come easily to the Sons' demographic, which is less comfortable with the vulnerability embedded in subscribing to behavioral dictates.

## Commitment and Conflict

In his 2013 essay, "The Faith of Our Sons and the Tragic Quest," Kevin Corn posits that it is the "collapse-from-within of [the Sons'] collective values, purpose, and meaning" which catalyzes the narrative's tragedy. Essentially, Corn suggests that the Sons' tragedy is linked to their inability to commit to a collective set of rules, and to their inability to ascribe agreed-upon meanings to the pillars of the club's fundamentalism. In observing the religious symbology of the motorcycle club, Corn compares the MC to a cult—specifically, he sees similarities between the Sons and the Mexican cult of Santa Muerte, or "Holy Death" (Corn 123). Corn argues that the club's colors, which feature a scythe-wielding reaper, allude to Santa Muerte, and that the requirement that patch holders never leave the clubhouse without their kuttes is a method for effacing the individual identities of the members within the collective of the club.

While I fully agree that the MC takes its structural inspiration from religious entities, I would argue that the MC is less cultish than it is monasterial. In order to get a sense of what the Sons' bylaws might have looked like, one might turn to the Rule of Saint Benedict (ca. 480–550 AD), the foundational text for much of Western monasticism. Benedict's Rule was written primarily as a pious guide for unaffiliated, autonomous religious communities, but it came to be constitutional for most Christian monasteries by the Middle Ages. The Rule is foremost concerned with brotherhood—it negotiates relationships amongst brothers of all ranks, describes a brother's proper attire under various circumstances, outlines ceremonial rites and orders, dictates a brother's responsibilities to travelers, and prescribes corrective actions against brothers who have transgressed. The Rule was primarily intended to inspire amiable communion amongst the brotherhood; however, this last aspect of the Rule—corrective actions against brothers who have transgressed—could (and should) have caused concern for any new prospect. The corrective actions proposed in the Rule are not particularly harsh or unfair, mostly consisting of excommunication practices, demotions, and obstacles to reinstatement. Yet the need to articulate corrective actions indicates that transgressions can and will happen within the brotherhood. Benedict acknowledged that fear of correction could discourage prospective brothers in the prologue of his Rule, writing, "if, prompted by the desire to attain to equity, anything be set forth somewhat strictly for the correction of vice or the preservation of charity, do not therefore in fear and terror flee back from the way of salvation of which the beginning cannot but be a narrow entrance" (Nursia). If "belief" is the fundamental core of the religious community, then rules and bylaws describe the individual's relationship to that fundamental core. Benedict recognized that commitment to a belief system becomes more difficult when behavioral expectations and corrective actions arise from that system. John Teller shares Benedict's cautionary tone, as in responding to the Emma Goldman quote he says, "true freedom requires sacrifice and pain. Most human beings only think they want freedom. In truth they yearn for the bondage of social order, rigid laws, materialism. The only freedom man really wants, is the freedom to become comfortable." The rejection of comfort and adherence to a strict moral code (even under the guise of anarchism) are essential to the formation of the group, as that common suffering bonds them together in celebration of the club and its ideals. Yet the club's ethical code promotes violence and represses expressiveness, which correlates negatively with commitment. In other words, the club's endorsement of these aspects of masculinity has set the club up to be undone by members who wish to see the "Sons live," but whose devotion to their own interpretation of the club's fundamentalism will lead them to lash out violently, even against their own brothers.

## *"Redwood bleeds": Expression, Violence and Women*

As in monastic life, MC patch holders are expected not to see themselves as individuals who are participating in a hobby-based social group, but rather to see the club as an essential extension of their identity (Harris). Yet the need to gather and agree upon social codes for profitable interaction generates tension between the member's commitment to the club and his responsibilities to the chapter in which he rides. Membership with an MC requires forging interpersonal relationships within the patch holder's chapter. Due in large part to the cohabitative nature of the MC and the self-allocation of the club to the fringes of society, these interpersonal relationships lead to opportunities for disclosure, vulnerability, and exposed moments of emotional crescendo. It is in these moments that fundamentalism and commitment collide for the patch holder—because of the nature of his relationship to the MC, this collision almost inevitably erupts in violence.

## Violence and Expression— Violence as Expression

A 2005 study led by Matthew Jakupac of the Seattle VA Medical Center investigated the relationship between the masculine norms of shame and fear of emotion in order to determine how those norms relate to violent tendencies. Jakupac found that when studied together, tendencies toward violence and emotional control may be causally linked. Jakupac argues that "although factors of masculinity may be relevant to understanding men's hostility and aggression, this relationship is partly accounted for by men's fear of emotions" (Jakupak 283). The study found that men's self-reported fear of emotions was directly related to their proneness to hostility and aggression, which suggests that "gender role socialization contributes to men's aggressive tendencies by limiting alternative emotional expressions and/or interfering with men's ability to tolerate vulnerable feelings" (Jakupak 284). Furthermore, the study supported theories which suggest that masculine aggression serves as a function for emotional avoidance and/or as a strategy to regain control (O'Neil and Harway). In other words, proneness for aggression and avoidance of emotion—the two masculine norms which factor most heavily in men's religiosity (and, un-coincidentally, the two factors which are most prevalent in the drama of the Sons)–are inherently connected. In *Sons of Anarchy*, Sutter again and again provides explosive violence as a means of avoiding emotional release and securing control over others.

Fear of emotion may be one reason that fundamentalism is more appealing to most men than is commitment—fundamentalist beliefs and the passion attached to those beliefs are more or less static; a strict adherence to scripture does not offer much opportunity for new emotional experiences. Yet the practicality of interacting with other members, with prospects and associates, with the community surrounding the club, and with members of the opposite sex all provide opportunities for emotional expressiveness. If the club is to sustain the personal investments of its masculine membership without cannibalizing itself, therefore, then it must provide context within which masculine expression is permissible, even if that expression is violent.

The challenge, of course, is that violence for the sake of violence is destructive. Unsanctioned violence might provide emotional release in the moment, but it threatens to destabilize the bonds and social order of the club. Violence must, therefore, be sanctioned by the group if the group is to cater to (and potentially temper) the hostility that arises from emotional control. At the crossroads of sanctioned violence and adherence to an ethical standard, the motorcycle club again meets the medieval monastery. Though hostility and ill-will was strictly prohibited by the Benedictine Rule, medieval monasteries had to deal with the fact that their membership was likewise pulled in conflicting directions with respect to emotion and aggression. Also like the modern motorcycle club, the medieval monastery was surrounded by a world in conflict, and that conflict often came to violent ends. Though monks generally preached against violence, there were occasions in which the monastery would sanction war, as long as it was considered just. Probably the most notable of these occasions came from the 12th-century Cistercian monk, Bernard of Clairvaux. Bernard has been hailed as the monk who launched the second crusade, after having been commissioned by the Pope to preach on the justice of the war. In a sermon called "Why Another Crusade?" Bernard writes:

> Fly then to arms; let a holy rage animate you in the fight, and let the Christian world resound with these words of the prophet, "Cursed be he who does not stain his sword with blood!" If the Lord calls you to the defense of His heritage think not that His hand has lost its power. Could He not send twelve legions of angels or breathe one word and all His enemies would crumble away into dust? But God has considered the sons of men, to open for them the road to His mercy [Clairvaux, *Why Another Crusade?*].

The appeal for holy war speaks directly to the masculine draw toward fundamentalism, as it depicts the group's core values as under attack, and the men to whom those values have been entrusted have been "chosen" as the defenders of divine truth.

*Sons of Anarchy* is replete with examples of just war—against the IRA, the One-Niners, the Mayans, and even against certain government agencies and officials. Those just wars help to negotiate members' commitment to the club through defense of the club's fundamental values, and allow the patch holders to circumvent emotional vulnerability and demonstrate their love for the club in valiant acts of anti-heroism. As the introspective (and often-melancholic) voice of reason throughout the series, Jax regrets the necessity of violence, but makes only minor moves to deter it. His most significant gesture away from violence points him toward another masculine norm, which is also correlative with religious fundamentalism—power over women.

## Scapegoating the Ol' Lady

By the show's sixth season, Jax has decided to pull the club out of the gun-running business in order to pursue an endeavor that is touted as ultimately more legitimate—pornography and prostitution. There is, of course, much to criticize in the show's depiction of the sex trade—the women of the trade tend to be flat, uninteresting, objectified characters whose only purpose is to provide sexual escapades and financial support for the club, and who also occasionally serve up challenges to the established females—namely, Gemma and Tara—who must cope with their husbands' intimate interactions with these women. Their existence, however, points to another significant finding in Ward and Cook's study—specifically, that stronger tendencies toward the masculine norm of "power over women" also correlates with religious fundamentalism, but not with commitment. In other words, a patriarchal attitude once again makes men more likely to brace onto a fundamental belief system, but less likely to manifest the moral and social codes of that belief system in their daily lives.

Yet scholars like Leslie A. Aarons have noted that once a woman has risen to the title of "Ol' Lady," her agency accelerates, and her influence in the club becomes more noticeable. Kerry Fine has observed that *SOA*'s heroines tend to subscribe to the same "just war" and violent expression as do their male counterparts. Indeed, Tara, Gemma, and even wives on the fringes like Donna and Lyla, hold heavy sway over the motives of their husbands, and those influences can be seen in club votes and in-the-moment decisions. Yet ol' ladies tend not to enjoy long lives with the Sons; Lyla, in fact, is the only wife who seems to escape the series with her life. *SOA* wives' influence, therefore, is less in their personal agency and more in their femininity. No one makes this clearer than Clay Morrow, Jax's stepfather and the dethroned former President of SAMCRO, when while attending mass in prison in the sixth season, Clay interrupts the priest's homily to preach on the redemptive power of the female: "I can't sit! I got the Lord in me! He wants me up, He wants me preaching, He wants me to spread the gospel ... pussy the healer, pussy the redeemer—Can I get a 'Amen' for pussy!" Once again, the sacred is conflated with the profane, as Christ is displaced by "pussy"—a synecdoche which reduces the female to an agent of sexuality and reinforces masculine power over her.

Yet Clay's celebration of the female as "healer" and "redeemer" is not entirely without sincerity. The show's female characters tend to be more protagonist than antagonist, and they often provide moments of escape for the male characters, allowing them to encounter emotion where that emotion would have been unacceptable in purely masculine circles. Prior to his attack on the prison nurse, for example, Otto buries his face in Tara's lap while he masturbates and breathes in his dead wife's perfume, and he is able to break down and weep. This is an important moment for both Otto and Tara; Tara begins to acknowledge her own draw toward depravity (evidenced by her own self-pleasuring as she recalls that moment at home in her bedroom), and Otto has given himself over to emotional release, which means that his violent attack on the infirmary nurse the following day is strategic, not reactionary.

Beyond a dictate for celibacy, the Benedictine Rule has little to say about relationships with women. St. Bernard of Clairvaux, however, is probably best known for his hyper-sexual descriptions of monastic life in his sermons on the Song of Songs. In the sermons, Bernard meditates on the Song of Solomon—a romantic poem about a bride's sexual encounter with her bridegroom. Bernard inverts gender roles and casts the monks as the bride and Christ as the bridegroom; he describes the intimate encounter with Christ as an ecstasy intended to maintain the loyalty of the brethren. In his *Sermon 61* for example, St. Bernard comments on a moment in the Song of Songs in which the bridegroom refers to his beloved as "My dove in the clefts of the rock," and suggests that the monks are like the bridegroom who seek the pleasure of Christ in their private spaces:

> He acts like a bridegroom, but as one who is shy, who shrinks from public view and wants to enjoy his pleasures in an out of the way spot, "in the clefts of the rock and the crannies of the wall." And when you consider the lovers themselves, think not of a man and a woman but of the Word and the soul. And if I should say Christ and the Church the same applies, except that the word Church signifies not one soul but the unity or rather unanimity of many. Nor must you think of the "clefts of the rock" and "the crannies of the wall" as hiding places for wicked carryings-on, or else some suspicion from the powers of darkness will straightway take hold of you [Clairvaux, *Sermons on the Song of Songs*].

St. Bernard winks at the notion that "the clefts of the rock and the crannies of the wall" would be places for lusty deeds, suggesting instead that those "clefts" are places for righteous pleasure. Yet Bernard goes on to compare the "clefts of the rock" to the "wounds of Christ," which the bridegroom wishes to enter. Christ's wounds were often conflated with vaginal imagery in Medieval Christian texts (Lochrie 190), so Bernard uses sexuality and desire to endorse a commitment to the monastic life. The desire to enter the clefts is desire to commit to the church, or so Bernard implies. Similarly, Clay's sarcastic praise for the redemptive female is a sermon that supports the moral pillars of MC life, as he taps into the masculine desire for power over women to suggest that to acquire "pussy" is to experience the liberation that is a the heart of the Sons' sacred text.

But to be like Christ is to be sacrificed. Fundamentalism tends to correlate with power over women, and so it is essential to the masculine narrative that individual females are dispossessed of their power over the men. According to philosopher and literary critic René Girard, communities in conflict will reach a moment of catharsis, in which the sacrifice of a "surrogate victim"–a scapegoat—bears the blame for the community's conflict, though the scapegoat is at least partly (and often entirely) innocent of the crimes for which she atones. Gesturing toward the Yom Kippur ritual of burdening a goat with the sins of the community and then sending it off to die in the wilderness, Girard writes in *Violence and the Sacred* that "all religious rituals spring from the surrogate victim, and all the great institutions of mankind, both secular and religious, spring from ritual.... It could hardly be otherwise, for the working basis of human thought, the process of 'symbolization,' is rooted in the surrogate victim" (Girard 306). The casting off of the scapegoat, according to Girard, is reflective of a subconscious "victimizing mechanism." Unlike typical sacrifices, which are enacted as rituals of gift-giving and worship, the victimizing mechanism causes a community to denigrate one of its members as a means for restoring harmony within the community.

The women who are sacrificed throughout the series each push the characters toward a more broadened awareness of the club's place within the world. From the burning alive of Tig's daughter, to the accidental shooting of Donna, and even the repeated sufferings of Jax's ex-wife Wendy, each deceased or mortified female pushes the male characters to reevaluate their relationship to the club and its principles. When Otto declares that "Redwood bleeds" as he ends the life of the infirmary nurse, he sees Tara as the SAMCRO chapter personified—she is the essence of the chapter, and in condemning her to life within the federal criminal system, he condemns all of the Redwood Originals.

## *The Patch Holder and the Higher Power*

Motorcycle club culture, as it is depicted in *Sons of Anarchy*, promotes violence and power over women, and discourages emotional expression. Coincidentally violence, power over women, and emotional control are also linked to men's attraction to religious fundamentalism, but they complicate men's ability to commit to the moral codes of their religion in their daily lives. Religious institutions expect daily commitment to certain beliefs and values; that commitment comes more easily to men who show fewer violent tendencies and greater emotional expression. Men who are attracted to fundamentalism, it could be concluded, are attracted to the motorcycle club "church" more than religious institutions because the MC allows them to adhere to clearly-articulated and (theoretically) unambiguous ideals, without having to sacrifice violence, patriarchy, or emotional control.

That isn't, however, to say that men who are attracted to fundamentalism are inherently flawed, or are incapable of committing to a collaboratively developed social code. It means only that this kind of masculinity is drawn in first by ideals. They are mission-driven; they strive for purity and simplicity in their values, and they respect clarity in their communications. They struggle when they perceive that the foundations of their beliefs have been misinterpreted or desecrated, and that struggle may lead more quickly to aggression than it would for some of their peers. They gather under shared symbols and observe shared ceremonial rites as a means of negotiating relationships and establishing community, and they are able to reconcile without much difficulty a sense of dominion over the women in their lives, and a sense that their lives absolutely depend on the essence of those women.

At its heart, the motorcycle club narrative is about man's relationship to higher power. When a biker wears the kutte, he is yielding his identity to a cause greater than himself. In weaving religious symbology throughout each episode of *Sons of Anarchy*, Kurt Sutter reminds the viewer again and again that there are larger forces at play in the biker narrative. What looks like profaning sacred objects—using them in violent or sexual acts—instead empowers them for an audience whose fundamentalist drives see sex and violence as reverential. For seven seasons, the Sons provided a tantalizing sanctuary in which to explore pious devotion alongside steamy transgression, and allowed a previously unacknowledged audience to step forward and be counted.

## Works Cited

Aarons, Leslie A. "When a Charming Woman Speaks." *Sons of Anarchy and Philosophy*, edited by G.A. Dun, J.T. Everl, & W. Irwin. Wiley, 2013, pp. 165–74.
Baston, C.D., P.A. Schoenrade, & W. Ventis. *The Religious Experience: A Social-Psychological Perspective*. Oxford University Press, 1993.
Clairvaux, Saint Bernard of. *Sermons on the Song of Songs*. Amazon Digital Services, 2013.
\_\_\_\_\_. *Why Another Crusade?* Amazon Digital Services. Accessed 31 May 2017.
Corn, Kevin. "That Faith of Our Sons and the Tragic Quest." *Sons of Anarchy and Philosophy*, edited by G.A. Dunn, J.T. Eberl, & W. Irwin. Wiley, 2013, pp. 117–27.
Cox, Nicole B., and Lauren J. DeCarvalho. "'Ride Free or Die' Trying: Hypermasculinity on FX's *Sons of Anarchy*. *Journal of Popular Culture*, vol. 49, no. 4, 2016, pp. 818–38.
De Vaus, D., and I. McAllister. "Gender Differences in Religion: A Test of the Structural Location Theory." *American Sociological Review*, vol. 52, no. 4, pp. 1385–1401.
"Fundamentalism." *Oxford Living Dictionaries*. https://en.oxforddictionaries.com/definition/fundamentalism. Accessed 31 May 2017.
Gilman, Greg. *The Wrap*. 29 October 2014. Accessed 3 June 2017.
Girard, Rene. *Violence and the Sacred*. A&C Black, 2005.
Haidt, Jonathan. *The Righteous Mind: Why Good People Are Divided by Politics and Religion*. Random House, 2013.
Harris, Kira J. "The Fierce Commitment to 1% Motorcycle Clubs." *Journal of Policing, Intelligence and Counter Terrorism*, vol. 11, 2014, pp. 73–83.
Hibberd, James. *Entertainment Weekly*. 6 December 2011. Accessed 31 May 2017.
Jakupak, Matthew. "Masculinity, Shame, and Fear of Emotions as Predictors of Men's Expressions of Anger and Hostility." *Psychology of Men & Masculinity*, vol. 6, no. 4, 2005, pp. 275–84.
Lochrie, Karma. "Mystical Acts, Queer Tendencies." *Constructing Medieval Sexuality*, edited by Karma Lochrie, Peggy McCracken, and James A. Schulz. University of Minnesota Press, 1997, pp. 180–200.
Long, V.O., and C.H. Heggen. "Clergy Perceptions of Spiritual Health for Adults, Men, and Women." *Counseling and Values*, vol. 32, no. 3, 1992, pp. 325–37.
Miller, A.S., and J.P. Hoffman. "Risk and Religion: An Explanation of Gender Differences in Religiosity." *Journal for the Scientific Study of Religion*, vol. 34, no. 1, 1995, pp. 63–75.
Nursia, Saint Benedict of. *The Rule of St. Benedict, Translated into English*. S.P.C.K., 1931.
O'Neil, J.M., and M. Harway. "A Multivariate Model Explaining Men's Violence toward Women." *Violence Against Women*, vol. 3, no. 2, 1997, pp. 182–203.
Sullins, D.P. "Gender and Religion: Deconstructing Universality, Constructing Complexity." *American Journal of Sociology*, vol. 112, no. 3, 2006, pp. 838–80.

Thompson, E.H. "Beneath the Status Characteristic: Gender Variations in Religiousness." *Journal for the Scientific Study of Religion*, vol. 30, no. 4, 1991, pp. 381–94.
Toto, Christian. *Breitbart*. 19 October 2014. Accessed 3 June 2017.
Ward, A. Zachary, and Stephen W. Cook. "The Complex Associations Between Conforming to Masculine Norms and Religiousness in Men." *Psychology of Men & Masculinity*, vol. 12, no. 1, 2011, pp. 42–54.
Webb, Eugene. "Girard, Sacrifice, and Religious Symbolism." *Journal of European Psychoanalysis. Humanities, Philosophy, Psychotherapies*, vol. 11, no. 1, 2002, pp. 17–18.

# Compilation Score and Trans-Diegetic Music
## *How Music Helps Give Voice to the Voiceless*

JESSICA SHINE

In her foreword to James Deaville's edited collection *Music in Television: Channels of Listening*, Claudia Gorbman notes that

> television is ... the nation's jukebox. Music is everywhere on television, endowed with all manner of signaling devices, emotive values, and rhetorical functions. Its ubiquity and variety entice us to reconsider distinctions between performance of music and music whose performers are invisible, to reevaluate notions of genre inherited from the movies, and to think about the fluctuating nature of audience identifications [ix].

*Sons of Anarchy* is a show rich with music; its pilot episode contained 16 songs, and season one featured 86 separate pieces of music. Almost all the music used in the seven seasons is pre-existing music, but the show also makes extensive use of specifically commissioned cover songs, and many of these cover songs are done by the same bands, which helps create a coherent sound for the show. With such a ubiquity of music it is little surprise then that the show's musical soundtrack became one of its defining features and lives on after the show as popular soundtrack albums. Throughout the series, this soundtrack invites the audience to question characters and their motives, to draw parallels between oppressed members of the show, and to undermine the authority of some of the show's leading figures.

In the diegetic world of the show, the Sons of Anarchy inhabit the fringes of society where they have constructed an alternative world of brotherhood and freedom that they fund through gun-running. While predominantly a white MC, SAMCRO comprises Scottish, Jewish, and Latino men, all of whom consider each other brothers; African American men, however, are barred from joining the club. In the patriarchal world of the club, women are the predominant outsiders. Though "old ladies" demonstrate considerable influence over their respective partners, the club is the primary consideration for most members. Women are excluded from "Church" and from any decision-making in relation to the club, and are often the victims of violence. In contrast to the fictional world, the show's soundtrack is surprisingly egalitarian. While predominantly comprised of hard-rock, Americana, and alternative-country, the soundtrack often incorporates themes, voices, and sounds that do not fit with the Club's manifesto. This essay analyses how the soundtrack, in combination with visual montage, often undermines, questions, and exposes the club's hypocritical philosophy under the stewardship of Clay, and foregrounds the true outsiders in the club and crosses the narrational divide between diegetic and non-diegetic.

## *The Pop Music Score*

As a medium, television differs from film. Kevin Donnelly notes: "Television is fragmented (Nelson 1997, p. 24) within a continuous 'flow' (Williams 1979, p. 78). This tessellated form obviates the need for lengthy sections of music to hold duration and build continuity and reaction through successive developments. Instead, what is required is that certain moments are emphasised, noted as significant, monumentalised and aestheticized" (331). The serial nature of television allows writers and directors to pace the action more slowly than films; TV shows are often allowed the freedom to dwell on moments of joy or anguish, and to develop these scenes beyond what is allowed in the restricted time-frame of a film. Television also allows for a great deal of intertextuality between episodes, for the development of episodic leitmotifs, and for the establishment of aesthetic and acoustic paradigms. Though it is important to assert that television shows may not always be analyzed by simply regurgitating film-music theory, an understanding of the compilation score and the use of pre-existing music in cinema helps to understand the use of such soundtracks in high-quality television. *Sons of Anarchy* fits easily within the remit of high-quality television and many of its episodes were feature length.[1]

It is now widely accepted in film and television music scholarship that a popular song can be as effective as a specifically composed score and that popular and pre-existing music can impact on the images and characters of a film. In some cases, compilation scores have become the driving force for marketers, or a signature characteristic of particular directors or franchises. Music supervisors are often requested to add songs from particular artists or labels to boost sales and artist profiles. The demands of marketing placed on those using compilation scores resembles, in many ways, the corporate pressure placed by studios on composers during the 60s and 70s to produce a "hit" pop song for the films for which they were composing, even if the pop song did not fit the narrative or aesthetic of the film. For television, compilation scores are far more common than specifically composed scores. The recent "Golden Age of Television" has also seen an increase in the demand for "hit" soundtracks for television shows. Melissa Locker notes that

> more recently, television shows have developed hit-filled soundtracks thanks to the work of music supervisors like Alexandra Patsavas on The OC and Grey's Anatomy. Patsavas built major plot points around songs: in The OC, Marissa's death was soundtracked by Imogen Heap's cover of Hallelujah, while Izzie's grief at Danny's death in Grey's played out to Snow Patrol's Chasing Cars. Today, music supervisor Chris Mollere continues the tradition on shows like Pretty Little Liars and The Vampire Diaries.

*Sons of Anarchy*'s soundtrack clearly retains some marketing elements; however, it is also an integral part of the show's aesthetic and is a key narrational element. Throughout the series, the *Sons'* soundtrack serves to add value to episodes and acts as the emotional core of scenes.

Though it might now seem entirely commonsensical, the realization that pre-existing music has its own cultural connotations and meanings and that these subsequently impact (directly or indirectly) the film or television show was a relatively late development in the analysis of film soundtracks. Estella Tinknell points out that "it was not until the mid 1960s that the pop soundtrack became more fully integrated into film texts in terms of narrative as well as spectacle, but this process brought with it a clear shift away from the conventions of the integrated musical, a shift that would inform the ways in which the soundtrack film produces meaning" (133). Two of the earliest films to utilize this new convention to its full effect were *The Graduate* (Nichols 1967) and *Easy Rider* (Hopper 1969). Mervyn Cooke argues that *The Graduate* "began the trend of using pop lyrics to suggest a character's otherwise unvoiced preoccupations" (409). Jeff Smith's *Sounds of Commerce* (1998) also convincingly argued that the compilation score and the pop score were as successful as the classical Hollywood score in providing emotional cues, augmenting film settings, and acting as a signifier of characters' feelings.

Throughout the 1990s the pop score was ubiquitous in popular cinema and became a lucrative source of financial revenue for filmmakers. In the same period, directors such as Danny Boyle and Baz Luhrman demonstrated how popular songs could both boost revenue for the films through soundtrack sales and, at the same time, be integral to the aesthetic of the films. In fact, often the more complementary the soundtrack was to the onscreen action, the more successful the soundtrack sales were.[2] In the 2000s to the present, which is widely regarded as a Golden Age of television, compilation scores are ubiquitous. Shows like *The Sopranos* (Chase 1999–2007), *Boardwalk Empire*[3] (Winter 2010–14), and *Breaking Bad* (Gilligan 2008–13) have all used compilation scoring, and have cultivated an audio-visual aesthetic that is heavily reliant on this interplay of pre-existing music and the image.

Cooke argues that the proliferation of the compilation score undermined traditionally composed film music (413) while Ian Inglis suggests that the pop score successfully displaced the composed score because "it performs its required tasks with equal (or greater) effectiveness" (5). Though compilation scores were not as efficient as composed scores at providing films with narrative continuity, pre-existing music offered directors opportunities to draw attention to the music and to create MTV-inspired montage sequences by linking seemingly unrelated events or by linking similar events that take place at separate places and times. Throughout *Sons of Anarchy*, pre-existing music is used, in combination with montage techniques, to create links between characters, to draw parallels between their struggles, and to undermine their diegetically vocalized intentions.

Many scholars also note that popular music can have not only an equal effect on the visual elements of the film as a traditional score but that, in some instances, it can be perceived as more noticeable. Jerrold Levinson argues that with appropriated, as opposed to composed, scores more attention is drawn to the music, both because it is often recognized as such and located by the viewer in cultural space, and also because the impression it gives of "chosenness,"[4] on the part of the implied filmmaker, is greater (145).

Lannin and Caley assert that pop songs have identical components to a film, which makes them extremely compatible media. These components of image, text, and sound interact between film and the song. They write that

> "image" in a pop song might be the "images" conjured by the lyrics, its iconic singer(s), its record-sleeve, the ubiquitous accompanying video-clip, its previous use in adverts or the "dream-images" it conjures up for the individual or collective consciousness—in other terms its hinterland of visual associations. The pop song adds its own suite of meanings to a films [sic], and how this heady mix is managed is of primary importance to whether the film succeeds in its endeavours [9–10].

For some songs in *Sons of Anarchy*, the lyrics are clearly the predominant reason for the choice of song, as they often resonate uncannily with the on-screen action. The show's creator, Kurt Sutter, commented on one particular song, Queen's "Bohemian Rhapsody" which played over a montage where Jax murders someone. He states that the lyrics and the song's story were the primary reason for choosing the song, as its musicality did not "fit" with the show's other use of music: "It doesn't really fit our model in terms of '60s music but the story behind that song feels very parallel to the show in terms of someone being condemned and looking for redemption. It's such a crazy ass song, and I throw these things at Bob" (qtd. in Bierly). That said, the show's music supervisor, Bob Thiele, did render the song in such a way that it would fit the show's musical aesthetic. He commissioned soundtrack regulars The Forest Rangers to cover the song. This use of songs that have very similar lyrics to the on-screen action has not always been warmly received by critics, despite the popularity of the soundtrack itself. While review sites like *AV Club* welcomed the montage with closely linked lyrics, *The Concourse* writer Susan Elizabeth Shepherd wrote an article entitled "Say Goodbye to Sons of Anarchy and its Lousy Soundtrack" (2014), in which she zealously critiqued almost every aspect of the show's soundtrack.

## *The Role of the Compilation Score*

Popular music is omnipresent in society, and genres of it evoke particular cultural associations and moods. Many soundtracks rely on these cultural resonances produced by various genres and these cultural associations often dictate how this music is utilized. Sometimes the expected associations are inverted and the resulting incongruity of the image-music combination produces a desirable effect. The way Americana, country music, and iconic popular songs are used in *Sons of Anarchy* often relies on the expected associations the audience will have with these songs/pieces of music, and these associations are often inverted or extended to new themes or characters.

Most of the songs featured in the show fall within the broad spectrum of indie/alternative hard-rock and Americana.[5] Many of these songs have a distinctly American sound, which helps give a sense of place to the show; however a thorough discussion of that aspect of the show's soundtrack is beyond the rubrics of this essay. This choice of music makes sense given the diegetic location of the show, its mainly male protagonists, and its apparently macho (often violent) aesthetic and themes. However, the music in the show is not simply a marketing device or a sonic mirror for the show's masculine imagery, it is also very much a part of the show's storytelling process. Rather than being consigned to background noise or filler between scenes, music is frequently the central focus of the scenes in which it is employed. Often, the diegetic sounds are totally muted or faded into the background and music becomes the narrational voice for lengthy montage sequences. These montage sequences, in turn, became one of the show's defining audio-visual characteristics. In Zack Handlen's review of the first episode ("Black Widower") of the *Sons*'s final season (7) he asks two questions: "Was there a musical montage?... Was there horrific violence?" In the body of the review, Handlen notes,

> Both of them [montages] served the same purpose as Sons' montages have done since time immemorial. Here's our ensemble; look at them doing a lot of mundane shit; here are some members of the ensemble who are not doing mundane shit; isn't it ironic how their violence contrasts against the pretty music. That last trick is no longer an effective one, because the element of surprise is completely gone. These days, any time a sad, sweet song kicks in, you know that murder will be along shortly. The fact that the gimmick doesn't work as well as it used to isn't really the fault of this particular series, but it is something you'd think someone would've caught on to by now. But then, maybe it was never supposed to be ironic, not really. Maybe this, at its heart, is Sutter's vision: horror and beauty without any clear distinction between the two.

Handlen's comments about the montage becoming "old" is justifiable, especially for a show that spanned seven seasons and incorporated a significant amount of music, but also because this particular audio-visual fusion of sonic "beauty" and visual violence being is also widely used in cinema.[6]

Hilary Lapedis writes:

> Pop songs in films use pop's own emotional conventions and, in so doing, place those films in a much wider context of popular culture than would be the case with a traditional score. Contrary, therefore, to Schoenberg's view that "music should never drag a meaning around with it," and Eisler's description of "abstract art par excellence," pop music, while having an existence separate from the visual system, nevertheless possesses its own codified meanings and associations. These meanings are drawn from shared conventions of musical meaning that are then associated with the visual system to which they are harnessed [370].

In many ways, these montages in *Sons of Anarchy* depend on the audience's prior associations with particular songs or, at the very least, a basic musical knowledge that a particular song would not traditionally be associated with violence. In these sequences, songs retain their original meaning which, when paired with visual violence or other material, is then imbued with new meanings. In *Sons of Anarchy*, the songs are often played right through from the beginning to the end, and up to five minutes of screen time can be dominated by one song; this allows the song to effectively retain its own narrative integrity and not purely be bent to the vision of the scene. This essay will analyze two montage sequences that do not conform to the show's established montage of "pretty song" overlaying horrific violence and instead, these two sequences add to the range of voices that appear in the show's soundtrack and add an extra layer of commentary that undermines and undercuts these acts of violence.

## Gemma's Confession

In season two, episode ten, "Balm," Patti Griffin's song "Mary" overlays a long montage sequence that is anchored by a distressing sequence where

Gemma Teller tells her son Jax and husband Clay that she has been gang-raped by a White Supremacist gang, spearheaded by a menacing character named Zobelle. The rape occurs because SAMCRO sell guns to African Americans. This storyline critiques and problematizes many elements of the biker gang culture depicted in the show. Firstly, even though Zobelle and Hale intend to wipe out the Sons, it is a woman whom they target to send a message to the MC, rather than one of its male members. Throughout the show, women are often the intended, but sometimes incidental, targets of violence that is not necessarily aimed directly at them. Often, women are harmed to hurt the men other men perceive as "owners" of those women. Equally, despite the fact that SAMCRO prohibit African American members in their manifesto, they are pitted against the Aryans because they sell to people of color. Neither women nor black people can be members of the club, yet both are victims of violence directed at the club. It is a feature of the show that those who are not members of the club suffer the most because of the club's actions. It is the marginalized outsiders who are aligned with the club that are the real victims.

The show often depicts Clay Morrow as a cunning, ruthless and judicious man who makes deals with people when it suits his club, and himself, the best. This is emblematic of his relationship with women and with African Americans. His respect for these marginalized groups is contingent on its benefit for him. In contrast, in this early season, Jax is depicted as having genuine respect for his mother and his love interest, Tara, and often attempts to put their needs ahead of his own. Before Gemma's confession, Jax had applied to go "nomad," effectively leaving his position as VP and hitting the road. This would have placed Jax further outside the club, perhaps not as outside as an "old lady" but much lower in the rankings than a resident club member. On hearing about the rape, however, Jax picks up his VP patch once more.

Gemma's confession takes place at the dining table in the house she and Clay share. Clay sits at the head of the table as usual, and Jax and Tara sit side by side across from Gemma. "Mary" by Patti Griffin plays from beginning to end. The singing voice of the singer is pitched in volume just below that of Gemma's, with the lyrics clearly audible as Gemma begins her story. As Gemma pauses her narrative the camera leaves her and moves to look at other characters whose women have suffered because of the club's actions. Piney, whose daughter-in-law was murdered on Clay's orders; Chibs, who is forced to deal with the IRA leader who stole his wife and daughter from him; and Unser, the decorated police chief who has been corrupted but who carries a torch for Gemma. The musical accompaniment means that this montage sequence does not link Gemma's suffering with that of the men featured in the montage but to the women whom those men lost as a direct result of their involvement with the club.

Griffin's song "Mary" repackages Jesus' narrative from the perspective of Mary. As Gemma speaks, the verses play. As the camera focuses on Gemma's face the lyrics become almost a part of the camera's gaze. The lyrics recall the image of Gemma, left tied up to a chain fence, soaking wet and covered in bruises and blood. As the camera pans from male to male, the lyrics begin to take on an ironic slant talking about how Mary stays while she loses her sons, how she stays loyal and true while it is the men who do the world proud. The lyrics suggest that men, in this instance Jesus, get the credit and glory, while women suffer loss after loss but remain faithful and loyal servants. For Gemma, it was in service to the club that she kept the rape secret, and it is in service to her son reveals her it. As Griffin's song fades slightly in volume, Gemma's voice fills the sonic space once more. The camera returns to the table where Gemma sits, and Gemma continues her narrative. The second montage occurs during the second verse of the song as we pan over Tig and Half-Sack as Tig mourns the moment he shot Donna and as Half-Sack soothes his testicles in the mud. The camera then returns to the table for the chorus. Once again Gemma's voice is pitched slightly louder than Griffin's and as the song recalls Jesus telling his mother that he can no longer stay, the camera lingers on Jax. After the third montage movement over Opie, whose wife was murdered on Clay's instructions, the camera returns to the table, where once more Jax is aligned with Jesus. The camera stays with the table for the remainder of the song. The rest of the scene is devoid of speech, and Griffin's voice swells, replacing Gemma's narrative. At the very end of the scene Jax picks up his patches and holds them in his hands and looks back at his mother, clearly indicating that she is the reason for his return to the club: unlike the other men, Jax does not put his own interests first. Jax, unlike the Jesus of Griffin's song, takes on the female role and returns to a life he hates to be with his mother.

What is significant about this scene is the dominance of the female voice. Apart from a brief moment in the second montage where Tig cries "I'm so sorry," the only voices heard are those of Gemma and Griffin. As the show ends and the Sons logo appears, it is still Griffin's voice that plays. While the effect of Clay's dominance, and by proxy, masculine dominance can be seen in the suffering of the characters in the montage sequences, his voice is absent; the only voices audible are those of the female outsiders. Despite the patriarchal nature of the show's diegesis, the soundscape gives precedence to the woman's voice. Though not a member of the club, Gemma repeatedly sacrifices herself for the club, even sacrificing her previous husband in the interests of the MC. Just like Mary, who sacrifices her son for the greater good, but who is often consigned to the sidelines in the narrative of Jesus, Gemma plays her part but is never truly a member. However, just as Griffin's song repackages the story and makes Mary the focus, *Sons of Anarchy* repackages

Gemma's story and gives her a greater power than she normally has. Gemma confesses on her terms and the men are completely silenced.

Simon Frith suggests that, through music, spectators are "drawn to identify not with the film characters themselves but with their emotions" and that these emotions are "signalled pre-eminently by music which can offer us emotional experience directly" (256). Here, however, it appears as if we are invited to do both. We are invited in this scene to see it from a female perspective, from Gemma's point of view. Certainly, there is nothing of Clay in the lyrics of the song, nor is there anything identifiably male in its delivery. The whole scene resonates with a feminine voice, its narrative is delivered from the female perspective because the lyrics and the voices frame the situation in favor of the female figure. The scene is not dominated by the male anger but by vulnerability and sadness, things not associated with the men of the Sons. Even when Jax slams his hand on the table, his actions are quickly overcome by his tender gesture as he kisses his mother's hands. Jax's subsequent decision to return to the club changes our perspective of him, and differentiates him from the male in the song. By aligning Jax with the female voice the show asks us to identify with him and with Gemma, but not with Clay.

## Uniting the Struggle of African Americans and Women

By season four the club has splintered and loyalty is divided between Jax and Clay. Jax's discovery that Gemma and Clay were together before his father's death and that his father had sired a child with a Northern Irish woman turns him briefly against his mother, but permanently against Clay. As Clay's hands continue to weaken from his arthritis he literally begins to lose his grip on the club.[7] His decision to get the club involved with a Mexican drug cartel backfires and the club takes heavy casualties. The MC is forced to align with their former rivals, a Mexican MC called the Mayans. Under his stewardship SAMCRO becomes less and less an MC who deal guns to fund an alternative life on the fringes of society and more a solely criminal enterprise. Though Clay strikes up an alliance with the Mayans, whom he calls "wetbacks," and seems to develop a type of friendship with Alvarez, it is clear that women are not the only outsiders in Clay's club.

Season four opens with the incarcerated members preparing to leave prison. Jax is shown to have cut his hair and acquired some new scars while in lock-up. Joshua James' song "Coal War" opens the episode and its lyric foreshadow the main themes of the season. As James sings that he will not cut his hair until the "Good Lord" returns we see that Jax has a new haircut.

The scene segues into a familiar montage sequence and cuts to Tara as she reads the letters which will eventually drive both Gemma and Jax to betray Clay. "Coal War" continues with its premonitory lyrics and as James sings that he will not open his eyes until people of all races are free and equal. This theme of race becomes the cornerstone of season four, as one of the central storylines hinges on the hidden racial identity of a SAMCRO member. As the club members leave prison they are to return to a very different Charming to the one they left. The town is now under the auspices of the San Joaquin County Sheriff, headed by the Lieutenant Eli Roosevelt, who is African American.

The new figure of Lincoln Potter, the U.S. Attorney, on the other hand, is as corrupt as season three's ATF Agent June Stahl. He manipulates Roosevelt into playing the race card with one of the MC members, Juice. Potter uncovers the fact that Juice's father was black, which means that Juice cannot be a member of the club. If the club members find out that Juice is African American he must leave the club but he has no desire to leave the club, as it is his only family. Eventually he capitulates to the pressure exerted on him by the attorney and steals some cocaine from the shipment. Unfortunately for him, he gets caught by one of the Prospects and, in a bid to save himself, shoots the Prospect in the head. Juice is unable to deal with his guilt and attempts to hang himself from a tree; this harrowing image recalls the historical imagery of lynchings.

The song chosen for this sequence is "Strange Fruit" which was made famous by Billie Holiday. "Strange Fruit" was originally a poem written by Abel Meeropol.[8] In its stanzas, which form the verses of the songs, the poem protested the savagery of racist lynchings in the U.S. It became a significant song for the anti-racist protest movements. In the original poem entitled "Bitter Fruit," Meeropol's description of the lynching victims mirror the show's own symbolism, particularly the references to crows which resonates with the Son's moniker SAMCRO, which is often abbreviated to CRO. The crow has also been a feature of much of the music used during all the seasons, including the title song. The song also reflects the moment where "Fly Low Carrion Crow" by the band Two Gallants plays in episode 11 of season two, where Jax reads his father's journal and learns of the true purpose of the club: freedom. Once more the imagery of a piece of music recalls another scene, and as Juice's body swings from the tree the scene reverberates with the imagery of Meeropol's "Strange Fruit" and the overall imagery of the show itself.

In this scene though it is not Billie Holiday's iconic voice that carries the song but Katey Sagal's. Sagal performs one song per season (Muse) which adds an unusual strand to the soundtrack. Sagal's singing voice is close to her speaking voice, and though, as Shepherd points out, "she's not singing in character, … it feels a little like she could be." The fact that it is the same voice performing the "non-diegetic" song and speaking in the diegetic world of the show is difficult to ignore and it breaks down the separation between the diegesis and the extra-diegetic soundtrack. This crossing of boundaries between the supposedly non-diegetic soundtrack and the action onscreen is indicative of the *Sons of Anarchy* soundtrack, and especially these montage sequences. Thiele notes that the band The Forest Rangers, whom Sagal sings with sometimes on the soundtrack, are like "another character on the show" (qtd. in Bierly). This problematizes a traditionally held distinction between diegetic and non-diegetic music.[9] Anahid Kassabian argues that "the distinction between diegetic and nondiegetic music thus obscures music's role in producing the diegesis itself" (43). This argument is particularly relevant for *Sons of Anarchy* as the onscreen action is frequently literally reflected by the lyrics of the song and the repetition of familiar voices, including the Forest Rangers and Katey Sagal, allows these cover songs to take on the feeling of a simultaneously external and internal narrator, and in some ways seems to produce, or at least influence the diegetic events. Thiele states, "If you look at screen time, we have a lot of lines. I think the instrumentalists in the band and the singers that we use are identifiable to the show. So the White Buffalo is one of our really familiar true voices. He sang that whole dark low, "Mama, I just killed a man"—and that's really what's happening on-screen. Kurt obviously knew what was gonna happen when he came up with this idea" (qtd. in Bierly). Sagal's vocals extend this problematization of the non-diegetic soundtrack by the instantly recognizable timbre of her voice, and the fact the themes, issues and emotions that Sagal vocalizes in her renditions of the songs directly relate to the characters on-screen.

Robynn Stilwell's article "The Fantastical Gap between Diegetic and Nondiegetic" discusses this gray area between diegetic and non-diegetic. She argues that this space is a liminal one between diegetic and non-diegetic and that it is "a place of destabilization and ambiguity" that "highlights a gap in our understanding" (186). She argues that traditionally the ideas of non-diegetic and diegetic have been viewed as "adjacent bubbles" between which there is little transfer (186). She and Jim Buhler, therefore, termed this threshold-like space as the "fantastical gap" arguing that this phrase captured both its "magic and its danger" (187). Sagal's rendition of "Strange Fruit" creates such a tension between diegetic and non-diegetic, existing in a liminal space in between. By utilizing Sagal's rendition of "Strange Fruit" rather than Holliday's this scene links the struggle of women to the struggle of African American characters in the show. Despite the fact Sagal is not singing in character, the recognizable timbre of her voice transforms the song from being a "non-diegetic" commentary on the scene by an unknown narrator to being a trans-diegetic vocalization by a character of things that they cannot vocalize in the diegetic world. The use of Sagal's voice here gives power to her character in one sense, but also reveals the fact that even the characters most loyal to the Sons are dissatisfied with the white patriarchal society that surrounds them.

## *Conclusion*

*Sons of Anarchy*, often unflinchingly, presents its audience with members of an MC that is a patriarchal and illegal organization. While viewers who were expecting sex, violence and crude jokes may be satisfied with the show, it certainly it offers much more. The show's emphasis on interrogating patriarchy, white supremacy and criminality is remarkable. It continually highlights the hypocrisy inherent in society with its arbitrary distinctions between law abiding citizens and the outlaws. Music helps highlight the MC's own hypocrisy of standing for freedom on the one hand and being the oppressors of women and African Americans on the other. The two montage sequences I have discussed reveal a disparity between what the characters say and what they feel. The montage sequences are a complex layer of narration that is applied over the show and allows the viewer access to a critical commentary on the diegetic events that seems to stem from the characters of the show itself. Ultimately, the show is carried by this tension between Jax, who truly believes in these early seasons in freedom for all, and Clay who believes in power. While the diegesis of the show may be a patriarchal, white dominated society, the soundtrack deconstructs and undermines it. Music not only augments the aesthetic and narrative development of the show but also its philosophical and political stance.

### NOTES

1. Feature length for television is about 90 minutes long.
2. The soundtrack for Danny Boyle's *Trainspotting* (Boyle 1996) was so popular that a second soundtrack was released that included songs that had failed to make the cut for the original motion picture soundtrack.
3. *Boardwalk Empire*'s first episode was directed by Martin Scorcese, who as a film director, notably used pre-existing and compilation scores for his films.
4. This is the term Levinson himself uses.
5. There are some notable exceptions, such as the bizarre choice of English folk song "Greensleeves," which is covered for the show by Katey Sagal and The Forest Rangers.
6. See for example Robynn Stilwell's "Hysterical Beethoven" ("Hysterical Beethoven" 2003).
7. Another rule of the club is that if you cannot ride, you cannot be a part of the club, or at least a leader.
8. Depsite the song's signifance for African American protests, Meeropol was actually a white poet and teacher who was prompted to write the poem after being horrified by a photograph of a lynching.
9. There is lots of work done on this area. I have written about the problems with this

arbitrary distinction in my work on *Peaky Blinders*, "'One Minute of Everything at Once': How Music Shapes the World of BBC's *Peaky Blinders*" in *Music on Screen: From Cinema Screens to Touchscreens. Musicology Research* 2 (Spring 2017), pp. 47–68, online.

## Works Cited

Bierly, Mandi. "'Sons of Anarchy' Music Supervisor Breaks Down Killer Queen Montage." EW.com. N.p., 10 Sept. 2014. Web. 25 May 2017.
Chase, David. *The Sopranos*. HBO, 1999. Film.
Cooke, M. *A History of Film Music*. Cambridge University Press, 2008. Web.
Deaville, James. *Music in Television: Channels of Listening*. Taylor & Francis, 2011. Print.
Donnelly, K.J. "Tracking British Television: Pop Music as Stock Soundtrack to the Small Screen." *Popular Music* 21.3 (2002): 331–43. *Cambridge University Press*. Web.
Frith, Simon. "Hearing Secret Harmonies." *Taking Popular Music Seriously: Selected Essays*. Hampshire: Ashgate, 2007. 239–56. Print. Ashgate Contemporary Thinkers on Critical Musicology.
Gilligan, Vince. *Breaking Bad*. AMC, 2008. Film.
Handlen, Zack. "Sons of Anarchy: 'Black Widower.'" *A.V. Club* 9 Sept. 2014. Web. 29 May 2017.
Inglis, I. *Popular Music and Film*. Wallflower, 2003. Web. Film Studies.
Kassabian, Anahid. *Hearing Film: Tracking Identifications in Contemporary Hollywood Film Music*. Routledge, 2002. Print.
Lannin, S., and M. Caley. *Pop Fiction: The Song in Cinema*. Intellect, 2005. Web. Intellect Books—Play Text Series.
Lapedis, Hilary. "Popping the Question: The Function and Effect of Popular Music in Cinema." *Popular Music* 18.3 (1999): 367–79. Print.
Levinson, J. *Contemplating Art: Essays in Aesthetics*. Clarendon Press, 2006. Web.
Locker, Melissa. "From Fargo to Hannibal, This Is a Golden Age for TV Music." *The Guardian* 5 Nov. 2014. *The Guardian*. Web. 29 May 2017.
Meeropol, Abel. *Bitter Fruit*. N.p., 1936. Print.
Muse, Heather. "Katey Sagal on Acting and Singing in 'Sons of Anarchy.'" *Rolling Stone* 2011. Web. 30 May 2017.
Shepard, Susan Elizabeth. "Say Goodbye to Sons of Anarchy and Its Lousy Soundtrack." *The Concourse*. N.p., n.d. Web. 29 May 2017.
Smith, J.P. *The Sounds of Commerce: Marketing Popular Film Music*. Columbia University Press, 1998. Web. Film and Culture.
Stilwell, Robynn J. "'The Fantastical Gap between Diegetic and Nondiegetic' [in] Beyond the Soundtrack: Representing Music in Cinema." In *Beyond the Soundtrack: Representing Music in Cinema*. Ed. Daniel Goldmark, Lawrence Kramer and Richard Leppert. University of California Press, 2007. 184–204. *Talis Aspire*. Web. 21 Apr. 2017.
\_\_\_\_\_. "Hysterical Beethoven." *Beethoven Forum* 10.2 (2003): 162–83. Print.
Tincknell, Estella. "The Soundtrack Movie, Nostalgia and Consumption." *Film's Musical Moments*. Edinburgh University Press, 2006. Web.
Winter, Terrence. *Boardwalk Empire*. HBO, 2010. Film.

PART 3. NO SEAT AT THE TABLE:
OUTLIERS IN SAMCRO'S WORLD

# Lover, Killer, Father, Friend
*The Complex Case of Nero Padilla*

ANDREW HOWE

*Sons of Anarchy* is a narrative crowded with alpha males and overt displays of masculinity. Despite the show's focus upon violence and dominance, as well as their fetishized accouterments (guns, bikes, and cuts), series creator Kurt Sutter and his team of writers injected nuance into this tale of criminal machismo, particularly when it came to certain characters. Aside from perhaps series protagonist Jackson Teller, no character enjoys a more complex portrayal than Nero Padilla (Jimmy Smits). Despite not appearing until the fifth season, Nero was quickly established as a nexus point combining numerous, and often competing, streams of masculinity. Nero owns the high-end brothel Diosa, demonstrating his entrepreneurial acumen. He also serves as a nurturing father figure to many of the women who work for him. In addition, he has a special-needs son from a previous relationship. He is a lover and confidant to Gemma Teller, giving her a shoulder to cry on. For her son Jax, he is a friend and mentor. However, he is also a criminal, proving quite capable of various forms of violence, including murder, in his affiliation with the Byz Lats, his street gang. He is a man of color in a world largely controlled by the ministrations of an Anglo gang (most of the show's groups of color—the Grim Bastards, the Mayans, the One-Niners—are located *outside* of Charming). And finally, he is the guardian of Jax's legacy, taking the Teller children (Thomas and Abel) away from Charming to a notionally better existence, one free from the fallout of violence. This essay examines Nero Padilla through a character analysis, exploring not only how these features work to establish his complexity as a character but also how they give him a position of privilege within the hyper-masculine world of *Sons of Anarchy* as one of very few characters not consumed by the engines of machismo and violence, able to come out the other side of the narrative with a positive future.

Very little criticism has been written about *Sons of Anarchy*; essentially none of it has focused on Nero, despite the critical role he plays in the latter half of the series. When we are first introduced to this character in "Sovereign," he is mid-intercourse with Gemma Teller, the dominant posture of the sexual position colloquially known as "doggy style" and his prominently displayed tattoos suggesting that he will be just another thug populating a narrative already filled with them. However, the fact that it is Jimmy Smits, critically acclaimed and popular star of both television and film, suggests that there may be more than meets the eye. Gemma did in fact pick up Nero in a bar; however, he is not just another one-night stand, becoming a mainstay in Jax's life, a series regular, and one of the moral centers of the series. This all comes later, however. Our first exposure to Nero is mid-coitus, and the next morning it is revealed that he is a pimp, owning the high-end brothel Diosa. His explanation to a hung-over Gemma–who does not remember their encounter from the night before—"I'm a companionater. I bring folks together. I'm all about the love"—plays upon stereotypes of both gender and ethnicity, something Gemma acknowledges in one of her retorts: "I must have been shit-faced to go for that whole rico sauve thing." As Hector Domínguez-Ruvalcaba notes, Hispanic masculinity is largely "an invention of modern colonialism, in which sensualizing means disempowerment" (3). One might think that Nero's characterization would fall into the trap of reducing him to a stereotype, given the circumstances of the initial character introduction. After this initial opening, however, the show's writers almost immediately begin undermining what assumptions we might have of this character and his initial markings of excessive masculinity and, through his tattoos, implied criminality. From the start, he is kind and considerate, a clear contrast to Clay, who toward the end of the prior season had beaten Gemma violently ("Hands"). Nero is a savvy businessman, throwing in with Jackson Teller but also one of the few characters who can stand up to Jax when the situation calls for it. He is neither a Romeo nor a simplistic thug, a refreshing break in a narrative with Hispanic characters deriving from one of two criminal outfits: the Mayans MC and the Galindo drug cartel. As Stephanie Larson notes, typical representations of Hispanic men in mainstream media often revolve around negative stereotypes: "Villainous representations of Hispanic men include sexually threatening males, criminals, gang members, drug dealers, and illegal aliens" (58). Such portrayals are part of a legacy of post–World War II fears regarding surges in Latin American immigration, bringing together texts as diverse as *West Side Story* and *Scarface*, *I Love Lucy* and *Breaking Bad*. The portrayal of Nero Padilla very much undermines fears involving Hispanic culture.

In Gemma, Nero identifies a fellow survivor, not only of the open-heart surgery that nearly claimed both of them but in the travails that attend a life of crime. Unlike Clay, for whom Gemma is a possession he wrested away from John Teller several decades prior, Nero allows Gemma to be who she needs to be, even when that means she cannot leave behind her life with Clay. Given the familial atmosphere of the MC, Gemma cannot avoid Clay, having to continue interacting with him despite her burgeoning relationship with Nero. It is interesting to note that, the closer Nero's business partnership with Jax becomes, the more difficult his relationship with Gemma proves to be. Drawn inexorably into the politics of the MC, he keeps his cool on several occasions when confronted by Clay. The triangle of Gemma, Nero, and Clay comes to a head when Gemma gets into a car accident, endangering her grandchildren ("Ablation"). Clay covers for Gemma, telling Jax that she was run off the road. Nero, the good angel, convinces her to tell the truth and face the consequences. For him, truthfulness is critical, and he demonstrates his leadership not through brute force or excessive display, as do most members of the MC, but through sage advice. Nero realizes that Jax will find out sooner or later, and as such it is best to be proactive in coming clean. He is a peacemaker, trying to heal Gemma's relationship with her son and daughter-in-law following her revelation about the car accident. He advocates for the latter when talking with Gemma about the future of her family: "You think any of this mercy might ever be able to spill over into Tara's cup? She's the mother of your grandson, Gem" ("Aon Rud Persanta"). Nero knows when to push Gemma and when to give her space, and how to steer her toward her better nature, even if she doesn't always take his advice. He is not the stereotype of the pimp or gangbanger or passionate Latin lover, instead a deep and cautious thinker with a strong moral compass. He has the courage to stand up not only to Clay, but to stand up for what he believes.

Nero is about the only character in *Sons of Anarchy* who knows how to handle Gemma. He realizes when she is vulnerable, and what he can do to alleviate her pain, at one point asking her to give him a ride so that he can see his son, his ulterior motive being to get her around children after she has been banned by Tara from seeing Abel and Thomas ("Andare Pescare"). Nero is emotionally supportive, such as when he consoles Gemma following Clay's death. Realizing that despite the depth of her hatred she has lost something definitional, he notes: "Good or bad, Clay was a huge piece of your life. It's going to take a minute" ("Aon Rud Persanta"). Finally, Nero protects Gemma, which sometimes involves hiding things from the MC, such as her location following Tara's death. The fact that he is usually 100 percent truthful with Jax suggests the depth of his love for her. It is interesting to note that, on occasion, he goes the other direction, telling Jax something that Gemma asked him to keep secret, such as when Gemma has a one-night stand with a much younger man who steals her purse and car. Realizing his own limitations in that he cannot solve this problem himself, Nero calls the MC

("Toad's Wild Ride"). In the ensuing search for the hustler, Nero refuses to judge Gemma for her reckless actions and also saves Jax from potential legal problems when he restrains the latter from killing the man in front of witnesses. Nero's grace only extends so far, however. Later, we see him beating up the hustler when he catches him trying to seduce another woman. Finally, Nero is wise enough to realize that, whereas Jax will never be able to leave his life of crime, Gemma has a chance, trying to convince her on several occasions to run away with him ("Wolfsangel" and "A Mother's Work"). Nero has one of the healthiest relationships with women of all the men in the series. His masculinity is predicated on equal partnership and he asks rather than instructs, ultimately resigned when Gemma rebuffs his attempts to leave behind the MC. Whereas Clay could not accept it when Gemma went against his designs, Nero is quietly resigned to let her forge her own path, even when he knows that it will end in trouble.

Aside from being a lover, Nero is also a father, literally to his son Lucius and figuratively to both Jackson Teller and his employees at Diosa. Soon after he meets Gemma, we find out that Nero has a son who suffers from degenerative spina bifida ("Authority Vested"). Although we don't see a lot of Lucius throughout the series, it is apparent that Nero and his son love each other and that much of the money he makes from Diosa goes to St. Emilio's Home for Physically Challenged Youth. Clearly, Nero is a loving father who dotes on his son, although he feels a measure of guilt for not realizing that his drug-addicted girlfriend had relapsed and was using during her pregnancy, leading to Lucius' health problems. When Nero confides this information to Jax, it solidifies their developing bond as Jax himself carries guilt over Wendy's mid-pregnancy drug use and the impact it had upon Abel's heart condition.

In this world of machismo and competition, Nero's son nearly becomes a liability on several occasions. In one, he is moved to a rare display of anger when one of his old gang members insults Lucius. Nero's measured and level-headed approach is occasionally subsumed throughout the series as his baser aggressive instincts are put on display, although unlike the other members of the MC they are quickly pulled back and do not spin out of control, leading to further damage and destruction. Two other examples of where Nero's position as a father of a special needs child are incorporated into threats are when the D.A. makes an implied threat about his son ("Sweet and Vaded"), and when Henry Lin—leader of the Lin Triads, a San Francisco–like gang—makes a direct threat ("Some Strange Eruption"). Certainly, the D.A.'s circumspect statement implies the possibility of foster care if Nero were to go to jail, whereas Lin's direct approach promises actual physical harm. Whether his allegiance to SAMCRO is rock solid or he realizes that the D.A. is bluffing (or both), Nero neither rises to the bait and retorts nor gives in to such prosecutorial tactics and testifies against Jax. In a world of excessive masculine displays of power and dominance, Nero is able to keep his cool and work his way through conflict in a relatively measured way, even when his son is used against him as a weapon.

Nero is also something of a father figure to his employees, most of whom are female and quite a bit younger. Even though he serves as their pimp, he has a policy of not sleeping with them, establishing a culture of respect that extends to the linguistic, insisting on several occasions that his employees be referred to as "escorts" rather than "prostitutes" ("Sweet and Vaded"). Nero is a good businessman, networking with local authorities and paying his girls well, resulting in political connections and employee loyalty. As he notes to Jax when they first meet: "It don't pay to be greedy. You know, you gotta treat your girls good. They stay happy. They all got regulars.... The money stays steady." ("Authority Vested"). Even though there is a paternalistic dimension to his view of "my girls," as he calls them, he views his employees as human beings deserving of respect and dignity, supporting them in a variety of ways. Often, in the hyper-sexualized world of internecine gang warfare, this support takes on serious implications, as many of the women who appear in Diosa and in other similar locations are used alternatively as sexual objects for gratification or pawns in the greater struggle between competing interests. Nero resists this approach even when the women involved are not his employees, such as when SAMCRO becomes involved with a sadistic ring of pornographers from Stockton. After witnessing the degrading conditions to which those working on these films are subjected, Nero assaults one of the filmmakers. His primary concern, however, is for the women who work at Diosa.

Routinely, Nero incurs significant risks in protecting his employees. When the members of his own gang—the Byz Lats—believe that one of his escorts spoke to the police, initiating a raid on Diosa, Nero risks his standing with his own crew by asking the MC to smuggle her out of town ("Stolen Huffy"). In running interference, Nero demonstrates that he is willing to risk his own business to ensure the safety of his employees. This is doubly true when Frankie shoots Lyla after the former takes hostages at Diosa. Even though it is Jax who owes Frankie money, Nero pays up nevertheless, giving the disgraced MC member the contents of his safe: $130,000 and several watches ("Ablation"). He does this more to save Lyla than for Jax's benefit, angrily lashing out at the latter in his failure to keep his promise of going straight: "You remember what you promised? We ain't even open yet, and I've got an employee with a bullet in her leg." When Jax says that he will handle it, Nero responds: "How you gonna handle it, more bullets?" Much as he did with Gemma, Nero knows when to push and when to back off. Jax is used to being in control and not having his actions questioned in the rigid hierarchy of the MC. Nero is not afraid to ask questions, however, putting Jax on his heels and making him receptive to a pivot involving Tara and his children. Nero concludes his verbal assault of Jax with a piece of advice that he gives, increasingly, throughout the latter seasons—"You need to accelerate the end game, Jax." Nero is friends with SAMCRO, but does not buy into their gratuitous hierarchy. He is a man who stands up for what he believes, even when that means standing up to Jax.

Nero's protection of two characters deserves particular attention. When she first appears in the season five episode "Orca Shrugged," Venus Van Dam is largely treated as comic relief, although the transgendered escort does allow an extra layer of masculinity to become manifest with Alexander "Tig" Trager, perhaps the only character in *Sons of Anarchy* with a masculinity as rich, nuanced, and varied as Nero's. Venus appears in two episodes of season six, during which the character is fleshed out and given a back-story. As a 15-year-old, Venus—at that point known as Vincent—was sexually abused by her mother. Nero took the youth in and served as a father figure. As Venus says: "Nero was the one who took me in, kept the wolves from my door. He never asked me for anything. My guardian angel" ("Salvage"). This storyline was brave for its time, especially given the hyper-masculine world of the show's setting. Nero helps Venus save her nephew from the same fate because Venus is, in his words: "familia." The same is true of Carla, who literally is Nero's half-sister, although who most likely harbors some attraction for him. Even though Carla is the one who arranged for the police raid on Diosa and subsequent arrest of SAMCRO members, Nero defends her, interceding and driving her home following a beatdown by Tara ("Stolen Huffy"). She, too, is familia, having helped him overcome his drug habit at some point in the past ("Small World"). He defends her even in death, even after she attempts to humiliate him one last time, crying over her body and whispering a prayer in Spanish ("Small World"). He even breaks into a large mausoleum at a cemetery so that her ashes can reside in a place of dignity and splendor ("Andare Pescare"). For Nero, the defense of women he views as vulnerable is paramount, a distinction that should without a doubt be noted as misogynist. Coming in this narrative, however, one built upon a premise of male power and dominance where women are objects to be used sexually until discarded or until they become an "old lady"—wife to one of the MC members, a higher order of property but property nonetheless—Nero's misogyny represents a counter-current in the outmoded gender politics of the show's male characters.

Finally, Nero is a father figure to Jax. By the time Nero is introduced into the narrative, Jax has finally cut ties to Clay and, by season five, his father's diary no longer plays a substantial role. Jax, however, still needs guidance, an interesting aspect of the show's larger view on masculinity and institutionalized power. With his supportive and calm demeanor, Nero is ready-made to step into the void as a father figure, or at least as an older brother figure. Initially, he helps Jax because of his feelings for Gemma, although he chalks it up to "networking" ("Sovereign"). However, the two develop an unshakeable bond that lasts until the end of the series, when Jax entrusts his sons to Nero while contemplating some final moves that might have fatal consequences. Both acknowledge this relationship, although it is interesting to note that they do so more to others than to each other. Jax admits Nero's importance when Gemma confronts her son about his mandate that she and Nero are banned from seeing each romantically ("Orca Shrugged"). Nero does the same when Gemma encourages him to help moderate Jax, although in characteristically humorous fashion he opines: "I'm too old to adopt" ("Aon Rud Persanta"). He also notes in this conversation that he trusts Jax to make the right choice. That is not to say that Nero doesn't clearly see and appreciate Jax's shortcomings, or pass up opportunities to give him advice. He understands Jax even better than does Gemma, telling her in the aftermath of Tara's death: "Your boy, he's unchained right now. He's looking for any excuse to rage" ("Poor Little Lambs"). Nero understands, as he was once very much like Jax.

From time to time, we are reminded of Nero's past, of the gang violence in which he partook and the time he spent in jail, experiences that allow him to speak with authority when it comes to Jax and his life choices. On multiple occasions, he encourages Jax to "get out" of this life. At the end of season five, he even makes a deal with Jax. After realizing that the journals Jax has been writing are for his sons, and that much like his father J. T., Jax does not believe he will survive his life of crime, Nero says: "You walk away, I'll walk away" ("J'ai Obtenu Cette"). Jax's enigmatic response, "have a good night," indicates that, whereas he respects Nero and recognizes the truth of his advice, he cannot break the chain of violence by just walking away. Instead, he will choose to solve his problems through violence albeit with a chronicling of his thoughts and attitudes that, someday, he hopes will guide his sons while *they* break free from the cycle. Nero never gives up, in the penultimate episode encouraging Wayne to journey to Oregon to intercede between mother and son, stating: "This isn't about saving Gemma. It's about saving Jax" ("Red Rose"). He realizes that Jax needs saving from himself, and is willing to enlist the aid of Wayne—with whom Nero is not exactly friendly—in order to mount a last ditch effort to save Jax.

Nero listens to Jax, gives him advice, and also allows him space when he perceives Jax needs it. He is also willing to stand up to Jax when necessary. José Limón notes that, in addition to negatives stereotypes of drug dealers and criminals, Latino characters are often depicted "as cowardly, apathetic, and dormant" (3). This is certainly not true of Nero, one of the few characters in the narrative who on a routine basis calls Jax to task. This tendency does not occur until the beginning of season six, after the two have developed a close relationship. Early in that season, he chides Jax for his relationship with Barosky, and then intercedes when Jax confronts Gemma, although he lets him take her back to the clubhouse ("Straw"). At this point in the narrative, Nero is willing to run interference for Gemma but still understands his place in things. By the end of the season, Nero's relationship with Jax and the events that have occurred have emboldened him to much more direct confrontation. After he finds out that Jax ordered Juice to kill Darvany, the mother of the school shooter and wife of Nero's cousin, he cites karma in an angry but measured confrontation: "You ever think, maybe, all these bad things that are happening to the mother of your children, just maybe that's because of some heinous thing that you did to another child's mother?" ("A Mother's Work").

No SAMCRO brother, throughout the course of the entire narrative, ever speaks so directly to Jax, testament to the fact that Nero is the father figure that Jax never knew in J.T. and never had in Clay. Indeed, season seven is filled with other moments of tension, and even outright conflict, between Nero and Jax, especially in the wake of Jax's move against Lin when the former orders a hit on Diosa, during the course of which 16 people are killed. This time, Nero's anger is white hot, his words delivered more in a rage than in a measured tone: "You've been lying to me, man, the whole time, to my face!" ("Some Strange Eruption"). Despite his developing frustration with Jax, however, Nero continues to support the MC. He has been accepted as a brother, and as such looks to support them and protect the club, even when that invites scrutiny and repercussion. Not realizing that he is in the clear, Nero cops to buying and giving the KG-9 to Darvany's son in order to protect Jax and SAMCRO ("Los Fantasmas"). Later, he helps nurse Juice through an overdose even after he realizes that Juice murdered Darvany, and consoles rather than confronts Jax when he finds out that Tara has absconded with Abel and Thomas ("You Are My Sunshine"). Even after the moves Jax has been making result in violence against his own friends and employees, Nero continues to put Jax ahead of himself, serving as a long-suffering and stable father figure in a narrative crowded with overt displays of masculine bonding often undermined by continually shifting political maneuvering.

There is another aspect of Nero Padilla that warrants discussion: he is a criminal. When we first see him naked with Gemma ("Sovereign"), his numerous prison tattoos indicate a past that we gradually discover involves assault and drug charges. Later in that episode, we see him interacting with his gang—the Byz Lats—although we do not yet realize their identity. As we soon find out, he is the only member of his original gang not dead or spending life in prison. As he tells Gemma: "Lucky bust. Spent my 30s in Chino. Gave up the needle. Picked up some books. Saw the bigger picture" ("Authority Vested"). Nero later mentions that he spent "3627 days in rehab" ("Toil and

Till"), a ten-year stint in prison that helped him acquire a new outlook on life, one that aids him in becoming a mentor to Jax. Despite his advice about walking away, however, slowly but surely Nero gets pulled back into his former life of crime, with both his old street gang and the MC. As he at one point explains, "It's hard to be a land baron on minimum wage" ("Andare Pescare"), and one wonders the degree to which the expensive care of Lucius, and the good wages he is paying his employees at Diosa, contribute to his increased business relationship with Jax and SAMCRO.

It is during this period that Nero's character is the most complex, as he negotiates between differing groups to which he owes allegiance and re-embraces a life of criminality where violence is sometimes required, yet maintains a strong moral compass and desire to protect the weak and innocent. Ultimately, Nero cannot escape his old life, drawn back into the politics of the Byz Lats when the latter try and steal some guns that Jax was going to sell to them at a discounted price ("To Thine Own Self"). Putting SAMCRO first, Nero confronts and kills two members of his gang, shooting the first one because he reaches for his gun and the second because he insults Gemma. Nero still has a moral imperative, and bluffs the second guy into reaching for his gun, stating: "I'm going to shoot you in the head in five seconds." As he walks out the door, he acknowledges to his old crew that he has turned a corner: "You putos wanted me back? Órale! I'm back" ("To Thine Own Self").

Later, the Byz Lats and SAMCRO come to each other's aid in the numerous turf wars and conflicts that arise over the last two seasons. With both groups, we see Nero's long dormant mean streak. He joins SAMCRO when they gun down a rival gang ("Playing with Monsters") and receives help from the MC in his battles with Dante, the head of a rival gang who has moved into an area controlled by the Byz Lats. Nero's change of attitude is very much evident when he chases down Dante, throwing him into a car with a pit bull and then holding the door closed while the dog savagely attacks his competitor ("J'ai Obtenu Cette"). Nero's killer instinct, however, is only on display when he is confronting other criminals. Unlike all the other gangs that appear in the narrative—including SAMCRO—Nero never turns his violence against civilians. In fact, he goes the other direction, consoling shop owners who are victimized during his turf war with Dante ("J'ai Obtenu Cette"). We even see compassion from Nero in dealing with other criminals. During the monologue that opens season six, when Jax is talking about writing a journal for his sons to read after he is gone, we see Nero overseeing his gang savagely beating a black youth, presumably a member of a rival gang attempting to make inroads into Byz Lat territory. After coldly watching the proceedings, Nero calls a stop to the beating, gives the youth a reassuring pat on the head, and lets him go, no doubt realizing that he is not the architect of the designs on Byz Lat turf ("Straw").

Ultimately, Nero has to choose sides between SAMCRO and the two Hispanic gangs in the narrative, the Byz Lats and the Mayans MC. In regards to the former, Nero sides with Jax in the aftermath of the school shooting. Matthew, the shooter, was the stepson of Nero's cousin and Byz Lat member Arcadio. Complicating matters is that the gun can be traced to SAMCRO. In the ensuing drama, Nero arranges for Arcadio and Darvany to hide out, but is forced to kill Arcadio when the latter has a confrontation with the MC, during the course of which Gemma is almost killed ("One One Six"). Nero also chooses SAMCRO over the Mayans. In a montage, we see him parleying with Alvarez, who clearly respects Nero and his attempts to mediate, keeping the violence from getting out of control ("Toil and Till"). However, he is ultimately forced to choose sides, telling Wendy in typically humorous fashion: "I'm going to revoke my diplomatic immunity" ("Toil and Till"). Nero cannot stay on the sidelines, drawn inexorably into the violence and conflict that typifies the latter seasons of *Sons of Anarchy*. However, the difference between him and Jax is that he benefits from age and perspective. As a key player in this world of hyper-masculinized criminality, he is willing to resort to violence, which is a necessary ingredient for success. However, he knows when to turn it on and when to turn it off, against whom it should be directed, and when to beat his sword into a ploughshare. Although he lacks the maturity to do the same, Jax at least has the vision to recognize this about Nero, which is why out of all of the figures in the narrative to which he can turn he entrusts his children to Nero, hoping that the latter's paternal instinct and sage advice will supplement the journal he leaves for his sons and be able to keep them from following in his footsteps.

Throughout the shifting alliances that predominate in *Sons of Anarchy*, the most consistent foil for Jackson Teller and SAMCRO is the Mayans MC. As Clara Rodriguez notes, historical depictions of Hispanic culture in American media reflect the changing political and economic factors of the time (8), and perhaps it is not too surprising to see a Hispanic gang serve as primary foil to a Caucasian one. This is why Nero is such a fascinating character in his interactions with SAMCRO. Nero's decisions are less informed by his situation within a historic masculinity than about his desire to be a good father, a supportive employer, a giving lover, and most of all a decent human being. However, in the context of the machismo that attends his identity as a pimp, gangster, and member of the Hispanic sub-culture, his appearance in this hyper-masculine narrative definitely contains overtones of machismo. Even though he cannot escape his past or the demands of the profession he has embraced, he employs violence as a means to a highly specific end: the purchase of his uncle's farm, which will allow him to relocate far from the violent end he is sure will come to SAMCRO. In the final season, Nero has conversations with both Gemma and Jax, at separate times making one final plea to the woman he loves and the young man to whom he has become something of a father figure. Choking up, pointing at the scar over his heart, a reminder of past traumas but also what drew Gemma to him, he implores her: "We deserve something better Gemma.... I got a serious love for you" ("Greensleeves"). Gemma can't escape her past actions, however, and neither can Jax, although he is able to see beyond his limitations and realize that Nero is the only hope for his sons to grow up outside the sphere of violence. Rare in *Sons of Anarchy*, Nero is a character who is *not* consumed by his violent and aggressive impulses. He is a lover who respects the rights of those he cares about to self-destruct and a killer who seeks to limit the scope and impact of violence; a loyal friend to even those who bring him harm, and a father figure to those in need. As Nero Padilla drives into the sunset, in addition to being a father to Lucius, he is also a father figure to Abel and Thomas, having made a solemn promise to Jackson Teller that he will do his best to shield the Teller boys from the world that claimed their father and grandfather ("Playing with Monsters").

## Works Cited

"Ablation," *Sons of Anarchy: The Complete Series*, written by Mike Daniels, directed by Karen Gaviola, 20th Century Fox, 2015.
"Andare Pescare," *Sons of Anarchy: The Complete Series*, written by Liz Sagal and Kurt Sutter, directed by Billy Gierhart, 20th Century Fox, 2015.
"Aon Rud Persanta," *Sons of Anarchy: The Complete Series*, written by Chris Collins and Kurt Sutter, directed by Peter Weller, 20th Century Fox, 2015.
"Authority Vested," *Sons of Anarchy: The Complete Series*, written by Regina Corrado, directed by Peter Weller, 20th Century Fox, 2015.
Dominguez-Ruvalcaba, Héctor, and Ignacio Corona. *Gender Violence at the U.S.-Mexico Border: Media Representation and Public Response*. University Press of Arizona, 2010.
"Greensleeves," *Sons of Anarchy: The Complete Series*, written by Gladys Rodriguez, Josh Botana, and Kurt Sutter, directed by Paris Barclay, 20th Century Fox, 2015.
"J'ai Obtenu Cette," *Sons of Anarchy: The Complete Series*, written by Kurt Sutter and Chris Collins, directed by Kurt Sutter, 20th Century Fox, 2015.
"John 8:32," *Sons of Anarchy: The Complete Series*, written by Kem Nunn and Kurt Sutter, directed by Guy Ferland, 20th Century Fox, 2015.
Larson, Stephanie. *Media & Minorities: The Politics of Race in News and Entertainment*. Rowman & Littlefield, 2006.
Limón, José. "Stereotyping and Chicano Resistance: An Historical Dimension." *Chicanos and Film: Essays on Chicano Representation and Resistance*. Edited by Chon Noriega. Garland, 1992.
"Los Fantasmas," *Sons of Anarchy: The Complete Series*, written by Roberto Patino and Kurt Sutter, directed by Peter Weller, 20th Century Fox, 2015.
"A Mother's Work," *Sons of Anarchy: The Complete Series*, written by Kurt Sutter and Chris Collins, directed by Kurt Sutter, 20th Century Fox, 2015.
"One One Six," *Sons of Anarchy: The Complete Series*, written by Chris Collins and Adria Lang, directed by Peter Weller, 20th Century Fox, 2015.
"Orca Shrugged," *Sons of Anarchy: The Complete Series*, written by Regina Corrado and Kurt Sutter, directed by Gwyneth Horder-Payton, 20th Century Fox, 2015.
"Playing with Monsters," *Sons of Anarchy: The Complete Series*, written by Peter Elkoff and Kurt Sutter, directed by Craig Yahata, 20th Century Fox, 2015.

"Poor Little Lambs," *Sons of Anarchy: The Complete Series*, written by Kem Nunn and Kurt Sutter, directed by Guy Ferland, 20th Century Fox, 2015.
"Red Rose," *Sons of Anarchy: The Complete Series*, written by Kurt Sutter and Charles Murray, directed by Paris Barclay, 20th Century Fox, 2015.
Rodriguez, Clara. *Latin Looks: Images of Latinas and Latinos in the United States Media*. Westview, 1997.
"Salvage," *Sons of Anarchy: The Complete Series*, written by Mike Daniels and Kurt Sutter, directed by Adam Arkin, 20th Century Fox, 2015.
"Small World," *Sons of Anarchy: The Complete Series*, written by Roberto Patino, directed by Adam Arkin, 20th Century Fox, 2015.
"Some Strange Eruption," *Sons of Anarchy: The Complete Series*, written by Roberto Patino and Kurt Sutter, directed by Peter Weller, 20th Century Fox, 2015.
"Sovereign," *Sons of Anarchy: The Complete Series*, written by Kurt Sutter, directed by Paris Barclay, 20th Century Fox, 2015.
"Stolen Huffy," *Sons of Anarchy: The Complete Series*, written by Chris Collins, directed by Paris Barclay, 20th Century Fox, 2015.
"Straw," *Sons of Anarchy: The Complete Series*, written by Kurt Sutter, directed by Paris Barclay, 20th Century Fox, 2015.
"Sweet and Vaded," *Sons of Anarchy: The Complete Series*, written by Kurt Sutter and Adria Lang, directed by Paris Barclay, 20th Century Fox, 2015.
"Toad's Wild Ride," *Sons of Anarchy: The Complete Series*, written by Kurt Sutter and Chris Collins, directed by Peter Weller, 20th Century Fox, 2015.
"To Thine Own Self," *Sons of Anarchy: The Complete Series*, written by Mike Daniels and Kurt Sutter, directed by Paris Barclay, 20th Century Fox, 2015.
"Toil and Till," *Sons of Anarchy: The Complete Series*, written by Charles Murray and Kurt Sutter, directed by Billy Gierhart, 20th Century Fox, 2015.
"Wolfsangel," *Sons of Anarchy: The Complete Series*, written by Kurt Sutter and Kem Nunn, directed by Billy Gierhart, 20th Century Fox, 2015.
"You Are My Sunshine," *Sons of Anarchy: The Complete Series*, written by Kem Nunn, Mike Daniels, and Kurt Sutter, directed by Paris Barclay, 20th Century Fox, 2015.

# Nero's Frontier
## Western and Latino Masculinity, Fatherhood and Family

MONICA MONTELONGO FLORES

The Western has long satisfied American desires for masculine-driven mythologies, where idealized men frame large and small screens, announcing their place on the frontier. Think of Gary Cooper's gait as he approaches four menacing gunmen in *High Noon* (1952), John Wayne's final exit from the homestead—body darkened against frontier light—in *The Searchers* (1956), or most recently the numerous male bodies lined in leather cuts in Kurt Sutter's *Sons of Anarchy* (2008–2014). What these bodies tell us is that the Western has historically imposed white masculine codes into its narratives, images, and messages. Yet, the treatment of racialized masculinity in the genre has categorically positioned non-white men as threats to "proper" white masculinity through patterns of violence, sexuality, and moral and ethical inferiority. Specifically, while white masculinity is constructed, performed, and celebrated in the Western, Mexican masculinity is often diminished in the genre through unilateral representation and disjointed cultural references.

It is understandable then that the hypermasculinity displayed in *Sons of Anarchy*, essentially a contemporary motorcycle Western, is dependent on the iconography of the genre, with its fixation on male bodies, male relationships, and their inscriptions on coveted—and battled—landscapes. Within the narrative, however, Neron "Nero" Padilla surfaces as a contradiction to the hegemonic white masculinity celebrated in the series. Played by Emmy award-winning actor Jimmy Smits, Nero Padilla is an ex-gang leader reforming his life to focus on legitimate, yet socially unsavory, business practices as the owner of an escort service. The father of a disabled son, Lucius, Padilla plans to leave his nefarious lifestyle and buy a farm to raise Lucius in the country, away from his past transgressions. Yet, the ex-gang leader is consistently pulled from this plan through his relationship with Gemma and affiliation with Jax and the MC.

Despite these challenges, Padilla's character questions many of the denigrated patterns of racialized masculinity in Western productions through his literal and figurative role as father and his participation in non-traditional familial kinship practices. Most notably, Nero's acceptance of a non-biological family counters the constant struggle of "blood" and "brotherhood" ever present in the series.[1] This acceptance of adoptive practices is understandable when viewed in context of Nero's allegorical name, a reference to Roman emperor Nero, a historical adoptee figure and emblem of societal power. However, Nero's character explodes the limitations of the Roman reference through culturally specific challenges to Western and Latino masculinities, namely machismo. The character's acceptance of two mother figures for Abel and Thomas, his figurative adoption of Jax Teller, and his questioning of the club's structures and masculine codes interrupt the idealized family values and absentee father patterns of the series.

## The Family Macho: Western Fathers

Nero's fracturing of fatherhood conventions is dependent on the reinscription of father figures in both the Western genre and in cultural representations of Latino masculinity. Fatherhood in the American Western typically presents the viewer with an opportunity to engage in the ideals of forging white masculinity and frontier life. *The Rifleman* (1958–1963) heralded Lucas McCain as the resilient widower, raising a young son to value Western morals and culture. Lucas's identity and obligations as a father were often used to balance the narrative's promise of a "Rifleman," where his moral authority often justified the violence of the series. Lucas does not draw first, never provoking instances of violence, but often engaging in them. Nevertheless, Lucas' abilities to effectively run his and his son's domestic space, doing general "housework," demonstrates the genre's ability to transcend the strict gender norms of the era, inviting adaptable fatherhood into its character dimensions. Yet, these mutable representations were often limited by racial boundaries, framing white paternity as racially, morally, and nationally dominant.

While *The Rifleman*'s resilient father figure allowed opportunities for varied representations of paternity in regards to gender conventions, Western notions of masculine freedom (and its associated violence) are often separate from "proper" father figures. George Steven's *Shane* (1953) imbues the pragmatic "necessary" violence of the frontier through the title character Shane, a reformed gunfighter roaming Wyoming territory. Shane's character is paired narratively opposite the character of Joe, the frontier father, working his cattle ranch with his wife and young son. When Joe is confronted with a gunfight in town, Shane knocks Joe unconscious in an attempt to save the patriarch from his inevitable loss and death. Instead, Shane takes Joe's place in the fight, winning and injuring himself in the process. As Shane rides out of town, too improper for domesticity, Joe's son yells for Shane to "Come back," begging for the masculinized balance between domesticity and frontier freedom later embodied by characters like the Rifleman.

These examples from 1950s Westerns prime our understandings of fatherhood and its role in the creation of U.S. masculinity, specifically white masculinity. Like *The Rifleman* and *Shane*, the frontier and the domestic space are still at odds in contemporary film and television. Specifically, the fathers in *Sons of Anarchy* either reject their families or invite conflict into the domestic space through their memberships in the MC. The series maps the thematic trajectory of domestic disaster beginning in season one with the tragic death of Opie's wife, Donna, and continues throughout the series with the fate of the Teller-Morrow family. The disintegration of these families largely reflects a long standing trope in the Western, where families work as an extension of nation building, a concept entangled in U.S. imagination and settled in the West.

Thus, the father's role in American Westerns has relied on upholding the gendered values and expectations of the frontier. In *Marriage, Violence, and the Nation in the American Literary West*, William R. Handley notes that often marriages in the genre emphasize a national anxiety regarding the "savagery" of the frontier, hoping instead "to perpetuate a 'civilized' genealogy in a region not known for American civility during western conquest and settlement" (3). Films like Fred Zinneman's *High Noon* (1952) use marriage as a metaphor for the desire for ethical civility on the frontier. The marriage of Marshal Will Kane and his young wife Amy Fowler frame the narrative of the film, as Kane searches for "special deputies" to help him protect the town from Frank Miller and his gang. Kane, still dressed in his matrimonial attire, is figuratively "married" to the West as he seeks to defend its civility.[2]

In *Sons of Anarchy*, the heroic cowboy figures are reversed, playing the outlaw father and husband. Unlike Will Kane, they seek to defend their families from the inside of criminal activities. Yet, both Will Kane and the men in *Sons of Anarchy* abide by a moral code, self-imposed and contrary to the dominant culture. Ramon F. Adams describes the code in *The Cowman & His Code of Ethics*, explaining, "Though the cowman might break every law of the territory, state and federal government, he took pride in upholding his own unwritten code" (13). Adams concludes, though, that individuals who break their codes are punishable by the same philosophy (13).

While the fathers in the MC hold their families subject to the same codes they abide, Nero challenges this philosophy repeatedly in the series. Though Jax Teller psychologically battles his fatherly role, unwittingly inflicting the code onto his oldest son Abel, Jax is unable to escape the requirements of the code. Nero questions the immutability of these codes, having restructured his life to balance the necessary pragmatics of such codes and the evolution of the frontier. In fact, Nero's pragmatic approach explains, in part, his openness to various familial forms, eventually serving as a surrogate father figure to Jax. While Nero directly rejects the notion of marrying Gemma (knowing the fates of her previous husbands), the bond between Nero and Jax is established without marital formality. It can be said, then, that families and family building are not necessarily institutionally formalized in a contemporary Western like *Sons of Anarchy*. Instead, adoptive fatherhood becomes a necessity due to the violence of the frontier. The characters seek family as much as they fracture family and, in some cases, the absence of a father is an unintended gift to the child.

## Blood and Blame: Fathering Sins

While adoptive fatherhood resonates as a challenge to classic forms of patriarchy in the Western genre, biological kinship maintains a stronghold not only in the genre, but largely in U.S. film and television. This is no different in *Sons of Anarchy*, where thematically "blood" (and its various meanings) resonates throughout the series. In fact, Nero's character reestablishes the significance of blood and fatherhood in an early interaction with Jax.

In the scene, Nero is behind the wheel of his black Ford F-150 with Jax in the passenger seat ("Authority Vested," season five, episode two). Through a series of shot-counter-shot exchanges, the men discuss and inquire about their respective businesses. Jax is interested in how lucratively Nero's escort service, Diosa, has performed, impressed by the ex-gangster's ability to maintain profitability outside of criminal activity. Nero's advisement, "It don't pay to be greedy," resonates as he asks Jax about the profits in criminal gun exchanges. Jax replies, "Percentages ... and blood." Notably, the conversation turns to the most recent dilemma, a murder charge due to a club member's "shoot first, ask questions later" approach. In an act of retaliation, the club member is forced to witness his daughter being brutally murdered. Here, Jax's reference to "blood" is understood in its fullest meaning, referring not only to the loss of life, but the loss of family.

While the scene's dialogue refers to the impacts of the MC lifestyle on club members' families, there are also constant visual reminders of fatherhood. Jax's "SO" "NS" rings are brought into the shot as the character lifts his hand to his face when he asks about Diosa's profits. The rings remind the viewer of Jax's deceased father, John Teller, Jax's own position as the son of two club presidents (John and stepson of Clay Morrow), and Jax's two sons, Abel and Thomas, whose births inspire him to seek legal avenues for club business.

Nero's character also carries a unique visual reference on his body, a tattoo of his son's name, "LUCIUS," written in script on the right side of his neck. While the name is partially obstructed by the character's shirt collar, it remains always in view, in opposition to the brief reminder of Jax's sons through his rings. Further, Nero's "LUCIUS" tattoo carries more visual weight than Jax's "Abel" tattoo, located on the character's chest. The "Abel" tattoo appears diminutive when compared to the Sons of Anarchy reaper covering Jax's back. The placement and position of Lucius' name signifies the impact and weight of his son's life on Nero. Here, Nero's fatherhood is constantly on display, reminding viewers of the character's affection for his son.

Nero's paternity is not only set apart from Jax, but also from another Latino character in the series, leader of the Mayans MC, Marcus Alvarez. Jimmy Smits' addition to *Sons of Anarchy* in season five relocates the problematic Latino father figure established in earlier seasons with Alvarez. Viewers recall the Mayans as the main antagonists in the first season. After Alvarez's son, Esai, bungles a hit on MC president Clay Morrow, the Mayan leader gives permission for the MC to kill his son as retribution ("Hell Followed," season one, episode nine). With an acoustic version of Creedence Clearwater Revival's "Fortunate Son" playing in the background, Alvarez sweetly consoles his son's disappointment and fears after failing his mission, telling him, "I love you, mijo" as he dies from a stab wound to the head inflicted by Sons of Anarchy member Happy.

Here, the Mayan club name works as a reference to both Mexican and American Indian presences in the Western. While at times camaraderie could be established between "good" or "innocent" racial Others and white settlers in these highly mythologized narratives, dark skinned bodies were typically portrayed in diminutive or even savage manners.[3] Charles Ramirez Berg explains the processes of Hollywood's racial stereotyping and its narrative function in *Latino Images in Film: Stereotypes, Subversion, and Resistance*, "not just Latinos but all people of color represent an inherent threat to the status quo simply because they are markedly different from the established WASP norm" (67). In a series where the white male protagonists grandly deflect from the conventions of WASP images in media, the racial characters are expected to press their negative stereotypes even further than the established Hollywood conventions.

Alvarez's willingness to sacrifice his child for the sake of his "tribe" reinforces and expands the stereotypes established in the genre through a portrayal of the often misrepresented history of child sacrifice in Mayan culture.

This misrepresentation has led to a stigmatizing of Latino/as, as ancestors of Mayans, situating contemporary Latino/as as inherently and perpetually violent. Calling Esai "mijo" (an endearing term in Spanish for "mi hijo" or "my son") as he's murdered declares Latino fatherhood to not only extend outlaw codes conceived by the Mayans, but presents the conflict of Latino masculinity and fatherhood in contemporary representations.

Nero's care for Lucius combats this prior introduction to Latino fatherhood in the series. In the sequence discussed earlier between Nero and Jax, Nero explains that he has to make a quick stop. As he exits the truck, he arranges a conspicuous black duffle bag, leading Jax to ask if he should leave the engine on. Like Jax, viewers assume Nero is engaging in some sort of illegal exchange. As the camera pans to follow Nero into the building, it stops on the sign reading "St. Emilio's Home for Physically Challenged Youth." As Jax watches from the street, Nero encourages his physically disabled son to walk across a grassy courtyard, embracing him and gifting a stuffed white bunny (which he pulls out of the black duffle bag) for his accomplishment. When compared to the unsteady camera movements in the shots in Nero's truck, the camera's smooth movement on Nero and Lucius indicates the stability of the relationship and Nero's role as father.

Nero and Lucius' relationship maintains a healthy balance despite Nero's inability, or perhaps unwillingness due to the dangers associated with his previous lifestyle, to care for his son within his own home. Further, the scene also opposes stereotypes concerning Latino fears of institutionalized assistance, showing Lucius as a happy child in an assisted living facility. Mostly, this scene demonstrates Nero's attempt to "save" his child from the mistakes of his past, which unfortunately (or fortunately) include Lucius living isolated from his father. This living situation appears as the only "middle ground" evidenced in the series involving the placement of children. Earlier in the season, Jax is willing to allow Abel to be adopted by a couple in Ireland in order to "save" him from the MC's activities, but that adoption attempt has disastrous results. Further, when Tara, with Jax's approval, attempts to take Abel and Thomas to live in Oregon, Gemma stands in opposition to the move, not wanting her grandchildren to leave Charming. Nero's living situation with Lucius reflects the character's pragmatic approach to parenting, separating him from the extreme "blood ties" mentality expressed by the Teller-Morrow family.

Nero's parenting approach also complicates a highly maintained cultural value within Latino society, specifically machismo. Machismo is a Latin American and Latino/a cultural system of codes and performances that invokes physical and sexual assertiveness and aggressions that operate to undermine not only women, but also men who do not uphold the qualities of machismo (Allatson 146). For these reasons, the role of the father is especially linked to notions of machismo due to the dissemination of gendered and cultural values through parenting expressions. Films like Gregory Nava's *Mi Familia* (1995) narratively investigate the impacts of machismo on family and self, generating complicated views of Latino masculinity in contemporary U.S. society. In more recent years, films like *La Mission* (2009) have pressed these narratives to include discussions of sexuality, exploring the expectations Latino fathers place on their sons.

The series introduction to Nero's character seemingly places him in the same tropes of Latino masculinity perpetuated by various media, showcasing Latinos as hypersexual and/or criminal. While recent research suggests an increase in Latino visibility on television and that representations are generally more favorable than previous portrayals, there is still a lack of complexity and a reliance on stereotypes in the media (Hernández 251–52). Viewers first see Nero's character engaging in sex with Gemma, while two young blonde women lay unconscious on the couches beside them. Following this introduction, viewers assume Nero is sexually aggressive with women, like many of the stereotyped Latino characters in cinematic history. Even Gemma makes this assumption after waking from an alcohol-induced sleep, pulling a gun on her future love interest, Nero. However, Nero immediately (and throughout the series) fractures these expectations of sexual aggression through his treatment of Gemma, even when jealousy would seem inevitable in the male dominant world of *Sons of Anarchy*.[4]

While Marcus Alvarez's character strictly upheld the conventions of machismo, Nero's character complicates the limitations of the gendered code. This is most evident in the character's acceptance of his role in his son's spina bifida diagnosis. As Nero and Jax drive away from the visit with Lucius, Jax asks about the cause of his son's illness. Nero replies "Neglect" and explains his son's mother was a drug user and he was uninvolved during the pregnancy. Significantly, Nero places blame on himself, rejecting the machismo tendency to blame women over men. Further, Nero does not speak diminutively of Lucius, calling him a "badass." This masculine referencing of Lucius both upholds and contests the expectations of machismo, where Nero seeks to masculinize his disabled son, but at the same time sees authoritative masculine qualities in the child despite his illness, a contradiction to the normative Latino masculine body expectations.

Not only does Nero reveal his paternal qualities in these scenes, the character invokes these qualities to publically arise in Jax. As Nero speaks about his son, Jax noticeably manipulates his "SO" "NS" rings in the foreground of the shot, indicating an acknowledgment of his children. Following his confession of neglect, Jax too admits he wasn't attentive during his ex-wife's pregnancy, leading to Abel's illness. What is significant however, is the term Jax uses to describe Wendy (Abel's biological mother). Jax calls Wendy a "junkie," while Nero simply states that his "ex" was "using." Nero avoids the stigmatizing labeling of Lucius' mother, while Jax fully employs it at multiple times in the series. While Jax claims to take responsibility for his part in Abel's illness, his usage of the term "junkie" suggests the machismo masculine order is still fully impacting his philosophies. In contrast, Nero resonates his earlier message by speaking in Spanish to Jax, "Pecados del padre, homes" (Sins of the father), reinforcing a meaning that suggest more than absence during pregnancy. This line indicts Nero's previous lifestyle as culpable for the misfortune of his son.

## Reforming Family: Fatherhood and Forgiveness

While much of the scenes discussed engage in Nero's role as the (biological) father of Lucius, these scenes more subtly display Nero's role as an adoptive father figure for Jax. In fact, no other father figure referenced in the series (John or Clay) have guided Jax toward positive approaches for growth and self-improvement outside of the MC. John's manuscript, in part, works as unchallengeable advice based on failed attempts to ascend the morals and codes of the same MC founded by the author. Here, viewers see the impacts of failed fatherhood, where Jax's relationship with John can never attain the pragmatic approach Nero applies to his parenting and lifestyle.

Nero's attempts at resuscitating humanity into the Teller-Morrow family demonstrate a major break from Western genre conventions, where racial Others are often villainized or portrayed as monstrous. In the scene discussed earlier, Nero's conversation with Jax suggests subtle attempts to advise the young outlaw without pressuring his choices or judgment. In fact, the scene plays like a father-son discussion of business, family, and even sex.[5] More importantly, the scene sets the foundation for Nero and Jax's relationship for the remainder of the series, where Nero acts as a mediator between extreme MC culture and fatherhood.

Yet, Nero's influence as a father figure is not only directed toward Jax. Nero invites Gemma to meet Lucius in order to introduce not only his son to his new girlfriend, but also his perspective as a father ("Andare Pescare," season five, episode nine). The scene begins with an establishing shot of Gemma and Nero sitting at an outdoor table with children playing in the foreground. The hurricane fence overlapping the shot reminds viewers of the many prison scenes throughout the series. The shot cuts to a close up of the couple, unobstructed by the fence, discussing the trajectories of their lives. Nero explains that he couldn't stay completely out of criminal activity, due to the restrictions of his "ex-junkie, ex-con" labeling and difficulties finding work. Gemma empathizes with Nero and implies her association with John and the MC began because she became pregnant two months into their relationship at the age of 18. Here, the fence used to overlap the beginning of the shot emphasizes the metaphorical "imprisonment" both characters have failed to escape.

Immediately following this discussion, Lucius arrives in a wheelchair to meet his father's "friend" Gemma. The child's interruption of their conversation represents the interruption of parenthood in both character's lives. Lucius' birth shifted the "ex-junkie, ex-con" identity stigmatizing Nero to include father. This shifting allowed the character to embrace more complicated understandings of self and identity. While Lucius' birth signifies a positive shift in Nero's identity, the birth of Gemma's child, Jax, helped to solidify her "imprisonment" with John and the MC. Nero's invitation to Gemma allows her to view Nero's positive experience in shifting his identity to include fatherhood.

Yet, this attempt to influence Gemma's worldview is not as productive as hoped. Later, Gemma takes Lucius a toy water gun as a gift, disappointing Nero's expectations ("Straw," season six, episode one). As Lucius unwraps the gift, he yells "This is awesome!" Nero unenthusiastically replies, "Yup. A gun ... awesome." Unlike Gemma, Nero rejects a violent future for his son, partly due to his son's limited life expectancy. Through this tragic turn, Lucius' illness has allowed him to escape the patterns set by his father.

Nevertheless, Nero maintains his alternative perspective to Gemma and Jax's strict "blood" family mentality. After Wendy relapses into drug use, Gemma and Nero help her recover ("Aon Rud Persanta," season six, episode 11). When Tara arrives to pick up her sons, Abel and Thomas, she is concerned by Wendy's presence in the home. Sensing her concern, Nero playfully asks "Abel, maybe you're going to grow up and be a doctor like your mom someday?" Carefully emphasizing Tara's position as Abel's mother, Nero tries to ease concerns regarding her familial role, indicating that despite Wendy's presence, Tara is in fact Abel's mother. His question also suggests Abel living a stable life, outside of MC culture, a desire he knows is important to Tara.

While Nero's acceptance of an adoptive mother for Abel challenges dominant ideologies of parenthood, his acceptance of two mothers through his acknowledgment of Wendy as the mother of Abel as well presses further on these notions. Unlike Gemma's rejection of one mother for another, Nero simultaneously accepts the unconventional parent paradigm, blurring the rigid parameters of adoption narratives. Marianne Novy describes three major "mythic" paradigms in *Imagining Adoption: Essays on Literature and Culture*: the "unhappy adoption," which leads to the search for birth parents, the "happy reunion," in which birth kin are reunited, and the "happy adoption" (1). In *Sons of Anarchy*, these three paradigms are constantly in conflict, overlapping throughout the narrative. Only Nero opposes these narratives, allowing for alternative family structures.

Moreover, Nero's character exposes the flawed thinking of the Teller-Morrow family, hoping to influence their abilities for forgiveness. Nero pleads with Gemma to forgive her daughter-in-law, Tara, and rebuild their familial bond, stating his current emotional suffering for never having "made it right" with his ex before her death ("Aon Rud Persanta," season six, episode 11). Gemma coldly refuses his plea, rejecting the possibility of forgiveness. Similarly, Nero attempts to influence Jax's cycle of aggression over compassion. Yet, Nero's attempts to "rescue" the adoptive Jax are often unproductive as well, when ultimately Jax chooses "blood" mentality over Nero's advisement. Jax's assertion, "I can't change" seemingly overpowers Nero's fatherly presence ("Papa's Goods," season seven, episode 13).

Perhaps most importantly, Nero's goal to raise his son on a farm in Norco rejects the association with criminal activity and transgression represented by urban spaces in Westerns. In the genre, rural space is romanticized in ways that elicit notions of freedom and renewal needed for nation building. Seeing this opportunity, Jax asks Nero to take his sons to his farm as well, indicating his hopes for Abel and Thomas to live outside of his transgressions. While, on the surface, it appears Nero's fatherly impact has failed, in fact, Jax's request indicates Nero's influence was, in some ways, successful.

## *Conclusion*

Though Western conventions would typically dictate Nero Padilla's character as highly villainous, the series manages to reverse this inscription of Mexican bodies on screen with his inclusion in the narrative. At the series end, Nero appears to be one of the only "salvageable" characters, expressing compassion and humanity through his care for his children. This includes Jax Teller, the defiant son he guided through passive influence rather than assertive and limiting codes of the frontier. Although Nero's presence did not adjust the Teller-Morrow family mentality, it does offer a mediator in a constantly battled West.

### Notes

1. While the non-biological ties are emphasized through membership in the MC, Nero accepts these ties without any formalized structure, such as club membership.
2. For a longer discussion of gender and race in *High Noon*, see my article "Helen's Hotel Room: The West, the Hotel, and the Mexican Female Body as Decolonial Sites in *High Noon*."
3. In fact, Ramirez Berg argues that the mistreatment or murder of "innocent" Native Americans in many of John Ford's Westerns represents a type of "villainy" despite being enacted by WASP characters (134).

4. For example, Nero is sympathetic toward Gemma following the events of her forced conjugal visit with Clay.
 5. Interestingly, Nero corrects Jax's judgment that his "cut" in the escort service may be too small, explaining that he "treats his girls right." While unsettling by realistic standards, in the world of *Sons of Anarchy* Nero's treatment of women is more ethical than the MC's history.

## Works Cited

Adams, Ramon F. *The Cowman and His Code of Ethics*, Encino Press, 1969. Print.
Allatson, Paul. *Key Terms in Latino/a Cultural and Literary Studies*. Malden, MA: Blackwell, 2007. Print.
Handley, William R. *Marriage, Violence, and the Nation in the American Literary West*. Cambridge University Press, 2009. Web.
Hernández, Leandra H. "Paternidad, Masculinidad, and Machismo: Evolving Representations of Mexican American Fathers in Film." In *Deconstructing Dads: Changing Images of Fathers in Popular Culture*. Eds. Laura Tropp and Janice Kelly. Lexington Books, 2016. Print.
*High Noon*. Dir. Fred Zinnemann. 1952.
*La Mission*. Dir. Peter Bratt. 2009.
*Mi Familia*. Dir. Gregory Nava. 1995.
Novy, Marianne, ed. *Imagining Adoption: Essays on Literature and Culture*. University of Michigan Press, 2011. Print.
Ramirez Berg, Charles. *Latino Images in Film: Stereotypes, Subversion, Resistance*. University of Texas Press, 2002. Print.
*The Rifleman*. ABC, 1958–1963.
*The Searchers*. Dir. John Ford. 1956.
*Shane*. Dir. George Stevens. 1953.
*Sons of Anarchy*. FX, 2008–2014.

# The Performative Crisis of Otto Delaney
## Destruction, Dematerialization and Masculine Identity

SUSAN FANETTI

According to Judith Butler, gender is constructed by its repeated, repetitive performance. Performative gender, specifically, is a stylized repetition of acts that imitate the dominant conventions of gender. "[T]he act that one does, the act that one performs is, in a sense, an act that's been going on before one arrived on the scene" ("Performative Acts" 526). When one acts "like a lady" or "mans up," there is extant, specific cultural coding that reifies and instantiates what those acts must be. The culture at large has already defined these behaviors.

Even so, the coding of gender is continually redefined, especially in more bounded and exclusive cultures and subcultures. The motorcycle club (MC) culture in which *Sons of Anarchy* (*SOA*) dwells, for instance, has defined masculinity to a sharp point. These are so-called "alpha males": violent outlaws for whom every part of their world is a performance of an almost atavistic masculinity so extreme that they are essentially apex predators among their own species. They are inked, leather-clad, boot-wearing (mostly), chain-dangling, Harley-riding, hard-drinking, gun-toting outlaws, exuding a powerful "manliness" that insulates them from outside reprisals for the lion's share of their bad deeds. Consequences come from within, for the most part, according to the code of the outlaw. These are men who believe in revenge and retaliation with a religious fervor.

Seen through this lens, Otto "Big Otto" Delaney, a longstanding member of SAMCRO, the Redwood mother charter of the Sons, who is incarcerated for nearly the full run of the series, is a fascinating study. From his first appearance early in the first season to his final in the sixth, he is set apart from the club, though his membership is key to many story arcs, including and especially the main series arc. In fact, the health and security of the club itself, even its very existence, rests heavily on his loyalty. Caged and stripped of his shield of leather, Otto is consistently subject to the reprisals his free brothers escape, and his lot becomes a metaphor for the chaotic fate of the club over the course of the series.

Separated from the MC and unable to engage in the cultural performance of its masculine rites, Otto is left vulnerable. It's no surprise, then, that in prison he is continually subject to attacks on his primitive, performative masculinity. Interestingly, Otto, while subjected to horrors by the legal apparatus he's caught in, is an agent, if not *the* agent, of most of his (literal) dematerialization. As his isolation from the club deepens, he again and again acts to assert his connection to the Sons and to make manifest the impact of its betrayals. Despite acts and circumstances in which his body is literally deconstructed, he maintains his agency of self. Even in his final act, at a point at which he appears to have been reduced to a state of pure abjection, Otto finds agency and turns the story in his own direction. It can be seen as a carnival in five acts.

# Big Otto: A Carnival in Five Acts

## Act I: Sacrifice

On Otto Delaney's character page in *Sons of Anarchy: The Official Collector's Edition*, there is a list, "Otto's Rap Sheet," which includes 13 different entries, starting from his six-year sentence, circa 1997, for murder and vehicle theft (Bennett 60). Each entry corresponds to something that Otto gave or lost in service to the club. In "Burnt and Purged Away" (season four, episode 12), Otto hands Bobby a yellow legal pad, covered in dense handwriting, which represents the same list, in his own words, starting with "March 1997—Broke Giordano's collarbone, two ribs" for which he got a "month in the hole" and had five months added to his sentence.

Bobby reads a few lines of that list, each item an instance of Otto's service and sacrifice. When Bobby expresses confusion about why he's reading, Otto takes it over and says, "It's my list, brother. It's all the things I've done for the club inside. Including the thing that got me life, and the thing that got me death." By the time of this meeting, late in the fourth season, Otto has sacrificed nearly everything for the Sons, including, in separate instances, both of his eyes. He has given up his freedom, his happiness, his life, his very body to the club. When he sits across that metal table in a sparse interrogation room and faces Bobby—in Otto's mind, a synecdoche for the club and its betrayal—he has lost his hope as well. But, unlike every other sacrifice he's made, his hope was not something he gave willingly. It was taken from him, and this is the key to Otto's dematerialization.

When we first meet Otto, in season one, he is calm, strong, invested, powerful as a dealmaker for the Sons on the inside—in fact, in his very first appearance, in "Giving Back" (season one, episode five), he is engaged in a prison brawl, protecting a club asset, beating off the man's attackers (he's protecting Chucky, a character who will become a fan favorite with a prominent recurring role throughout the rest of the series). Otto is composed, self-possessed, and entirely materialized as a SAMCRO patch, even without access to his kutte. Though we never see Otto's bare torso, so only see the ink on his hands, arms, and neck, we can assume, because it's consistent with the club code, that he bears a Reaper on his body. It's important that we don't see it—at some point in the series, we see the Reaper on every other patch of note—because it suggests that there is a distance between Otto and the club even at that early point during which we have repeated signals of his importance. But he bears the logo "SOA" on the left side of his neck, right over his pulse point, and Otto is often filmed from that angle, so we can never forget that he is club. In the same way, his wife's name, Luann, is inked very prominently on his left forearm, and whenever he talks about her—and in the single scene of the series in which they are together—that ink features heavily. Luann is a pivot point for his loyalty to his brothers because he has entrusted them with her protection and care while he cannot meet this need himself. Again, care of family is the mark of humanity these violent men cling to. Like all his brothers, Otto is literally inscribed with the cultural meanings of his club and his place there.

But according to R.W. Connell, "[t]he surface on which cultural meanings are inscribed is not featureless, and it does not stay still" (51), and this is certainly the case for Otto. His body is a constantly changing surface, and the inscriptions on it fade and change as the series progresses. Though he gains tattoos throughout the seasons, we see less of his important ink, even that placed so prominently on his neck, as his isolation from the club and his subjugation to the institutional machine of the prison erase his identity and reinscribe him not as a member of SAMCRO but as a prisoner of the state.

Foucault calls discipline "a political anatomy of detail" ("Docile Bodies" 182) and explains that "for the disciplined man, as for the true believer, no detail is unimportant, but not so much for the naming that it conceals within it as for the hold it provides for the power that wishes to seize it" (183). He is speaking particularly of soldiers here and the obsessive attention to detail that marks military culture, but the idea applies to prisoners, and to outlaw club culture as well, as both are militaristic in their operations and reflect rigidly similar ideas about power and discipline. Though civilian societal structures of law and order send men (and women) to prison, the system of power within that space does not reflect civilian society. It, too, is a space of atavistic performances of power and gender.

For Otto, both a disciplined man (prisoner) and a true believer (patch), this political anatomy of detail creates a gap of identity through which he falls. Willingly disciplined into the club's ways of meaning, a true believer in that indelible code, when he is incarcerated, the prison culture strives to write its code over him. On the outside, he was Big Otto, powerful member of a powerful club. Inside, as long as he's still Big Otto, still recognized as a member and still agent in their operations and protection, he maintains and performs the details of his identity even as prison carves itself into his body.

But as the club seeks more from him and offers less, that identity begins to fade, and prison inscribes itself over who he was. Because club identity is mediated strongly, if not solely, through the gendered coding of virile masculinity, Otto's masculinity is the surface on which prison writes itself and overwrites his self.

## Act II: Crisis

R.W. Connell argues that "gender is vulnerable when the performance cannot be sustained" (54). Michel Foucault tells us that "the means of coercion make those on whom they are applied clearly visible" ("Correct Training" 189). Discussing Foucault, Judith Butler explains that "cultural values emerge as the result of an inscription on the body, understood as a medium, indeed a blank page; in order for this inscription to signify, however, that medium itself must be destroyed" (*Gender Trouble* 166). These ideas converge on a single point: the control of identity. Who has power over the body has the ability to sustain its inscription, and thus the self's performance—its *comprehensibility*. For an outlaw biker, performance of gender *is* self.

As a member of SAMCRO, Otto's masculinity is entirely and extremely coded in his physical strength and his power of influence—he is a man because he is strong, because he is fearsome, because he *protects*—and as long as he can continue to perform those functions, he remains inscrutable to the prison institution. His jailers can act on him—confine his movements, extend his sentence, allow other inmates to beat him, beat him themselves—but they cannot shape him. When his connection to the club wanes, however, so does his sense of himself and his power over his inscription.

The seed of Otto's crisis is sown late in the first season. June Stahl, an ATF agent fixated on bringing down the Sons, arrests Luann on a drug charge and uses that as a lever to trick Otto into giving her information about the club. Telling him she has no interest in taking down the club and just wants to get the case off her desk, Stahl gets Otto to agree to give her old information that he believes is useless in exchange for his wife being cleared of all charges ("Better Half," season one, episode ten). When the club gets word to him that Stahl means to use his "dead" information to establish history for a RICO charge, he acts out, with sudden, vicious violence, to make his statement null.

It's important that it's Luann, in a conjugal visit, who brings him this information. We see, as they share a tender marital moment, Otto in a fully masculine-coded, heterosexual performance, and we see him on both sides of the hypermasculine scale. He is gentle with Luann, holding her as she weeps, kissing her, calming her, and instructing her to stay strong. Watching from the other side of the observation window, Stahl is sarcastic and dismissive of the tender scene, clearly reading vulnerability—weakness—in Otto's tender care of his wife.

When he has saved Luann and she has returned to the free world, Otto exploits Stahl's misreading of his strength. He asks her to come close to help him read the prepared statement, because he doesn't have his glasses with him—a performance signaling weakness and need. Completely disarmed by her own sense of victory and power, Stahl comes close, and Otto explodes with extreme, bloody violence, writing his power on her body.

As he's subdued and beaten in retaliation, Otto laughs.

This scene is crucial to understanding Otto as a Son, as a mate, as a man—and as a prisoner. We see him perform every masculine identity he has. In that scene, he protects his club and his wife, both. He shows his soft side—his capacity for love and tenderness and deep emotion—and his steely side—his loyalty to his club, his capacity for extreme, unrepentant violence, and his code of retaliation. That he performs violence on a woman immediately after performing tenderness on one is further evidence of the reinscribing power of the legal apparatus—Otto doesn't read Stahl as a woman. He reads her as an agent of his incarceration.

This scene in which we see every dimension of Otto Delaney performed is also the moment that his connection to the club and the identity he's forged in its leather and ink begins to fray. Two important things have happened, in the midst of this performance: Otto has signaled to the club, and to himself, that Luann is the most important presence in his life. Not the Sons. He has shown that he is willing to give information up to save her. Information he thought dead, yes, but information nonetheless. To save his wife, he is willing to rat, and, as Sonny Barger explains, in an outlaw MC, "which is based on brotherhood, freedom, and your word, a rat is the true enemy" (229). There is no one lower in the club's eyes than a traitor in their midst, and now the point on which Otto might turn has been noted.

Conversely, Otto has learned that the club cannot or will not protect

Luann to the extent she needs. He has left her in the care of his brothers, trusted them to keep her safe and well, and their actions, and their neglect, put her at risk. After a decade spent in prison, Otto comprehends completely how profound the danger of a prison sentence would be for Luann.

When Luann tells him, during their fleeting moment of tenderness, of the real danger to the club, Otto acts to turn back the damage he might have done. He acts swiftly, only moments after learning of the RICO trap, decisively, and at great risk to himself. He protects his club. The Sons forgive him. But the stain of the rat, the idea that Otto's loyalty has a limit, is indelible. Otto and the Sons both now understand the limits of their brotherhood, and that potent seed implants in the narrative until it grows into a crisis.

That crisis matures in the second season, when Stahl goes after Luann again, this time in retaliation for the beating Otto dealt her and the loss of her RICO case and its career-making potential. In the second episode of the season, "Small Tears"—with a narrative that focuses on club women as both a chief source of the brothers' strength and their greatest vulnerability, not to mention the grave risk the club presents to those women—Otto tells Jax that the seizure of Luann's porn studio is Stahl "pissing in my mouth for what I did to her, and I did that for SAMCRO." He's worried that Luann will have to "go back in front of the cameras again"—as a porn star herself—and he'd promised her she'd never have to do that.

In this scene—another scene that opens with prison violence in the foreground—Otto again imbricates all his masculine signifiers—violence, strength, protection, virility, heterosexuality (this writ especially large in a conversation about his porn star wife and his promise to shield her), loyalty, sacrifice, and family. He harkens to the club's promise to him—to take care of his wife—as he concretizes his performance of his promise to the club—to do whatever he had to do inside to serve and protect their interests.

But the club fails utterly to protect Luann. Indeed, in its attempts to protect her, it creates the ultimate danger, and she is killed. Without his wife, knowing that she was lost to violence he and the Sons catalyzed, Otto begins to lose the threads of connection he had to the club, and to his sense of agency and self. Though he continues to act in service of the club, those acts become increasingly violent and reckless. By the second season finale, "Na Tiobloidi," Otto has lost his right eye and his vision has been reduced to ten-percent. He shows Jax the empty, drooping scar of a socket, a visceral physical sign of his sacrifice. Jax tells him it's "time for retribution, bro."

But Otto, by this point, has become defined by nothing else. His body is a medium for acts of retribution, as both subject and object thereof. Otto lives, literally, in a world of "an eye for an eye." And that world has blinded him.

## Act III: Retribution

Perhaps there is no clearer indication of Otto's waning significance to the club than his near-total absence from the narrative in the third season. His last act of the second season, in the season finale, is to collect payback for SAMCRO and for his own eye, and then he disappears completely, from the screen and from the club's notice, until the *third*-season finale, "NS." But he acts there in his old role of dealmaker, working from the inside to help the club set up a partnership with the Putlovas, a Russian crime syndicate. Though mostly blind, he appears in this episode at least partially restored, in body and identity. He wears glasses, remediating his diminished sight, and the club ink on his neck features prominently again. Even his humor has returned, though darker in tone. He laughs as he tells Clay and Jax that the legal apparatus has declared him to "continue to exhibit a pattern of aggressive behavior" and that he will "be on the Row" (Death Row, that is) soon. He says this with an air of wry resignation. Otto has lost hope, but he clings to the last thread of identity he has: his club. Now he lives to serve the Sons in the most basic way: it's the only thing he has left to live for.

Despite everything Otto has done for the club, despite the way his sacrifice is inscribed on his body, carving deeper with every new incident, the Sons continue to lean on him to serve their needs. In fact, they *exploit* his hopelessness. After Jax is attacked and badly injured during a brief stint in prison, the club looks to Otto to exact revenge—to the extreme extent that Otto *slits his wrists* so that he'll be taken to the infirmary, where he'll be given an opportunity to kill Jax's attacker ("Out," season four, episode one). And so begins the end stage of Otto's decline: he is not only willing to *risk* harm to serve the club but willing to *inflict* self-harm. He is so weakened by self-inflicted blood loss that, as he plunges a scalpel into his target's ear, he has to lean against the wall, wearing nothing but the blood-soaked bandages around his cut wrists and a blood-spattered hospital gown hanging loosely over a body much *less* than it once had been.

When next we see Otto, he is lying prostrate in a cell hardly bigger than the narrow cot on which he rests. The bandages over his wrists are still blood-soaked, and he has obviously also been beaten since we last saw him. Too weak to stand, still wearing the same gown, covered in his blood and in his latest victim's, his body filthy and his hair in greasy tangles, without his glasses, thus basically blind, he is the very image of abjection. In "Approaching Abjection," the first chapter of *Powers of Horror*, Julia Kristeva explains the ways the body's fluids and excretions reflect on the self: "These bodily fluids, this defilement, this shit are what life withstands, hardly and with difficulty, on the part of death, There, I am at the border of my condition as a living being. My body extricates itself, as being alive, from that border. Such wastes drop so that I might live, until, from loss to loss, nothing remains in me and my entire body falls beyond the limit—*cadere*, cadaver" (3). Otto cannot extricate himself, not from his coffin-sized cell, not from the blood of his service and sacrifice, not from his subjection and exploitation at the hands of both the prison system and the club to which he has sworn his fealty. In that cell, after he has opened his own wrists and invited his own corpse to reckon with him in service to the club, Otto is at the border of his life and death. Entirely abject, entirely subjected, he is, for the first time, beyond the limit of self. "Abject. It is something rejected from which one does not part, from which one does not protect oneself as from an object" (Kristeva 4). Abjection is the utter rejection of what one essentially *is*, what one cannot help but be, what one cannot escape. Captive, trapped with nothing but a body the control over which he has sacrificed utterly, Otto is reduced to passivity. He can no longer protect himself. His identity—one founded entirely on a code of masculinity—is forfeit.

Into this moment, Lincoln Potter, State Assistant District Attorney, steps. And he brings with him the agent that will undo Otto, and nearly the Sons as well.

"Out," the fourth season premiere, in which Otto kills Jax's attacker, also marks the point of no return for the club. Every move made from that point on further ensures the crisis the club will face at the end of the series, and it all runs hand in hand with Otto's crisis of loyalty and sacrifice. When Otto discovers that the Sons have betrayed him, he asserts the last dregs of his agency in the service of ultimate retribution, marking his essential nature as a Son by seeking to tear down the space in which that nature was expressed.

Potter exploits Otto's weakened state and twists the facts of Luann's death and the Sons'—specifically, Bobby's—lies about the circumstances of her death and the retribution Otto demanded, turning truths into a lie about the club's betrayal. Bobby did betray Otto, but the club did not. Or, rather, it did—the Sons neglected him, they neglected their duty to protect Luann, they exploited his loyalty without performing any act of loyalty to him—and the one remaining faith Otto had was that they had exacted revenge for Luann's murder.

But they had not. In service of their own needs, they had allowed Luann's murder to go unavenged. Potter uses that truth like a cudgel and finally breaks Otto's bond to the club completely. He goes full rat and gives Bobby up, signaling the end of his fealty and sacrifice to the Sons. In the episode "Burnt and Purged Away," when Otto hands Bobby his list of sacrifices, his parting words are "Time for you to start a list, Bobby." The implication is that Otto has nothing left to add to his own list. He will act no more as a Son. He has nothing more to give.

But ultimately, that's not true, because it isn't the Sons of Anarchy he wants to hurt. It's SAMCRO—his own charter, his own brotherhood, the men who swore they would do the things that he could not, protect the woman that he could not. These are the men who betrayed him, even discounting Potter's twisting of the facts of Luann's death. When he learns, in the fifth season, that his statement could destroy the entire club, he acts again, in extreme, sudden violence again, to save the Sons but hurt SAMCRO. The last words of significant dialogue Otto speaks are "Sons live. Redwood bleeds" ("Crucifixed," season five, episode ten). The club will live on, but he means to deal his own charter a crippling blow.

He acts to implicate Jax's old lady, Tara, in his latest kill, paying back the club's dereliction of their duty to Luann by putting Jax's own woman's freedom at stake. In the preceding episodes, while Otto sets this trap, he consistently draws parallels between Luann and Tara, even asking Tara to stand as a surrogate for Luann so that he can remember her touch. When he takes his retribution, Tara serves as Luann's surrogate again. The club took Otto's old lady; he takes Jax's. As Jax is by now the club president, Otto's act against Tara becomes a metaphor for the club's inability to protect what it says it most values: family.

"Sons live. Redwood bleeds" serve as his last words because after that, Otto ensures that he will never speak again. In another interrogation room, facing another statement against the Sons, observed again through a two-way mirror by an agent with a personal vendetta against him, Otto again acts in extreme, sudden, bloody violence—this time on himself—and silences himself in the most permanent, visceral way he can. Discussing that episode, "J'ai Obtenu Cette," the fifth season finale, showrunner Kurt Sutter (who plays Otto) explains that "I thought with a guy as fucked up and damaged as Otto, what better way to say 'I'm not talking'" (Porter). Already blinded in prison while serving his club, Otto silences himself in yet another act of service to a club that has forgotten him.

The title of this episode is in French. It translates to English as "I Got This," a phrase which, by the end of the fifth season, has become poignantly synonymous in the show's mythos with a supreme act of sacrifice wrapped in bitter betrayal. SAMCRO is crumbling because its members are no longer a family. They perform the acts of their masculine identity, but they have lost the meaning of brotherhood.

## Act IV: Reversal

The agent with a personal vendetta in the fifth season is Lee Toric, who takes over the role of Otto's chief tormentor from Lincoln Potter. Toric is the brother of the innocent Otto killed in his act against Tara and the Sons. Toric introduces himself to Otto in his tiny Death Row cell, where Otto again lies prostrate, again still covered in the blood of his latest kill, again bearing the marks of a savage beating. Guards burst into the cell and again beat a passive, broken Otto, and then Toric, dressed nattily, in contrast to Otto's decrepit state, introduces himself, speaking the first words of the scene: "Can you hear my voice, Mr. Delaney?" ("To Thine Own Self," season five, episode 12). Functionally blind and physically broken, Otto still manages a defeated laugh. He tells Toric that he should have "kept going"—kept the beating up until he was dead. But that's not the revenge Toric wants. He wants Otto to suffer even greater torments than he yet has.

When Otto acts out to silence himself permanently and gorily, Toric, observing from the other side of the mirror, at first shows grudging respect: "Way to commit, Otto," ("J'ai Obtenu Cette"). But he responds in deed with extreme malice, and he does so directly on the stage of Otto's scanty remaining masculine identity. In the warlike way of masculine power assertion, Toric sets guards upon Otto for a daily routine of torture by anal rape. For the rest of Otto's appearances, the show does not flinch from showing these acts and their consequences.

Considering the condition of Otto's body and the torture to which he has been, and especially that to which he is now, subjected, we must finally turn to Mikhail Bakhtin and the carnival, from which the heading of this section derives. Otto's body has become a grotesquerie, even a carnival itself. In *Rabelais and His World*, Bakhtin describes the grotesque body as

> a body in the act of becoming. It is never finished, never complete; it is continually built, created, and build and creates another body.... This is why the essential role belong to those parts of the grotesque body in which it outgrows its own self, transgressing its own body, in which it conceives a new, second body: the bowels and the phallus. These two areas play the leading role in the grotesque image.... Next to the bowels and the genital organs in the mouth, through which enters the worlds to be swallowed up. And next is the anus. All these convexities and orifices have a common characteristic; it is within them that the confines between bodies and the world are overcome: there is an interchange and interorientation [233–34].

In the Bakhtinian construction, the grotesque body dwells in the space of potential, which is the carnivalesque. There is power in that space, the power of rebuilding, renewal, reinscription. But always in the act of becoming, the grotesque body is also always in the act of unmaking, leaving behind what it was before. Kristeva tells us that the grotesque is also the abject: "If dung signifies the other side of the border, the place where I am not and which permits me to be, the corpse, the most sickening of wastes, is a border that has encroached upon everything" ("Abjection" 34). The act of rape, so viscerally, intimately connected with all the physical sites of abjection and grotesquerie, is an act of unmaking. Framed in this way, to be raped is to be abjected—to be unmade.

In "Engendering Rape," Kim Shayo Buchanan discusses the conventional understanding of the gendered power dynamics of prison rape, the stereotype of the hypermasculine (read: violent) male prisoner and the institutional "heterosexist understanding of sexuality" (1681) that sees the raped prisoner as feminized. She notes that male guards are also stereotyped as hypermasculine but notes that their position, their "*identity* as law enforcers confers upon their violence a legitimacy that is not accorded to violence by inmates" (1683, emphasis mine). This understanding of the dynamics of prison rape, particularly male-guard-on-male-inmate prison rape, situates the act not only on the space of gender and power but on legitimacy. What happens to Otto, then, not only subjugates his body and his manhood but his very identity.

The phallus is the physical weapon of rape and also, as Jacques Lacan explains, "the signifier that is destined to designate meaning effects as a whole, insofar as the signifier conditions them by its presence as signifier" ("The Signification of the Phallus" 579). The effects of this presence include "a deviation of man's needs due to the fact that he speaks: to the extent that his needs are subjected to demand, they come back to him in an alienated form" (579). Lacan goes on assert that demand "in itself bears on something other than the satisfaction it calls for. It is demand for a presence or an absence" (579). Rape, as a violent act of phallic signification, is also that Lacanian demand. It is force, and coercion—not merely physical coercion, but a "coercion of materialization" (Farmer 106) that obviates the raped man's ability to signify. For Otto, speechless and blind, the lack of self-signification is especially acute.

The daily routine of rape perpetrated on Otto is more than simply an act of power or even of coercion. It is torture—not institutionalized torture, that which is enacted in order to produce information or actions, but punitive, retaliatory torture, intended primarily as its own end—though it's key to note that Toric does use Otto's situation as a lever against Clay, threatening the same kind of torture if he doesn't comply. In "A Theoretical Introduction to the Functions of Psychoanalysis in Criminology," Lacan considers the diminishing usefulness of torture in a world that recognizes human rights and no longer conflates sin and law, suggesting that a man "abstracted from his social consistency was no longer believable ... it was necessary to know his motivations, along with his motives ... and these motivations and motives had to be comprehensible—comprehensible to everyone" (113). But a prison, certainly the prison of the *SOA* world, is not a place of human rights. In the case of Lee Toric's raping of Otto by institutional proxy, we can see an Old Testament sense of justice in play. Toric has no need to understand Otto, and Otto can no longer be comprehensible. He is beyond his social consistency, beyond the limit of his identity, beyond the bounds of his materiality.

Janine Natalya Clark notes that from feminist and gender theory perspectives, rape is acknowledged to be "an expression of *gendered* power and patriarchy" ("A Crime of Identity" 147, emphasis original), but she pushes that idea beyond the common constructions of rape as an assertion of power and argues that rape is an attack on the very core of self—the gendered self. She explains male rape as an attack on "the victim's sense of masculine self" (148) and suggests that more than a domination and assertion of power, male rape is a crime of identity: "part of what makes male rape a crime of identity is the way in which the victim responds to and interprets the act of violation ... rape is not just a violation of the victim but also of societal expectations of what it means to be a man" (150). This is perhaps an especially poignant violation for Otto, whose (masculine) identity has been undergoing constant events of rupture for years. By this point, rape is more than a violation of his sense of self. It is erasure.

Scholars' descriptions of this violent violation, this rending of self, are generally as ferocious as the act they describe. Ann Cahill, in *Rethinking Rape*, calls it a "violent destabilizing of the existing self" (132). Setting this in gendered terms, Angela Farmer notes that when a man is raped in prison,

> it is said that he has "been punk'd," he's getting "punk'd." The action occurs to him—on his body; he is passive, *therefore feminized* ... he is said to be "made someone's bitch" or "made someone's wife." On the other hand, the aggressor is active and maintains his status as subject and therefore masculine ... the more violent the encounter, the more feminized the victim, the more the aggressor can therefore retain his status as masculine ["The Worst Fate" 108, emphasis mine].

Sasha Gear agrees with this reading of male rape as a violent unmaking of gendered identity, going so far as to label it "demolished masculinity" and "imposed womanhood" ("Behind the Bars of Masculinity" 216). This is the plight Otto finds himself in at the end of his story: abandoned, betrayed, broken, subjected, abjected, silenced, blinded, and unmanned. Lee Toric, who is both the primary agent of Otto's final abasements and a passive observer of them, writes his own masculinity on Otto's bare, grotesque body. In an act of revenge that Otto should comprehend and relate to, one coded as retroactive protection for a beloved, deceased female family member, Toric erases Otto's own code of masculinity.

## Act V: Reclamation

But Otto's story is not yet over, and it's the club that gives him a chance for a final moment of agency—one he performs through another act of extreme, sudden, bloody violence. In "Wolfsangel," the fourth episode of the sixth season, Otto is again in the prison infirmary. He is entirely passive, strapped to a gurney. There is fresh blood on his clothes. He is without his glasses. His body, once so robust and powerful, is now small and frail. He's aged decades in the few years of the series timeline. He is no longer Big Otto.

Clay, the former SAMCRO president—either a direct or indirect agent of many of the club's betrayals of Otto and now subject himself to club reprisals—is also a prisoner. He comes into the infirmary (Toric has set up this meeting as a concrete threat, so that Clay can see what he faces if he doesn't flip on the Sons) and is appalled at Otto's condition. He's appalled, of course, because he hasn't seen or had word of his brother in a long time. Otto was forgotten when his usefulness dwindled, even before he became a club antagonist.

But in that brief, crucial moment, connecting with an also-disenfranchised brother, Otto reclaims that brotherhood, and with it his identity, if not his place. Clay leans over Otto's gurney and apologizes. Otto, long beyond the power of speech, weeps and nods. Clay eases a blade into Otto's bound hand and says, "No more, brother," signifying both the brotherhood and the salvation of it. Otto's *SOA* neck tattoo, over his pulse point, is clearly visible. Again, at last, Otto has agency. He reclaims his body, his self, and his fate. He decides.

When he is alone again with Lee Toric, he acts again to exact revenge and to save the club. He does it in a way that throws everything back in the face of his tormentor and proves that he has not, in fact, despite everything, been broken—or, if he had, he has been remade. As he did long before with Agent Stahl, Otto uses the perception of his weakness against Toric. Unable to speak, he scrawls a vile note about Toric's sister across the page on which he was meant to write his statement against the club. When rage distracts Toric, Otto uses his chance to reclaim his agency, his masculinity, his identity—and his destiny.

Through all the seasons of Otto's travails, SAMCRO, too, has been unraveling—betrayals, deaths, and failures that reflect and intersect with his own. Even after all his sacrifices, all his losses, his suffering, when the club finally acts *for him*, giving him the tools to exact revenge and end his torment, Otto is able to reclaim the last vestige of a brotherhood that remains visible on his body and inscribed on his psyche. In regaining that comprehension of a masculine identity that had been written over but not erased, Otto is able to perform a final act of self-assertion.

Kurt Sutter explains in *Entertainment Weekly* that Otto's end could be no other way: "There's only one way this guy can go out. After all the violence he's perpetrated ... he just has to go out bloody and violently. He can't go out peacefully" (qtd. in Bierly). In *Sons of Anarchy: The Official Collector's Edition*, he describes Otto's fate as the "whole idea of live free and ride free, of freedom and camaraderie, all of that can end up quite honestly being the antithesis of that. You are in a box and you are in pain. You are living in fear, and you are swallowed up by the violence that you have sworn to live by" (qtd. in Bennett 60). I agree with Sutter on both counts, but I read more in Otto's end than simply fatalism. If that were solely the case, then a more fitting end would have been the one Otto challenged Toric to deal him upon their very first meeting: being beaten to death in the box of his Death Row cell.

Instead, Otto dies fully agent. For the first time since he bit off his own tongue, he is the actor and not the victim. His body, dematerialized to a husk over the course of years of sacrifice, loss, and betrayal, becomes materially powerful again, and when he is killed for his act of vengeance, he opens his arms and welcomes an end he has earned. Sutter refers to a joke by FX Networks CEO John Landgraf that "by the end of the series, Otto is just a middle finger" (qtd. in Bennett 60), but this is significant. The middle finger is not just a digit, an appendage. It is a metaphor. For rejection. For contempt. For rebellion. For an aggressive—and thus conventionally masculine—assertion of self beyond what is civilly inscribed. What remains of Otto at the end is the very identity that made him a Son in the first place.

WORKS CITED

Bakhtin, M.M. "From *Rabelais and His World* (1965)." *The Bakhtin Reader*, edited by Pam Morris. Arnold, 1994, pp. 227–44.
Barger, Sonny, with Keith and Kent Zimmerman. *Hell's Angel: The Life and Times of Sonny Barger and the Hell's Angels Motorcycle Club*. Harper, 2001.
Bennett, Tara. *Sons of Anarchy: The Official Collector's Edition*. Time, 2014.
Bierly, Mandi. "'Sons of Anarchy': Kurt Sutter and Cast Talk 'Wolfsangel' Shockers." *Entertain Weekly*, 1 October 2013, http://ew.com/article/2013/10/01/sons-of-anarchy-kurt-sutter-wolfsangel/. Accessed 4 May 2017.
Buchanan, Kim Shayo. "Engendering Rape." *UCLA Law Review*, vol. 59, 2012, pp. 1630–1688.
Butler, Judith. *Gender Trouble: Feminism and the Subversion of Identity*. Routledge, 1999.
\_\_\_\_\_. "Performative Acts and Gender Constitution: An Essay in Phenomenology and Feminist Theory." *Theatre Journal*, vol. 40, no. 4, 1988, pp. 519–31.
Cahill, Ann J. *Rethinking Rape*. Cornell University Press, 2001.
Clark, Janine Natalya. "A Crime of Identity: Rape and Its Neglected Victims." *Journal of Human Rights*, vol. 13, 2014, pp. 146–69.
Connell, R.W. *Masculinities*. 2nd ed. University of California Press, 2005.
Farmer, Angela. "The Worst Fate: Male Rape as Masculinity Epideixis in James Dickey's *Deliverance* and the American Prison Narrative." *Atenea*, vol. 28, no. 1, 2008, pp. 103–15.
Foucault, Michel. "Docile Bodies." Rabinow, pp. 179–87.
\_\_\_\_\_. "The Means of Correct Training." Rabinow, pp. 188–205.
Gear, Sasha. "Behind the Bars of Masculinity: Male Rape and Homophobia in and About South Africa's Men's Prisons." *Sexualities*, vol. 10, no. 2, 2007, pp. 209–27.
Kristeva, Julia. "Approaching Abjection." *Powers of Horror*. Columbia University Press, 1982, pp. 1–31.
Lacan, Jacques. "The Signification of the Phallus." *Écrits*. Translated by Bruce Fink. Norton, 2002, pp. 575–84.
\_\_\_\_\_. "A Theoretical Introduction to the Functions of Psychoanalysis in Criminology." *Écrits*, 102–22.

Porter, Rick. "'Sons of Anarchy' Creator Kurt Sutter Discusses the Season 5 Finale, Jax's Dilemma, and Otto's Tongue." *ScreenerTV*, 5 December 2012, http://screenertv.com/news-features/sons-of-anarchy-creator-kurt-sutter-discusses-the-season-5-finale-jaxs-dilemma-and-ottos-tongue/. Accessed 4 May 2017.

Rabinow, Paul, editor. *The Foucault Reader*. Pantheon, 1984.

Sutter, Kurt, creator. *Sons of Anarchy.* SutterInk and FX Network, 2008–2014.

PART 4. TRANSGRESSING BROTHERHOOD:
TIG AND VENUS

# Attempting Redemption with Tig and Venus

LAURIE NORRIS

Kurt Sutter seems to have a fraught relationship with what society demands of "manhood." As Shawn Ryan recalls of his former staff writer on the FX network's breakout series, *The Shield*, "'there are two Kurt Sutters. There's the outlaw rebel he likes the world to see, and there's a more sensitive, thoughtful Kurt. It's not that the rebel is an act. It's more like a wish-fulfillment deviation and way to mask the pain from what he was as a kid and a young adult'" (Hedegaard). The tension between these "two Kurts" drives the emotional engines of his own flagship series for the network, *Sons of Anarchy*. The story of a young man, born into an outlaw culture and groomed to one day lead its violent and criminal motorcycle club, *Sons* is also ultimately a story about trying to figure out how to be a man. It is a story about the struggle to reconcile the demands of society and self on the journey toward figuring out who "you" really are. Sutter's dual, dueling selves provide a model for how this story will play out. His was a tumultuous labor, so the world he built around his characters is equally turbulent. *Sons of Anarchy* is, for this reason and others we will examine in this essay, a very violent show. Its Sons of Anarchy Motorcycle Club[1] members are very violent men. Most of these men see their world in very clear-cut terms: one needs power to survive the tumult, and power only comes through aggression, so powerful men must also be aggressive men. These outlaws, then, in trying to rebel against a mainstream world that has failed them repeatedly, ultimately reify and reenact hegemonic masculinity, a toxic paradigm that grinds down any edges of difference from their identities and forces them to conform, ironically, to an unhealthy but uniform vision of supposedly authentic manhood: stoic, cold, hard, and violent. According to series star, Charlie Hunnam, who plays Sutter's conflicted protagonist Jax Teller,

> It's a very hard show to make. I'm operating from a place of being borderline sociopathic most of the time playing a guy who almost invariably handles every obstacle with violence. You play a character like that in the burning sun for 16 hours a day, five days a week, and then a real-life problem gets presented in the midst of doing that, and at that moment my default setting is like "All right, well, maybe I'll just punch this fucking cunt in the face. Maybe see how he feels about that," you know [Bierly 24].

*Sons'* Shakespearian[2] fantasia's pull is so powerful that it even begins to change how the real life people who bring the story to the screen interact with the real world. That's the danger of the toxic masculinity on display in the show; it is pervasive, like a virus. That is also part of its appeal. As Michael L. Wayne notes, "the particular appeal of hyper-masculine FX dramas with violent overtones are the [sic] often linked to the growing sense of 'white masculinity in crisis'" (Wayne 206).[3] There is an attractive side to *Sons'* world and its brutal simplicity. We keep watching because of the drama inherent in Jax Teller's struggle with the bold dictates of his community and the small, quiet voice inside him telling him that "really real" manhood should resist the fascist logic of the Sons' hegemonic masculinity. Kurt Sutter's personal battles are writ large across Jax Teller's narrative; his is the small, quiet voice in his character's head.

His is also the voice and the hand guiding the show as it attempts to depict and challenge the toxicity of this hyper-masculine FX drama. Combining the occasional real-world psychological analog with elements of his own approach to identity, Sutter uses two particular and atypical characters, Tig and Venus, to rewrite what identity can mean within the confines of *Sons'* outlaw motorcycle culture. Tig's sexuality, always presented as somehow "queer" if never explicitly "Queer," combines with Venus' arc to demonstrate how *Sons of Anarchy* tries to right its own wrongs with regards to nonconforming gender identities and sexualities. Sutter and his team attempt to atone for their mistakes as well as SAMCRO's. Without betraying the series' exploitation roots, they find a way to redeem two broken and flawed people by expanding the show's scope of who "real" men and women can be. Importantly, it is also through these characters' redemption that the show creates its most ironically wholesome and sincere image of romantic love, suggesting that a queered sexuality might be the most effective strategy for healing toxic gender relations.

Sutter, arguably too aware of how his dark side can take over and dominate the art he makes, has stated frequently that he believes in owning up to the mistakes his volatile personality leads him into. He feels the lure of violence and aggression as strongly as his characters, but, unlike many of them, he attempts to make amends when his aggression hurts others. As he told Erik Hedegaard for *Rolling Stone,*

If I didn't apologize, I'd have no fucking friends.... I'm not the kind that can let shit roll off my back. I can be in a room where 999 people love me and I will focus and obsess about the one dude who doesn't. I did not get filled as a kid. I am forever hungry. I want to find that one guy and find out why he doesn't like me. But it's not about changing his mind. I wanna fuckin' chop his head off. But then afterward, if I was wrong, I have no problem apologizing [Hedegaard].

He echoes this sentiment in an interview with Lacey Rose of *The Hollywood Reporter*: "'I've made a lot of mistakes, and for the most part I tend to learn from them,' he says sinking deeper into the couch. 'I think I became aware of my impact on people and the need for me to not move through the world swinging the sword as ferociously as I have. That doesn't mean that I don't swing the sword anymore; I just have a lot more sense of whose head I'm chopping off.... I just can't have my head up my ass about the impact of the shit that I'm saying anymore'" (Rose). This willingness to admit to and learn from his errors is at the heart of the way Sutter uses *Sons* to work through how his characters grapple with their sense of self. Though the show appears at first glance to glamorize and valorize the toxicity at the heart of SAMCRO's traditional way of being "manly," closer readings reveal the ways Sutter and his team acknowledge their world's flaws. *Sons* models both the ultimate negative trajectory as well as possible routes out of its toxic hegemonic masculinity.

Tig is this model condensed into a single character. When the series starts, Alex "Tig" Trager is the sergeant-at-arms for SAMCRO, meaning he is responsible for enacting the disciplinary justice decreed by the club's president. This "man of mayhem," alternately *Sons*' vicious attack dog and charmingly psychotic oddball, is arguably the club's most lethal member.[4] He is also responsible for much of the trouble plaguing the club at the show's outset. Picking up in a sort of *en media res* of a long simmering conflict between the club and another outlaw MC, Tig drags SAMCRO into his sexuality via two dead bodies, unintentional victims of that club war. Staying at the warehouse where the Sons stored their guns, these two women are unknowingly murdered by a fire bombing that decimates the building. As Tig had been sleeping with them both before their deaths and his DNA, still on the women's bodies, is in various police databases thanks to prior arrests, it is Tig's sexual choices that land SAMCRO in their first dramatic quagmire of the series' run. Immediately, we are asked to think of him as a sexual figure, a bit of a deviant, and a fool. Taken alongside his title as sergeant-at-arms and the ferocious violence he brings to the role, Tig becomes a model for *Sons*' toxic masculinity taken to its logical extremes. He is aggressive and weird and aggressively weird.

This weirdness is consistently filtered through Tig's sexuality, reinforcing the sense that there is something a little "queer" about him that must be balanced out by ever more violent displays of aggression if he is to remain acceptable within the rigid parameters of SAMCRO's gender hegemony. The most pronounced instance of this queerness couched in violence happens, almost off-handedly, in the middle of an episode in the program's first season. In season one, episode seven, "Old Bones," as Tig and then-president Clay Morrow stealthily burn the decades-old remains of a former club friend turned snitch, Tig reveals that he has enjoyed "cold packing" before. The scene pauses, if only briefly, at this admission of his sexual defilement of a corpse, makes it into a joke akin to "oh, that's just Tig being good ol' Tig," and moves on, back to the drama of betrayal and loyalty at hand. While the audience may be aghast to learn that Tig considers sex with a dead body to be an acceptable if not entirely normal act, the other characters take the revelation as but one in a series of odd things they perhaps wish they didn't know about their friend.

Though it seems safe to assume that Sutter would not himself own to necrophilia, he does reassert and reinsert his own personal struggles into Tig's weirdness, if not his explicit sexuality, in a second season episode. In season two, episode ten, "Balm," Tig and Half-Sack, a young club member, head into the California desert on an American Indian reservation on a mission for the club. While there, both men take hallucinogenic mushrooms. Though an experienced drug user,[5] the mushrooms have a profound effect on Tig, who reveals his pediophobia, or fear of dolls, while under their influence. This new character quirk comes straight from Kurt Sutter's psyche, as it is a fear he deals with as well. Rather than simply include this new detail as quirk for quirk's sake or just to add on yet another thing that makes Tig seem weirder, Sutter uses his own fear transposed onto this character as a means of forcing the man to begin processing the negative emotions he had been bottling up since the start of the series. While high on these mushrooms, Tig breaks down in front of row after row of porcelain dolls, imagining each of them as a woman he murdered at the climax of season one. Killing her instead of her husband, a brother Son, has wracked Tig with guilt he has not be able to express or deal with in any way. Through his fear of the dolls, he is forced to confront that guilt. Because, though SAMCRO refuses to allow its men to address their emotions, like Tig's guilt, any time such dark feelings break out, such emotions explode into the story in frightening and unhealthy ways. Manifesting through drug-induced fear visions is just the tip of the inappropriate emotional iceberg for Tig's overwhelming guilt.

When next we see him, Tig has switched from hallucinogenic mushrooms to vodka for breakfast, waiting at the start of the next episode in Gemma Teller's kitchen, completely drunk and barely holding himself together as he tries to deny that anything is wrong. Gemma, wife of club president and mother to show protagonist, is a surrogate mother figure for all of the characters on the show. She is also, as the alpha Old Lady for the

MC, a highly sexualized figure, wielding both her maternal status and her sexuality to maintain a feminine form of power in SAMCRO's aggressively gendered society. As such, when Tig drunkenly comes onto her at the start of season two, episode 11, "Service," following his mushroom freak-out, the scene underscores the subtext that something is "off" about Tig's sexuality as well as his emotions. He stops the encounter[6] when reminded of its oedipal undertones by the numerous family photographs on the walls around the pair. The emotional spiral that began through his pediophobia comes to its full as Tig runs away from Gemma and then confronts the husband of the woman he killed. Trager allows the furious and grief-stricken Son to beat him savagely, but, according to the perverted logic of *Sons'* world, the assault becomes almost cathartic, the source of healing for the two men and their fractured motorcycle club as both are finally allowed to release their pent-up emotions. The release is only temporary, however, as both men continue on their tragic trajectories. For Tig, his life doesn't begin to turn around until Venus appears and becomes a stabilizing presence in it.

Venus Van Dam[7] is brought into SAMCRO's world in season five, episode five, "Orca Shrugged," to be a shocking and funny visual punchline to one of their regular jokes about proper masculinity, though the characters themselves likely wouldn't see it that way. The club, caught up in another criminal enterprise on the brink of discovery and punishment, decides to solve this particular quandary by blackmailing a local politician, Allen Biacone. They drug him, and, while he is passed out unconscious at his office, they bring in Venus for an illicit photo shoot. Played by cisgender male actor Walton Goggins,[8] in a breastplate that would make any drag queen envious, Venus appears in full black latex dominatrix gear, riding crop included. The club proceeds to direct Venus in the mock "boudoir" photo shoot as she poses in sexually explicit positions with the unconscious Biacone. All the while club members surround the edges of the office, laughing hysterically at their great joke that anyone would voluntarily engage in such intimate acts with such a "woman." Venus, here, is merely a tool for furthering the club's ends, deprived of dignity or depth by the way the scene is set up. Though their dialogue suggests a friendly camaraderie, the scene itself does not view Venus as a friend of the club or even as a woman. She is merely her sex, her penis and her breasts. Even as Tig lusts after her, the derision directed at him by his fellow Sons for thinking such a figure could be attractive underlines how the scene, and ultimately the show, views Venus and her non-normative self.

Part of the joke here, the idea that this politician will be so ashamed of these pictures of him with someone like Venus, is also being played on Tig. His atypical sexuality has been long established by this point in the series, so his attraction to Venus plays as just another instance of Tig being queer, if very adamantly not "Queer." He allows the rest of the club to make jokes about him because he knows he can prove his manhood and his worth to them through the acts of extreme and often horrific violence he is willing to commit for them. He is allowed his sexual deviance because his deviant violence is so useful. Similarly, Venus is not physically attacked or abused despite her "deviance" because it, too, is so useful for the club. Their otherness is reduced to jokes and thus assimilated into SAMCRO's otherwise strictly policed gender world.

Though Venus and Tig's differences from the hyper-masculine heterosexist norm of the club will continue to be policed, the show itself appears to reconsider its initial choice to treat them, particularly Venus, as a joke. In a series known more for bombastic excess, Kurt Sutter and his crew walk back their transphobic portrayal of Venus by subtly integrating her into the club's world and slowly, but organically, building up a sincere and healthy romance between her and Tig. By the series finale, *Sons of Anarchy*'s closet friend of Mister Mayhem[9] finds a loving and equal partnership with the show's most unusual old lady.[10]

This transition begins in earnest in season six, episode six, "Salvage." The episode retcons Venus into the deeper history of SAMCRO while extending the back story for Nero, played by Jimmy Smits, a father-figure for the show's protagonist who was introduced in season five around the same time as Venus. In "Salvage," Venus runs to Nero for help when her estranged family begins threatening her. To explain this otherwise sudden and heretofore unknown deep connection between these two relatively new characters, the show decides that Nero had helped to raise Venus as a child because her mother had been one of his prostitutes working for him at his brothel, Diosa.[11] When, in present day, Venus appears at Diosa, she is met by Gemma Teller, the protagonist's ferocious mother and Nero's lover. Our first sign that the show is trying to change the way it treats Venus comes during this encounter. Gemma, played by Kurt Sutter's real life wife Katey Segal, often acts as the voice of the show. If Gemma likes someone, the show likes them, too. However, if Gemma distrusts, dislikes, or just can't be bothered to deal with someone, that is a sure sign that the show doesn't care very much about the character. Thus, when Gemma decides to comfort Venus and welcome her into the SAMCRO family, we know that the show is trying to make amends for how it treated her back in season five.

The following episode, season six, episode seven, "Sweet and Vaded," devotes most of its time to Venus' story, further deepening her both as a character and her ties to the club, and reintroduces Tig's sexual attraction to her. Continuing from where "Salvage" leaves off, Venus explains that her vile and toxic mother, Alice, had essentially kidnapped Venus' son, Joey. When the boy was born, shortly after Venus had begun her transition, the family decided to raise him to believe that Venus was his aunt and not his father.

Because she was in no emotional or financial position to raise him herself, Venus agreed to Alice's demands. Now, though, Venus has learned that the sexual abuse she experienced as a child is being forced on Joey, and she turns to SAMCRO for help rescuing him. Despite the countless illegal and unethical things the club does on a daily basis, protecting children has always been a constant element in how they and the show define "correct" masculinity and femininity. It is the line they will not cross, their moral Rubicon. When Jax learns that Alice had also been creating child pornography of the numerous children she abused, the show's protagonist then sides with Venus in the dispute. The whole episode culminates in a confrontation between Alice and Venus with the club supporting the daughter. As Alice viciously taunts her child about her gender identity, Jax shoots the older woman in the face, the hyper-masculine white knight to the extremely violent rescue. Jax's action also provides an excuse for Tig to comfort Venus, as she turns away in shock with the gun blast. This is the backdrop against which the show transforms Tig's fetishistic crush into honest affection and Venus from punchline to member of the family, the highest honor SAMCRO is capable of bestowing. With bloodshed, *Sons of Anarchy* stops sexualizing Venus for her differences and starts seeing her as a real, full character.

This change in how the show positions Venus is incredibly important. As Karine Espineira points out, most transgender people, and certainly transgender characters in media, typically see "themselves dispossessed of their gender and loaded with sexuality[, rendering] invisible their critiques of the gender order and of sexism" (Espineira 323). These people are reduced down to nothing but their genitalia and are looked at only through the lens of what their genitals can do to satisfy the desires of others. This is exactly how Venus was treated by the Sons in "Orca Shrugged." The show refused to acknowledge the irony of using a character, whose existence proves SAMCRO's hardline view of gender to be an illusion, as a tool for the club to intimidate someone because of that illusion. Put another way, it wasn't until later that Sutter and his team realized that Venus could help tell their story about redemption because she offers another way of understanding how gender can be lived. By choosing to live openly as what she feels is her authentic self, to present to the world a self that matches what she feels like on the inside instead of abiding by a gender assigned to her at birth by someone else, Venus demonstrates the fluidity of the construct. She embodies the idea at the heart of Jax's emotional struggle; people can change, even down to the very core of their being. No one has to be what someone else tells them they are.

*Sons of Anarchy* dealt with this struggle from its very first episode. Because Jax, the protagonist and scion of the eponymous motorcycle club, understands it in relationship to his father and his homosocial bonds with the men of the club, the show typically presents this struggle of identity through forms of masculinity. Cox and DeCarvalho explain the results this way: on the show, "authentic masculinity is supposed to be one's ability to control his emotions and his mental psyche. Men's overt control over their emotions serves as a response to the crisis in masculinity,[12] in such a way that is helps alleviate the anxiety created by a perceived lack of control" (Cox and DeCarvalho 822). This obsession with self-control leads Jax and SAMCRO into one dangerously bad decision after another, which in turn leads into a sort of violent one-upmanship as the only acceptable emotion a club member can express is anger. While the characters battle to prove their manhood by beating it out of someone else, the show itself complicates the hypermasculine heterosexist paradigm such violence begets. Again, we turn to Cox and DeCarvalho's work with the show, as they note that

> the Sons' acts of violence are not always shown as a perfect solution or performance of masculine identity. The series, in this way, complicates traditional understanding of the crisis in masculinity. The violence on-screen often creates more problems, and, sometimes, members are not successful in their mission at all. These latter outcomes call into question the club's view of violence as the answer, and question the very foundation of violent masculinity [Cox and DeCarvalho 826].

This suggests that while the show presents images of men who consider their violence, racism, and misogyny to be "correct," the show itself has been trying to call such toxic behaviors into question. Sutter and his team have tried to show deleterious effects of SAMCRO's heterosexist, white supremacist hypermasculinity. The series exists because its protagonist himself has begun to doubt his community's gendered traditions. Now, with the more complex and considered characterization for Venus, the show seems to be trying to correct its misstep with her original introduction in a way that works to underscore their complication of SAMCRO's gender politics rather than make the show expressly complicit in them. With this new stance toward Venus, and the changes her presence begin in Tig, the show counters its presentation to viewers of "an onslaught of white, heterosexist characters ... with characters and events that call into question the value (or cost) of enacting hegemonic masculinity—both for men and the women around them" (Cox and DeCarvalho 822). The line is very fine between what the club believes and what the show believes, but Venus and Tig's transformations are arguably the most pronounced examples of *Sons of Anarchy* distancing itself from and complicating the views of the Sons of Anarchy Motorcycle Club.

This is not to suggest, however, that these transformations are immediate or happen just in the two episodes devoted to Venus' family problems. They are the beginning of a process that plays out in stolen moments across the remainder of the series. Rather, with Venus established as an accepted member of the SAMCRO extended family, and her non-normative gender identity affirmed by the club's willingness to commit violence on her behalf as that identity is being expressly challenged by an outsider, the show now uses her to explore Tig's non-normative masculinity. This begins at the end of "Sweet and Vaded" when his crush on her is reestablished by the show. It picks back up in the next season when Venus returns to the narrative in season seven, episode four, "Poor Little Lambs." Here Venus provides the club a link to their target of the week, a shady pastor foolish enough to double cross the club. Venus knows how to get in contact with this man, so the MC turns to her for help. She remains on the edges of the episode's plot until, during a shoot-out with the crooked preacher, Tig is gut shot. Unable to stop or get to a proper doctor, Tig eventually falls into Venus' arms. As she tends to him and comforts him while he thinks he is slowly bleeding to death, he kisses her. It is passionate yet sweet, unusually so for the show. The way the kiss is staged underlines how it is meant to represent more than mere titillation or even the last act of a dying man. The scene is romantic, if a bit melancholy, the first kiss between new lovers. The scene tells us that we are meant to take the bourgeoning romance between these two broken and battered souls sincerely. It is *Sons of Anarchy*'s version of the birth of true love.

When we next see the two together, in season seven, episode ten, "Faith and Despondency," Tig and Venus are in a legitimate long-term romantic relationship. It is implied that they have been sleeping together since the events of "Poor Little Lambs," but they are still trying to figure out how to navigate what is clearly a new situation for both of them. As the episode begins, Tig is in a dark place emotionally and taking some of his distress out on Venus. By episode's end, Venus confronts him for treating her like an exotic plaything, simultaneously calling out the show for doing the same thing to her when she entered its world. The show makes its current stance clear, however, through what happens next. Venus is allowed to declare how comfortable and happy with herself she is now that she is living openly in all aspects of her life. That the show supports her comes through in how the scene puts her in a positive light, literally and figuratively, and Tig in a negative one for having made Venus question her choices as a woman and as his partner. Tig's behavior has been wrong, the scene tells us, wrong but not unforgivable. Venus confesses that she has fallen in love with Tig, risking being vulnerable in a world that does everything it can to take advantage of such perceived weakness. Rather than exploit Venus, to take advantage of her vulnerability and honesty in the way SAMCRO's typical hyper-masculinity would have him do, Tig apologizes to her. He reciprocates her vulnerability by admitting that, just as she has seen him at his worst and still loves him, he wants to be with her because he loves her as well. He repositions himself as the "freak" in their relationship and her as the partner accepting someone "different," reversing most narratives about romance for transgender partners and SAMCRO's toxic worldview that renders all emotional interactions as transactional opportunities to exert or reinforce a heterosexist hypermasculinity.

The series finale leaves us to wonder how Tig and Venus will make their way in the world together "after" the show's cameras stop rolling. Season seven, episode 13, "Papa's Goods," finds Tig literally leaning on Venus, using her for physical, moral, and emotional support the midst of the darkness of the episode, their mutual affection a source of hope and comfort for them both. As the episode swirls in deaths and violence, brutally tying up the last few narrative loose ends, these two find solace and happiness in each other. Theirs is arguably the only happy ending for anyone on the series. That loving embrace inspires us to wonder what the future would hold for characters like these in such a brutal world. I like to think that the show suggests they will live perfectly imperfectly together, each helping the other heal from the many traumas haunting them both. Perhaps their bond might even inspire them to try to heal the wider world around them. If, as Mauk, Perry and Muñoz-Laboy note, after witnessing transgender women being treated as second class citizens, a number of the men [participating in their sociological study on romantic relationships between cisgender men and transgender women] expanded their community activism ... and regularly marched in [LGBT parades] as a means of publically supporting [transgender women] in their struggle for social and economic justice" (Mauk et al. 800), then perhaps Alexander "Tig" Trager might also march beside Venus Van Dam in Charming, California's, first annual LGBT pride parade. It would be a beautifully surreal and somehow fitting image, Tig leading a cavalcade of Sons down the streets of their small northern California town. Highly unlikely and probably preposterous, that even such a flight of fancy could come out from where *Sons of Anarchy* began proves how far the show ultimately went to challenge the toxic notions of what it means to be a man in a community where gender and identity have been traditionally so dangerously policed.

NOTES

1. From here on out, this will be shortened to the accepted acronym according to both the show and criticism about the show, SAMCRO.

2. Sutter has oft mentioned the Shakespearian roots of his show in interviews. Speaking with Lynette Rice about his influences while creating the series, he recalls, "'During research of motorcycle clubs, I became aware of how quickly they shifted from war vets blowing off steam to what law enforcement categorizes as organized crime,' explains Sutter, who appears regularly on screen as Otto, the incarcerated member of the club who has a bitter history with the Sons. 'I wondered what the first guy who put on a [vest and patches] to blow off steam thought about their outlaw evolution. That guy became John Teller, and that's when the Hamlet archetype came to me'" (Rice, "TV's Wildest Ride"). For more information on and a deeper reading of these Shakespearian elements, please see Jessica Walker's essay in this collection, "'Incapable of His Own Distress': Genderbending Ophelia."

3. Wayne's article focuses on the ways that masculinities have been racialized on FX shows like *Sons* and *The Shield*. Though the issue is much broader than my focus here allows for, his reading of the numerous ways that "masculine" and "White," and very particular ver-

sions of both concepts, are conflated in these programs is vital reading. In particular, I direct your attention to the way he discusses how "the deployment of multiple white masculinities provides white audiences with the opportunity to both take pleasure in overt expressions of racial superiority and generally disavow the existence of structural racism" (Wayne 207).

4. According to the show's fan-run wiki website, *SAMCROpedia*, Tig is responsible for 26 murders over the course of the series, second only to Jax Teller. Most of Tig's victims were shot, though the character was given to a flair for the dramatic in some of his murders: he executed a rival gang member in a hospital by injecting him with cyanide (season three, episode six, "The Push"); he strangled with a chain the man who murdered his daughter (season five, episode one, "Sovereign"); he drowned a pornographer in a bathtub filled with urine (season six, episode one, "Straw").

5. In fact, Tig is present for this mission because of his experience with hallucinogenic mushrooms in particular. He is meant to help test the quality of the product before the club agrees to help its grower distribute them along with the homemade bullets that originally attracted SAMCRO's attentions.

6. It should be noted that the sexualized encounter is consensual, in as much as both adults are willing participants. Tig's inebriation does make his ability to consent questionable, but he is not forcing himself on Gemma. She maintains her own sexual agency throughout the scene.

7. Early on in the show's run, season two, episode seven, "Gilead," another Venus makes an appearance. Though Venus Bell, referred to as a "transvestite" also known as Vincent Bell, shares a name with the character that appears in season five, episode five, this seems to be the extent of the similarities. Bell was a black woman played by black drag performer and actor, Jazzmun, and was connected neither to SAMCRO or Nero's Diosa but with one of the various Black street gangs populating the outer edges of *Son's* world. Her presence, though, echoes Van Dam's introduction later on: Bell is dismissed by most of the members of SAMCRO as a "tranny snitch" even as Clay Morrow, then head of the club, consistently refers to her by her preferred pronouns. Opie, a tragic figure within the show and husband to the woman Tig murders in season one, consistently misgenders Bell and refers to her by her dead name.

8. Goggins, a series regular on *The Shield*, presents an unusual form of masculinity in most of his acting roles. He is a relatively small man, slight and lithe of frame, so he does not fit the physically dominating and imposing image preferred by those who subscribe to toxic forms of masculinity. Almost in spite of his physical differences from the typical hypermasculine action star, Goggins is known for his magnetic and charismatic swagger, particularly in the role that made him famous on another important FX series, as Boyd Crowder on *Justified*. Goggins unusual performance of masculinity brings to mind a point that Solomon and Kurtz-Costes make when discussing how audiences receive mediated images of transgender women characters played by cisgender men. They write that "although recent portrayals of trans women have become more sympathetic, they may still reinforce negative ideas. For instance, casting a well-known or highly masculine cisgender man to play a trans woman, even if the role is a sympathetic one, reinforces the notion that trans women are really cisgender men pretending to be women" (Solomon and Kurtz-Costes). One potential avenue for future research on the impact of images of transgender people in the media could look at how the casting of actors who present as both "highly masculine" and non-normative simultaneously affects the way viewers respond to their characters.

9. "Mister Mayhem" is the club's code word for death. The members of SAMCRO who have murdered someone on behalf of the club wear a "Men of Mayhem" patch on their kuttes as literal badges of honor.

10. "Old lady" is the term used by outlaw biker gangs to refer to a member's primary romantic partner. Gemma Teller was first Clay Morrow's old lady, then Nero's. Tara was Jax Teller's old lady. Venus is the only significant romantic partner Tig has over the course of the show, though he is frequently shown interacting with the various "crow eaters," women who hang around with the club and regularly engage in sexual acts with members but who are not considered primary partners for any of the men.

11. That the brothel is named "Diosa," which means "goddess" in Spanish, is meant to

convey the idea that Nero, as a pimp, respects and values his women unlike most men in the sex trade. Along with Venus' sudden reappearance and the emotional impact of their story together, details like *diosa* are meant to position Nero as an antidote of sorts to the deadly version of manhood modeled by the other men in the life of Jax Teller, *Sons* protagonist.

12. They define the crisis in masculinity as a response to shifting power dynamics in society and the growing awareness of the ways men have traditionally reaped the benefit of privilege in those power dynamics. They write that "as the logic goes, because women have advanced in politics, education, and economics, and have witness changing roles in the home, this creates a culture of men who feel powerless and anxious about their place in society" (Cox and DeCarvalho 820). Thus, masculinity becomes toxic because it "is not just about exerting control over one's self; it is also about asserting control over others" (Cox and DeCarvalho 830). Similarly, Sexton notes that "taking refuge in traditional masculinity is a coping mechanism that works only so much as it deadens a man and his emotions. In it most pure state, masculinity is a hardening shell meant to protect men from the disappointments and travails of life, a self-delusion that preserves them from feeling overwhelmed by the odds against them" (Sexton 25).

## Works Cited

"Balm." *Sons of Anarchy*. FX, 10 November 2009. Television.
Bierly, Mandi. "'Sons of Anarchy' Reaches the Last Fork in the Road." *Entertainment Weekly*, 10 October 2014, http://ew.com/article/2014/10/03/sons-anarchy-cover-story/. Accessed 8 May 2017.
Cox, Nicole B., and Lauren J. DeCarvalho. "'Ride Free or Die' Trying: Hypermasculinity on FX's *Sons of Anarchy*." *The Journal of Popular Culture*, vol. 49, no. 4, 2016. Web. 25 October 2016.
Espineira, Karine. "Transgender and Transsexual People's Sexuality in the Media." *Parallax*, vol. 22, no. 3, 2016, pp. 323–29. Accessed 28 April 2017.
"Faith and Despondency." *Sons of Anarchy*. FX, 11 November 2014. Television.
"Gilead." *Sons of Anarchy*. FX, 20 October 2009. Television.
Hedegaard, Erik. "The Original Son of Anarchy." *Rolling Stone*, 9 October 2014, pp. 52–55. Web. Accessed 8 May 2017.
Mauk, Daniel, Ashley Perry, and Miguel Muñoz-Laboy. "Exploring the Desires and Sexual Culture of Men Who Have Sex with Male-to-Female Transgender Women." *Archives of Sexual Behavior*, vol. 42, 2013, pp. 793–803.
"Old Bones." *Sons of Anarchy*. FX, 15 October 2008. Television.
"Orca Shrugged." *Sons of Anarchy*. FX, 9 October 2012. Television.
"Papa's Goods." *Sons of Anarchy*. FX, 9 December 2014. Television.
"Pilot." *Sons of Anarchy*. FX, 3 September 2008. Television.
"Poor Little Lambs." *Sons of Anarchy*. FX, 30 September 2014. Television.
Rice, Lynette. "TV's Wildest Ride." *Entertainment Weekly* 30 November 2012, pp. 30–35.
Rose, Lacey. "'I'm a Dark Mother---er." *The Hollywood Reporter* 4 September 2015, pp. 34–39.
"Salvage." *Sons of Anarchy*. FX, 15 October 2012. Television.
"Service." *Sons of Anarchy*. FX, 17 November 2009. Television.
Sexton, Jared Yates. "Donald Trump's Toxic Masculinity." *The New York Times* 13 October 2016, Late Edition ed., p. 25. https://www.nytimes.com/2016/10/13/opinion/donald-trumps-toxic-masculinity.html. Accessed 8 May 2017.
Solomon, Haley E., and Beth Kurtz-Costes. "Media's Influence on Perceptions of Trans Women." *Sexual Research and Social Policy*, 2017. https://link.springer.com/article/10.1007/s13178-017-0280-2. Accessed 8 May 2017.
"Sweet and Vaded." *Sons of Anarchy*. FX, 22 October 2013. Television.
"Tig Trager." *SAMCROpedia*. http://sonsofanarchy.wikia.com/wiki/Tig_Trager. Accessed 8 May 2017.
Wayne, Michael L. "Ambivalent Anti-Heroes and Racist Rednecks on Basic Cable: Post-Race Ideology and White Masculinities on FX." *Journal of Popular Television*, vol. 2, no. 2, 2014, pp. 205–25.

# Riding Crisscross
## Venus Van Dam and the Politics of Transgender Representation

### Peter Nagy

In the past seven years or so, the spotlight on transgender men and women on television has grown considerably. We have enjoyed a recent wave of shows that involve or center on transgender characters, including *Transparent* (Mort Pfeffermann), *Orange is the New Black* (Sophia Burset), *Glee* (Unique Adams), *Ugly Betty* (Alex Meade), and even *American Horror Story* (Liz Taylor). Amidst the current trend of trans-inclusive shows, Kurt Sutter's *Sons of Anarchy* (2008–2014) is one of the most surprising—and perhaps one of the most problematic. *Sons*, which ran on FX from 2008 to 2014 tells the story of the Sons of Anarchy Motorcycle Club (SAMCRO), an outlaw motorcycle club housed in the fictional town of Charming, California. It focuses specifically on Jackson "Jax" Teller (played by Charlie Hunnam), the son of a founding member whose ambivalence about his criminal heritage, struggle to reclaim his manhood from a dominating mother, and love of his brothers (the fellow members of SAMCRO) comprise the show's central drama. Thematically *Sons* explores the deep-seated vulnerability and toxicity of mostly white small-town American men, those who see themselves as marginalized and who reclaim their masculinity through crime, violence, and general badassery.

As a show about a brotherhood of renegade bikers—a fraternity that has a long tradition of being brutally homophobic and misogynistic—one might expect *Sons* to celebrate only the most rigidly masculine men. After all, it draws on the image of the biker, a fantasy of male potency that has never strayed too far outside the boundaries of conventional manhood, even in the early days when the figure was celebrated, in films like *The Wild One* (1953) and *Easy Rider* (1969), as part of a progressive counterculture. But in its fifth season, the writers behind *Sons of Anarchy* defied this trend by introducing a character who seemed to challenge the gender binary at the root of motorcycle masculinity: Venus Van Dam (played by Walton Goggins), a transwoman whose name combines one of the most recognizable embodiments of conventional femininity, the goddess of love, with one of the most beloved icons of macho masculinity, Jean-Claude Van Damme.

While Venus originally appears in the series as a harmful stereotype who serves as little more than a dehumanizing spoof of transgender women, in the last two seasons, she grows into a multidimensional character through whom the show explores connections between the cisgender male biker, the outlaw who lives outside the rules of mainstream society, and the transgender woman, the gender outlaw who, as Kate Bornstein claims, lives outside the rules of the gender-sex system. *Sons* accomplishes this, in part, by aligning Venus with Jax, depicting both as lost innocents, as tragic sons who have been raised in toxic family environments and have paid the price for straying—or in Jax's case, trying to stray—from the course of normative manhood. In the final season, *Sons* boldly pushes this connection, even going as far as to explore a romantic relationship between Venus and one of the members of the motorcycle club, Alexander "Tig" Trager (played by Kim Coates).

But even as it pushes the boundaries of motorcycle masculinity and the biker genre, *Sons* ultimately falls short of offering a humanizing exploration of transgender womanhood. As I show, even though the series portrays Venus in a sympathetic light, it depicts her subject position as a superficial masquerade, a feminine surface through which an essential manhood always threatens to erupt. *Sons* reveals its interest in transgender representation to be a smokescreen of sorts, a flirtation with gender non-conformity through which it reinforces the gender binary it superficially challenges. In this way, the show cashes in on the trend of exploring transgender lives without truly challenging conventional manhood, and while still avowing cisgender manhood as an immutable subject position, one that cannot be renounced or transitioned away from, even if one is, like Venus, a "man who knows she's a woman" ("Faith and Despondency").

To understand the politics of transgender representation in *Sons*, it is important, first, to touch on the show's account of masculinity. *Sons* is a fantasy about contemporary white American masculinity. It critiques and romanticizes the deep vulnerability of men who feel powerless and who perceive their manhood—their agency, independence, and self-possession—as imperiled in a changing social order. As Nicole B. Cox and Lauren J. Decarvalho have shown, the series explores the brutality of such men: the rage they feel in the face of emasculating conditions; the spectacular violence through which they seek to reassert their agency; and the fraternities they form in order to experience affectionate, loving relationships with brothers who share their rage and propensity for violence.

In short, the series is about men who cry and kill together. But it is also about the role that women play in shaping such men. Kerry Fine has argued for a more complex understanding of the show's depiction of women, claiming that *Sons* challenges the gender binary by assigning traditionally masculine qualities—toughness, aggression, even brutality—to its female protagonists. But in my estimate, the show is ultimately antifeminist. Apart from its incessant sexual objectification of women, it reinforces men's anxieties about women's power and influence by reproducing the stereotype of the controlling mother. Recently the media has been obsessed with footage of Grigoriy Kichigin, a Russian MMA cage fighter whose mother climbed into the ring and slapped him on the face as he lay bloody on the floor after a brutal loss. *Sons* perpetuates this very image. It is a series preoccupied with displays of male power and the spectacle of emasculation, one associated with mothers who want their sons to dominate and who shame them for failing to do so. This dynamic surfaces most fully in Jax's mother, Gemma Teller Morrow (played by Katey Sagal), who serves as a contrast to the "good father," an ideal associated with Jax's dead father, the former leader of the Sons who died mysteriously before he could realize his dream of turning the club away from crime and violence.

The show suggests that in a world devoid of such fathers, the fate of young men like Jax—who alternates, throughout the series, between attempting to realize his father's dream and trying to escape the toxic outlaw lifestyle altogether—lies in the hands of women like Gemma, who emotionally manipulates her son and attempts to dominate his life so she can turn him into the next leader of the motorcycle club: the patriarch she believes he should be. In this way, *Sons of Anarchy* displaces men's anxieties about the status of white manhood onto women, whom it vilifies as the psychic root of their impotence and rage. The show suggests that women are responsible for the lost innocence of American sons, who must free themselves from their mothers so that they may repossess their manhood.

Given that *Sons* claims that men must liberate themselves from invasive women, it comes as a great surprise, then, that the show portrays an individual who does the exact opposite. But in its final seasons, the writers introduce us to Venus Van Dam, a person born as a man who sees and presents herself as a woman. Initially Venus appears to be a problematic depiction of transgender womanhood. First, there is the ethical issue of a transwoman being played a cisgender man, actor Walton Goggins. As some have argued, this is in itself an exploitation of transgender identity, which, in this case, serves the career of a non-trans actor in a show that mostly revolves around the lives and experiences of cisgender characters. Moreover, as those like transgender actress Jen Richards have rightly pointed out, the performance of a transwoman by a cisgender actor perpetuates the dangerous notion that transgender women are simply men in drag (Thomas).

Unfortunately this idea seems to be precisely what *Sons* perpetuates through Venus early in the show. When Venus first appears she functions as a transphobic joke. In season five, episode five, "Orca Shrugged," the Sons hire Venus in order to blackmail an insurance broker. She is a sex worker, an employee of Nero, the former Latino gang member (played by Jimmy Smits) who owns an escort agency and forms a romantic relationship with Gemma over the course of a few seasons. Venus shows up sporting large breast implants with hard nipples that stick out through a blue and green dress. While some transwomen do get implants, Venus's seem less an attempt at verisimilitude than a comical exaggeration of feminine artifice. Her appearance exaggerates her femininity to the point of absurdity, as if to say it were an obvious ruse. Venus also acts hypersexual. She makes sexual puns and passes at Jax that are meant to be ridiculous and over the top: "My lips are sealed. Although I might open them up a little bit for you," she says to Jax at one point ("Orca Shrugged"). The jokes continues as the Sons pay Venus to gag, bind, and ride the pale and obese body of the unconscious insurance broker (the Sons knock him out with drugs). They laugh and take emasculating photos of her on top of him, playing the role of dominatrix, wearing a leather costume that undercuts her femininity by showing her large biceps and her muscular buttock in a black thong. The joke goes a step further when a young man, the broker's stepson, accidentally stumbles on the scene. The Sons pay him to look the other way with sexual services from Venus, who, grabbing the young man through his pants, asks, "Have you ever had your dick sucked by a southern girl with a huge cock?" The bikers laugh as they trick the young man into receiving fellatio from a transgender woman as payment, assuring him that it's something they themselves have done. "Doesn't mean you're gay, man. We've all been there," Jax says.

The original depiction of Venus thus perpetuates what Julia Serano identifies as the common media image of transwomen as hypersexual and hyperfeminine. Venus has not had gender reassignment surgery, which is a genuine preference for some transgender women (*Whipping Girl* 15–16). But the purpose of her mentioning her "cock" is to sensationalize and eroticize her fluidity, to reduce her to a "chick with a dick." But in season six, Venus seems to transform into a less reductive and more sincere representation of transgender womanhood. Episode seven, "Sweet and Vaded," deepens her storyline. In a desperate situation, Venus reaches out to Gemma, who brings her to the Sons. Venus tells Jax and the others that she has a nephew, Joey, who needs to be rescued. She explains that since the death of his mother, Lula, Joey has been living with her mother, Alice, who has a history of sexual abusing children. Venus has experienced this abuse first hand. She explains that when she was ten years old and began to discover her true gender identity, her mother would get her "drunk" and try to "straighten [her] out," eventually using her as part of a "lucrative child pornography service" ("Sweet and Vaded"). Here, the writers draw on the stereotype of the gender nonconformist as a tragic victim. But they do so in order to portray Venus as a sympathetic character with a story of her own. Venus's tragic backstory endears her to the Sons, particularly Jax. She reveals that she has endured an abusive mother, Alice, who raped her at an early age, in order to "straighten" her out, to prohibit her from transitioning into a woman. Consistent with the show's perception of mothers as enforcers of normative manhood, Alice cannot abide a son who refuses phallic manhood. Venus implies that the goal of the sexual abuse she has endured was to force her to accept a body that the mother could exploit for her own pleasure and gain—the "lucrative child pornography service" that started with Venus ("Sweet and Vaded").

In addition to offering a sympathetic portrait of a transgender woman—one that addresses, if through exaggerated circumstance, the abuse that suffer gender non-conforming individuals suffer from an early age—the tragic backstory figures Venus as a mirror for Jax, who struggles with his own disastrous upbringing. Like Venus, Jax has been raised by a mother in a toxic environment. He has not been the subject of sexual abuse. But he, too, has born the burden of a mother who, in the absence of his father, lays claim to his manhood and manipulates him in order to shape him into the man she believes he should be. In this sense, the show sets up a parallel between the gender outlaw and the outlaw biker, seeing both as victims of villainous mothers they struggle separate themselves from in order to shape their own lives.

Venus's struggle and experience of victimization enables the Sons to take her seriously and to validate her identity. Jax promises to help. "I guess I'm a sucker for a pretty face," he says ("Sweet and Vaded"). The boldness of this portrayal should not be understated. The depiction of the male outlaw acknowledging and coming to the aid of the gender outlaw is a positive gesture that affirms (albeit through the normative scenario of male heroics) the possibility of connection between cisgender men and transgender women. This connection unfortunately depends, in this account, on a misogynistic rejection of mothers as destructive influences. But, importantly, *Sons* also suggests that to the extent that young men are bound together by the wounds they endure within family structures that perpetuate patriarchal manhood, cisgender men can acknowledge, even identify with transgender women.

*Sons* is, however, ambivalent about Venus. In subsequent scenes, the show cycles between furthering its sympathetic portrayal of Venus and her connection to Jax and returning to reductive stereotypes about transgender women. After Venus explains her situation, she and the Sons drive to the house where she grew up. They confront Alice, who reveals that Joey is, in fact, Venus's son, not her nephew. Alice refuses to give up the boy. She warns him that Venus is a "mutation" who will "fill his head with lies," and then takes off with him in a car while the Sons fight off a few of the male family members who try to intervene. A car chase scene ensues in which Venus, Jax, Trig, and Gemma hop into a truck and pursue Alice. During the chase, Jax demands the truth from Venus, who explains that Joey is indeed her son, the product of a drunken night of sex with Lula, one of her former best friends. Venus apologizes for lying but insists that she isn't quite ready to tell Joey that he is her son. But when a couple of men who have been following them suddenly rear-end their truck, her tone suddenly shifts. Venus erupts and takes actions. She angrily screams "Goddamn it!" in a deep, masculine voice before reflexively grabbing a handgun and unloading it with Schwarzenegger-like fury through a back window that shatters. Her wrath shocks Jax, Trig, and Gemma, forcing them to pull over. On the side of the road, Jax confronts Venus about her actions:

> JAX: What the hell is the matter with you?
> VENUS: I'm sorry, Jackson. But I'm afraid Vincent's rage has become uncorked.
> JAX: Well, at the risk of where this might go, please put the cork back in.... No more Vincent ["Sweet and Vaded"].

Venus's macho outburst and the subsequent exchange with Jax reveals a lot about the show's account of transgender subjectivity. Consistent with the original reduction of Venus to a "chick with a dick," in this scenario transgender womanhood is simply a cover for an essential masculinity, one whose undeniable anger and violence breaks through the precarious artifice of Venus's femininity. The transphobic language supports this notion. Venus's use of the word "uncorked" to describe the sudden return of her former male identity, Vincent Noon, suggests that her transition is incomplete, that her womanhood merely plugs up a male persona that refuses to be sealed off. It also suggests that male rage is natural and immutable. Vincent is a powerful monstrosity that always lurks just underneath the surface. At any moment, he can break free from the flimsy cage of transgender womanhood. Moreover, the eruption of his rage—a rage that the show sees as specific to men—blurs the boundaries between manhood and womanhood in a way that the Sons cannot abide. Put more simply, Jax and the Sons can only accommodate the transgender woman insofar as she fulfills the role of a conventionally feminine woman, a "pretty face" in need of male heroics. Venus is forced to put the cork back in order to sustain this narrative. In addition to its transphobic implications, "uncorked" is homophobic. When Jax asks Venus to put the cork back in (him), he plays on the homoerotic implications of the language in a glib conflation of trans womanhood and male homosexuality. The joke is that putting the cork back in—damning up the violent male persona—entails plugging up the male body sexually, as if trans womanhood necessarily entailed gay male intercourse (getting or putting a plug in the ass), or as if it were a subject position interchangeable with being a gay man.

However, the exchange doesn't derail the show's depiction of a connection between Jax and Venus. Eventually Venus and the Sons track Alice down to a child portrait studio, the family business that acts as a front for her child pornography ring. When they enter, they find Joey drugged out on a couch. Venus confronts Alice, who says, "when he finds out what you are.... This boy is gonna blow his brains out before his balls completely drop." Alice sees Venus as a destructive father, a "freak of the fringe" who will force her lifestyle onto her son and, in doing so, poison him with hate and self-destructiveness. Her diatribe strikes a chord in Jax, who puts a violent end to the speech before wiping away his tears ("Sweet and Vaded").

In this scene, the show indulges the viewer with bit of anti-transphobic vengeance. It displays a sympathetic Jax who protects Venus from further emotional abuse, from a transphobic mother who continues to berate her from deviating from patriarchal manhood. His actions derive from his sense of connection to Venus not only as the victim of a controlling mother but as a protective father who wants to shield his sons (he has two sons from two different mothers) from his toxic upbringing, to preserve in them the innocence he has lost. In one of its most progressive moments, the show also seems to imply that that the liberation of cisgender men and the freedom of transgender women depend on each other. Affectionately stroking her unconscious son, Venus explains to Jax that in order to escape her upbringing she had to be "reborn" as a woman, and that she hopes "something comes along to liberate my son from that fate." Jax responds, "Yeah. I hope so." Through this brief exchange, the writers depict transgender womanhood as a subject position through which a former son can escape the "doom" of the heteronormative family. It is an avenue of identification through which one can liberate himself from the destructive fate of normative manhood—from the hateful, violent, and destructive manhood that mothers such as Alice and Gemma seek to manipulate. Jax's "hope"—that Venus's son, and his own sons, will gain the freedom that Venus has found—rests on his recognition of transgender womanhood as a form of liberation. In other words, Venus, a man reborn as a woman, enables Jax to visualize and feel some optimism about the possibility of freeing oneself and one's sons from toxic masculinity ("Sweet and Vaded").

In its seventh and last season, *Sons* advances the connection between the social outlaw and the gender outlaw by depicting the two as romantically involved. Venus has developed a relationship with Alexander "Tig" Trager, the Son who has had eyes for her since her first appearance. In earlier seasons

**164 Part 4. Transgressing Brotherhood**

Tig's attraction to Venus serves as a joke that exaggerates his sexual adventurousness. But the relationship between Tig and Venus evolves into a sincere and emotionally complicated dynamic. Episode ten, "Faith and Despondency," explores how Venus's self-presentation becomes an obstacle for Tig. The opening scene shows the two getting dressed the morning after a night of passion. Venus doesn't have any makeup on, and she doesn't realize that this makes Tig uncomfortable. He claims he's all right, but acts cold and quickly leaves without promising to return. Wondering what went wrong, Venus looks into a mirror and sees that her facial hair has grown back. She realizes her stubble has scared off Tig. When he returns later that night, Venus confronts him about his discomfort. She confesses that she has fallen in love with Tig, who is with her, she assumes, only to prove his sexual adventurousness. Venus knows that nothing can come of her feelings because of her "crisscross," specifically her refusal to remove her penis. "I don't want the surgery," she says. "I don't want to undo what God has given me." Tig admits his hesitance. He has difficulty reconciling his feelings for Venus with the fact that she still has male genitalia. Yet it won't stop him from loving her. "'Cause you are my, my sweet ... my beautiful Venus," Tig says ("Faith and Despondency").

At one level, the writers offer, in this scene, a daring portrayal of love and compassion between a cisgender man and a transgender woman. Venus has fallen in love with Tig but sees such love as impossible. She assumes that Tig is a chaser, a cisgender man who fetishizes her and seeks her out as an exotic thrill in order to show that he lives "outside the box." Venus wants more, but she believes her "complicated identity" prohibits it. Venus is a woman with a penis, one which she refuses to have surgically removed because she doesn't want to "undo what God has given me." She loves her "crisscross," her gender fluid identity. She sees herself as "beautiful" but is pessimistic about the possibility of finding love. She does not expect Tig to accept her ("Faith and Despondency").

Tig's response to Venus is perhaps the most touching moment in all of *SOA*. Tig sees the relationship as also his "crisscross," a connection through which he rides against the grain of hardboiled biker masculinity by being emotionally vulnerable. He allows Venus to see "everything," all the emotional baggage he hides underneath the tough exterior of his biker persona, including his wounds, fears, and self-hatred. He is amazed by Venus, who loves him despite all the flaws she sees. But she is right. Her fluid gender presents an obstacle. Tig can't get "close" because he is unable to reconcile his "normal" attraction to women with the fact that Venus still has a penis. He "can't hook it up." But he wants to. Regardless of the difficulties, he wants Venus to be his woman, and to go "anywhere" or "anyplace" with her. Suggesting that she go get "cleaned up," put on a "pretty dress" and put "flowers" in her hair, Tig affectionately affirms Venus's femininity and the normalcy of their relationship. He, too, sees Venus as the "sweet" and "beautiful" woman she knows she is ("Faith and Despondency").

By this account, *Sons* presents us with a tender, affirmative, and optimistic depiction of love between a cisgender male biker and a transgender woman. It represents as viable the relationship between a man who is, in many respects, normatively masculine (physically tough, violent, sexually insatiable, promiscuous) and a transgender woman whose identity blurs the gender binary without undermining her femininity—the makeup, dress, and flowers through which she presents herself.

Yet, the representation of Venus as "crisscross" isn't as progressive as it seems. In one sense, Venus's desire to keep her male genitalia validates a particular mode of transgender self-fashioning that pushes the envelope of her relationship with Tig, a cisgender man in love not only with a transwoman, but one who refuses gender reassignment surgery. But in another, her decision reinforces the show's idealization of phallic manhood by insisting that one's penis should not renounced, even by a man who sees himself as a woman. Venus refuses surgery because it would "undo what God has given me" ("Faith and Despondency"). Her language idealizes male genitalia as a natural and God-given part that one who is born a man should embrace and honor. Her words also echo the show's insistence that manhood should not—or cannot—be undone. Just as the writers portray Venus as unable to erase the psychological traces of her former male identity, the uncorked rage of Vincent Noon, so, too, do they depict her, in this scenario, as unwilling—or unable—to erase the physical vestiges of her manhood.

In this way, the show also seems to undercut its portrayal of transgender womanhood as liberation from the "doom" of heteronormative manhood ("Orca Shrugged"). Initially the writers portray Venus's male genitals—that which her mother, Alice, sexually abused and exploited for economic gain—as a source of pain, trauma, and rage that her rebirth as a woman enabled her to escape. Her male body was a cage that her mother tried to lock her in. She freed herself from that cage by becoming Venus. Her refusal to remove the penis in this instance thus suggests that as much as the writers see transgender womanhood as an escape from the toxic conditions that create angry, destructive men, they cannot allow Venus to repudiate the kind of manhood that the show ultimately values. Understood in this context, *Sons* seems able to acknowledge transgender womanhood as a genuine and liberating subject position only insofar as such womanhood does not threaten the erasure of manhood. Thus, even as the show flirts with gender non-conformity, with a son who crosses into womanhood in order to overcome the wounds and the violence of normative manhood, it cannot allow that son from committing what it perceives as the most cardinal of all sins: self-emasculation.

As Julia Serano claims, in a patriarchal society "there is no greater perceived threat than the existences of trans women, who despite being born male and inheriting male privilege 'choose' to be female instead" (15). Through Venus, *Sons of Anarchy* welcomes the "threat" of transwomen into the world of the biker, one of the most sacred fantasies about the potency and rugged individualism of white American masculinity. In doing so, *Sons* pushes the boundaries of the biker genre and motorcycle masculinity, challenging, to a limited degree, the homophobic and misogynistic roots of both. But as a show that disseminates images of masculinity to millions of cisgender heterosexual men, *Sons* misses an enormous opportunity to humanize transgender women. It also fails to develop its bold proposition that there can be meaningful avenues of identification, even love, between transwomen and cisgender men.

While the expansion of transgender representation does not necessarily entail social and political gains for transgender individuals, shows like *Sons* have potential to increase visibility and awareness about social and psychological lives of gender non-conforming individuals. They also can help to shape social change by providing a stage for trans rights advocacy, as exemplified by the emergence of *Orange Is the New Black*'s Laverne Cox (Sophia Burset) as an icon of the Trans Rights movement. It is, therefore, important that we continue to deconstruct the politics of transgender representation and demand more humane depictions of trans lives.

## Works Cited

Bornstein, Kate. *Gender Outlaw: On Men, Women, and the Rest of Us*. Routledge, 1994.
Cox, Nicole B., and Lauren J. Decarvalho. "'Ride Free or Die' Trying: Hypermasculinity on FX's *Sons of Anarchy*." *The Journal of Popular Culture*, vol. 49, no. 4, 2016, pp. 818–38.
Fine, Kerry. "She Hits Like a Man, but She Kisses Like a Girl: TV Heroines, Femininity, Violence, and Intimacy." *Western American Literature*, vol. 47 no. 2, 2012, pp. 152–73.
Serano, Julia. *Whipping Girl: a Transsexual Woman on Sexism and the Scapegoating of Femininity*. Seal Press, 2007.
Thomas, June. "Is it Ever OK to Cast a Cisgender Actor in a Transgender Role?" *Slate* Sept. 2016. *Slate* Web. 5 May. 2017.

## List of Episodes

"Faith and Despondency." *Sons of Anarchy*, season 6, episode 10, FX, 11 Nov. 2014. *Netflix*.
"Orca Shrugged." *Sons of Anarchy*, season 5, episode 5, FX, 9 Oct. 2012. *Netflix*.
"Sweet and Vaded." *Sons of Anarchy*, season 6, episode 7, FX, 22 Oct. 2013. *Netflix*.

# About the Contributors

Jamie L. **Brummer** teaches English and coaches soccer at Christian Brothers High School in Memphis, Tennessee. His academic interests include Cormac McCarthy, the American Western and issues of masculinity.

Susan **Fanetti** is a professor of English at California State University, Sacramento. She teaches courses on popular literature and culture, English language arts pedagogy, literary theory, and American literature. Her research follows the same intersecting lines, with a particular focus on gender in popular culture.

Monica Montelongo **Flores** is an assistant professor of multiethnic American literature in the department of English at California State University, Stanislaus. Her specializations include U.S. literature, film and media studies, and Latina/o cultural studies.

Andrew **Howe** is a professor of history at La Sierra University, where he teaches courses in American history, popular culture, and film/television studies. He has published on fan-generated art involving *Game of Thrones*, the transformation of the Mohican myth in *Avatar*, and the anticipation of the late 20th century culture wars in the television show *Voyagers!*

Christian **Jimenez** has presented at a number of professional conferences at Rider, Rutgers, New York University, Drew University, and the State University of New York. His major research interests include narrative, gender, religion, and the apocalypse.

Jossalyn G. **Larson** is an assistant teaching professor with the Department of English and Technical Communication at Missouri University of Science & Technology. Her research interests include rhetoric, religious symbology, science writing, and philosophy (and the interplay of those domains), as well as writing pedagogy.

Shawna **Marks** is a doctoral candidate at the University of Adelaide, Australia. Her research explores the intersection between male-dominated sporting culture and sexual violence, and sport as a microcosm of hypermasculine culture in conjunction with theories of masculinity, heterosexuality and sexual ethics.

## About the Contributors

Peter **Nagy** is an assistant professor of English at Cedar Crest College. His work focuses on U.S. modernism, masculinity, feminism, queer theory, and psychoanalysis. He has published academically and in general-interest magazines.

Laurie **Norris** is a doctoral candidate in English at the University of Georgia. She focuses on the rhetoric of style in popular culture, and the aesthetics of so-called Prestige Television and the implications of what that which we deem prestigious reveals about contemporary America.

Jamieson **Ryan** is a doctoral student at Queen's University, Canada. His research interests, and work thus far, have been focused on sport, masculinity, popular culture, trauma and trauma theory, and bereavement.

Jessica **Shine** is a lecturer in the Department of Multimedia at Cork Institute of Technology. Her research focuses on the use of sound and music in film and television with a particular interest in soundscapes, aesthetics and narrative. She has presented at a range of international conferences.

Jessica **Walker** is an assistant professor of English at Alabama A&M University, where she teaches medieval and Renaissance literature, literature on film, and the history of the English language. Her publications include essays on 17th-century women's discourse in Neil Gaiman and Terry Pratchett's *Good Omens*, among other topics.

# Index

Abel Teller (character) 34–35, 51, 52, 61, 68, 70, 75, 107, 109, 110, 114, 117, 120, 122, 123, 12, 125–126, 127–128
abjection 131, 136–141, 143
"Ablation" (episode) 109, 111
Act of Contrition 80
addiction 18, 52, 110
adoption, informal 113, 119–129
African American characters 12, 39, 39–48, 53, 94, 99, 101–103, 104
agency, concept of 2, 39–41, 47, 88, 131, 135, 137, 141–142, 155, 158
aggression: as masculinity 26–27, 86–87, 90, 128, 145–147, 159; sexual 124–125
A.J. Weston (character) 30
"Albification" (episode) 10, 30, 71
Alice (character) 150–151, 160–165
*American Horror Story* 157
Americana 94, 97
anarchism 82, 83, 85
"Andare Pescare" (episode) 43, 109, 122, 115, 117, 126
anger 12, 20, 26, 46, 101, 110, 114, 162
antifeminism 159
antihero(es) 1, 78, 87
anxiety: cultural 56, 121; emotional 71; masculine 25, 40, 55, 57, 59, 152
"Aon Rud Persanta" (episode) 109, 113, 127, 128
apology 142, 146, 153, 162
Arcadio (character) 116
Asian characters 42, 45–49
August Marks (character) 31
"Authority Vested" (episode) 72, 74, 110, 111, 114, 122

Bakhtin, Mikhail 138, 143
"Balm" (episode) 98, 148
Barger, Sonny 2, 34
betrayal 30, 41, 43, 67, 68, 70, 102, 131, 132, 137, 138, 141–143, 146, 148
"Better Half" (episode) 134
"Bitter Fruit," Abel Meeropol 102

"Black Widower" (episode) 97
blackmail 12, 30, 149, 160
*Boardwalk Empire* 96, 104
Bobby Munson (character) 42
"Bohemian Rhapsody" 96
"Booster" (episode) 71, 72
Boyle, Danny 95, 104
*Breaking Bad* 40, 61, 96, 108
bromance 9, 23
bromosociality 9–23
brutality 14, 22, 25, 40, 52, 122, 146, 154, 157–159
"Burnt and Purged Away" (episode) 75, 131, 137
Butler, Judith 51, 58, 59, 130, 133
bylaws, club 12, 83–85
The Byz Lats 58, 107, 111, 114–116

"Capybara" (episode) 69, 70, 74
Cara Cara 17–18, 43, 55
carnivalesque, concept of 131–143
cartels, in *SOA*: 30, 101; Galindo 108; Putlova 136; True/Real IRA 37
Catholicism 79, 80
Charming, CA 24, 25, 27–29, 31, 32–33, 35, 42, 43–47, 51, 56, 60, 102, 107, 124, 157
Cherry (character) 15
Chibs Telford (character) 29, 32, 33, 45, 61, 99
Chucky (character) 132
cisgender 6, 149, 154, 155, 158, 159–160, 161, 163–166
Clay Morrow (character) 10, 14–15, 17, 31 36, 39, 42, 43, 47, 51, 52, 54–61, 65–68, 70–73, 74–75, 88–89, 94, 99–101, 102, 104, 108–110, 112, 114, 123, 126, 129, 136, 140, 141, 148, 155
"Coal War," Joshua James 101–102
Coates, Kim 6, 158
code: club 35, 37, 71, 122, 124; culture 41, 74; gender 3–6, 28, 33, 70, 119, 120, 125; institutional 27; moral 80, 85, 88, 90, 121
commitment: to club 69, 72, 84, 87; to identity 44; to religion 78, 80–82, 84–86, 88

169

# Index

competition, in men 13–15, 17, 18, 22, 26, 78, 110
confession 45, 80, 83, 98, 99, 125
conflict 12–14, 17–22, 24, 28–29, 30, 51, 58, 59, 61, 68, 70, 73, 74, 79, 81, 83, 84–86, 89, 111, 114–116, 121, 124, 127, 147
control: of club 39, 111; and power 24, 27, 28; of self 3, 11, 13, 73, 78, 8–81, 133, 137, 152, 156; of women 43, 48, 86, 90
Coones, Rusty 2
counterculture 157
courage 5, 13, 109
cowboy(s) 53, 61, 71, 121
criminal 31, 37, 42, 44, 67–69, 77, 90, 101, 104, 107, 108, 113–116, 121–122, 125, 126, 128, 145, 149, 157
"Crucifixed" (episode) 77, 83, 138
Crusades 87
cut(s) (*also* kuttes) 1, 2, 4, 7, 24, 28, 29, 30, 35, 36, 53, 68, 75, 84, 91, 107, 119, 129, 132, 155

Damon Pope (character) 14, 31, 53, 72–73
damsel 3, 6
danger 4, 5, 35, 46, 52, 59, 67, 68, 71, 72, 74, 103, 124, 135, 152, 154
Darby (character) 30
daughter(s) 14, 19, 21, 44, 45, 51, 67, 70, 90, 99, 109, 122, 128, 151, 155
Dawn Trager (character) 14
deviance, sexual 6, 16, 18, 147, 150
Devil's Tribe 17
Diosa 17, 18, 58, 60, 107, 109, 110, 111, 112, 114, 115, 122, 150, 155, 156
discipline 24, 132–133
doctor(s) 24, 26, 27, 29, 36, 127; Tara as 18, 25, 34, 35, 77, 127
domesticity 46, 53, 59, 60, 61, 70, 71, 120, 121
dominance 11, 13–15, 19, 22, 27, 62, 100, 107, 111, 112
dominatrix 149, 160
Donna Winston (character) 31, 36, 37, 67, 68–69, 70–71, 73, 75, 88, 90, 100, 121
drag 149, 155, 160
drugs: addiction 52, 78, 110; charges 114, 133; trafficking 42, 30, 50, 53, 79, 101, 102, 108, 113, 114; use 45, 112, 125, 127 use of alcohol 125; use of methamphetamine 52, 78; use of mushrooms/psychedelics 148, 149, 155
drunkenness 148–149, 161, 162

*Easy Rider* 95, 157
Eli Roosevelt (character) 29, 30, 102
emasculation 60, 159, 165
enemies 27, 31, 47, 51, 55, 68, 70, 87
Ethan Zobelle (character) 30, 37, 53, 99
"Eureka" (episode) 70

Facebook 78
"Fa Guan" (episode) 29

"Faith and Despondency" (episode) 153, 158, 164, 165
"Falx Cerebri" (episode) 70, 74
family 3, 4, 5, 9, 10, 21, 22, 29, 36, 44, 47, 46, 59, 60, 61, 67–74, 75, 102, 109, 119–128, 132, 135, 138, 141, 149, 150–152, 158, 161, 162
"Los Fantasmas" (episode) 114
father(s) 5, 10, 12, 30, 33, 44, 48, 50–62, 66–73, 74, 83, 102, 107–117, 119–129, 150, 151, 159, 161, 163
F.B.I. 37
feminism 29, 31, 34, 35, 51, 58, 60, 141
The First Nine 51
"Fix" (episode) 71, 72
"Fly Low Carrion Crow," Two Gallants 102
The Forest Rangers 97, 103, 104
forgiveness 52, 54, 73, 126–128, 135
"Fortunate Son," Creedence Clearwater Revival 123
Foucault, Michel 24, 58, 132, 133
Frankie Diamonds (character) 2
fraternity 157
freedom 24, 28, 48, 68, 69, 85, 93, 94, 102, 104, 120, 121, 128, 131, 134, 138, 143, 163
Freud, Sigmund 51
friendship 10, 11, 75, 101
"Fruit for the Crows" (episode) 80
"Fun Town" (episode) 27
fundamentalism 77–92
FX Network 1, 24, 25, 61, 77, 78, 143, 145, 146, 154, 155, 157

gangs *see* Byz Lats, Mayans, One-Niners
Gemma Teller Morrow (character) 14, 16, 29, 34, 36, 37, 40, 41, 43, 54, 55, 58, 66, 70, 74, 75, 78, 87–88, 98–101, 102, 107–111, 113–117, 120, 122, 124–129, 148–149, 150, 155, 159, 160, 162, 163
gender reassignment surgery 160, 165
ghost(s) 51–53, 61, 66, 74
"Gilead" (episode) 71, 155
"Giving Back" (episode) 36, 68, 69, 72, 132
*Glee* 157
God 79, 80, 82, 87, 164, 164
goddess 58, 155, 158
Goggins, Walton 6, 149, 158, 159
Goldman, Emma 82–84
*The Graduate* 95
grandchildren 74, 109, 124
Great Recession 3
"Greensleeves" (episode) 117
The Grim Bastards 42, 45, 107
grotesque, concept of 139–141
guilt 12, 16, 72, 79, 80, 102, 110, 148
gun(s): running 29, 40, 52, 54–56, 87, 93, 99, 101, 115, 122, 147; as symbol 107, 130, 162; violence 19, 62, 116, 119, 120, 121, 125, 151

# Index

Half-Sack (character) 36, 100, 148
*Hamlet*, as influence 1, 6, 42, 50, 53, 65–76, 154
"Hands" (episode) 35, 71, 108
Happy Lowman (character) 2, 61, 123
Harley-Davidson motorcycle(s) 58, 60, 65, 68, 130
heart disease, surgery 108, 110, 117
Hector Salazar (character) 31
"Hell Followed" (episode) 69
Hells Angels 1, 2, 5
Henry Lin (character) 31, 110
hero(es) 30, 46, 49, 52, 53, 59–61, 65, 66, 88, 121, 161, 162; tragic 65–76, 83, 84
heteronormativity 2, 165
*High Noon* 119, 121
Hispanic/Latinx characters 6, 20, 33, 39, 41, 42, 44, 47, 48, 93, 109, 116, 160
home 3, 16, 36, 46, 69, 70, 74, 75, 88, 112, 119, 127, 156
homophobia 26, 36, 157, 162, 166
homosociality 9–23
hostility 27, 86, 91
Hunnam, Charlie 145, 157
Hurst, Ryan 6
hypermasculinity 1–7, 25, 26, 29, 34, 60, 61, 66, 67, 71, 79, 80, 107, 112, 116, 119, 134, 140, 146, 150, 151–155

identity 2, 5, 6, 16, 26–33, 35, 36, 40–44, 50–63, 68, 74, 85, 91, 102, 116, 120, 127, 130–144, 146, 151–154, 159, 161, 162, 164, 165
Ima Tite (character) 18, 20–21
impotence 159
incarceration *see* prison
ink 2, 6, 132, 134, 136; *see also* tattoo(s)
innocent(s) 67, 72, 89, 115, 123, 128, 138, 158
insanity *see* madness
institutional workers in *SOA*: healthcare 27, 29; law enforcement 12, 25–28, 32, 35, 36

Jackson "Jax" Teller (character) 10, 14, 15, 16, 18, 25, 30, 34, 35, 36, 37, 39, 44–47, 48, 50–62, 66–67, 68, 70–75, 77, 81–82, 83, 87, 96, 99–102, 104, 107, 107–117, 120, 122–129, 135, 136, 145, 146, 151, 152, 155, 156, 157, 158, 160–163
Jacob Hale Jr. (character) 56, 99
"J'ai Obtenu Cette" (episode) 113, 115, 138, 139
jail *see* prison
Jazzmun 155
John "J.T." Teller (character) 10, 34, 51, 52–54, 66, 74, 82, 83, 85, 109, 123, 154
journal: Jax's 113, 115, 116; J.T.'s 66, 102
Juan Carlos "Juice" Ortiz (character) 15–16, 30–33, 36, 37, 40, 44–47, 61, 79–80, 83, 102, 114

June Stahl (character) 29, 31, 34, 43, 53, 70, 71, 73, 102, 133–135, 142
just war, concept of 87, 88

Kellan Ashby (character) 79
Kichigin, Grigoriy 159
Kristeva, Julia 136–137, 139
kutte *see* cut
Kyle Hobart (character) 68, 69, 72

Labrava, David 2, 76
Laroy (character) 44
"Laying Pipe" (episode) 72
League of American Nationalists (L.O.A.N.) 14, 30, 37, 53, 55
legitimacy 27, 28, 140
Lenny the Pimp (character) 2
letters, J.T.'s 54, 102
liberty, concept of 82
Lincoln Potter (character) 30, 102, 137, 138
loyalty 2, 6, 12, 47, 69–70, 72, 74, 79, 89, 101, 111, 131, 132, 134, 135, 137, 148
Luann Delaney (character) 77, 132–135, 137–138
Lucius Padilla (character) 60, 61, 65, 110, 115, 117, 119, 123–127
Luhrman, Baz 74, 95
Lyla Winston (character) 41, 71–72, 75, 88, 111

machismo 33, 97, 107, 110, 116, 120, 124–126, 129, 158, 162
Mack, Christy 21
madness 67, 70–72, 75
Madonna/whore 18
manliness 72, 130
Marcus Alvarez (character) 31, 44–47, 101, 116, 123, 125
marriage 56, 61, 62, 67, 79, 71, 121
"Mary," Patty Griffin 98–100
masculinity: hegemonic 24–38; non-white 31, 39–49; 119–129; toxic 5, 25, 26, 35–36, 37, 67–69, 145–147, 150, 152–156, 157–159, 165; white 31–33, 37, 39–49, 56–57, 62, 104, 119–124, 146, 151, 154, 155, 158, 159, 166
The Mayans MC 33, 34, 37, 44, 46, 47, 55, 87, 101, 107, 108, 116, 123, 124
medieval era 68, 69, 74, 79, 86, 87, 89, 91
mercy, concept of 46, 71, 87, 109
*Mi Familia* 125
military 4, 9, 11, 17, 22, 55, 73, 132–133
misrepresentation 123–124
*La Mission* 125
monasticism 77–92
montage, use of 34, 75, 94, 96–100, 102–104, 116
mother(s) 11, 14, 16, 18, 34, 41, 44, 49, 61, 67, 69, 73, 74, 77, 78, 99, 100–101, 109, 110, 112, 113, 114, 120, 125–126, 127, 148, 150, 157, 159–161, 163, 165
"A Mother's Work" (episode) 44, 114

murder 12, 14, 15, 16, 19, 21, 30, 58, 67, 70, 71, 72, 73, 78, 79, 96, 98, 99, 100, 107, 114, 122, 124, 128, 131, 137, 148, 155
music, in *SOA* 93–106

"Na Tiobloidi" (episode) 135
Nero Padilla (character) 6, 51, 57–60, 61, 74, 107–118, 119–129, 150, 155, 156, 160
Nomad 1, 2, 53, 99
"NS" (episode) 71, 136

Oakland, CA 1, 2, 46
objectification, of women 9, 11, 15–18, 21–22, 87, 159; Crow Eaters 15, 155
"Old Bones" (episode) 36, 148
old lady/ies 33, 34, 51, 54, 57, 77, 94, 99, 112, 138, 148, 155
One-Niners 30, 33, 44, 46, 87, 107
"One One Six" (episode) 116
Opie Winston (character) 6, 10, 14, 31, 34, 36, 37, 41, 61, 65–76, 100, 121, 155
*Orange Is the New Black* 157, 166
"Orca Shrugged" (episode) 112, 113, 149 151, 160, 165
The Other, as a concept 29–33, 53
Otto Delaney (character) 6, 73, 77, 83, 88, 90, 130–144, 154
"Out" (episode) 136, 137
outlaw 1–4, 13–14, 25, 27, 30, 37, 44, 45, 50, 53, 54, 56, 61, 67, 68, 104, 121, 124, 126, 130, 132, 133, 134, 145–147, 154, 155, 157, 158, 159, 161, 163

parenthood 71, 124–125, 126–127
patch 2, 4, 5, 6, 53, 78, 79, 81, 84, 85, 87, 90, 99, 100, 132, 133, 154, 155
patriarchy 4, 5, 43, 48, 69, 70, 74, 81, 90, 94, 104, 121, 122, 141, 159, 161, 163, 166
Patterson (character) 29, 62
pediophobia (fear of dolls) 148–149
Perlman, Ron 54
phallus 55, 139, 140, 161, 165
"Pilot" (episode) 35, 51, 52, 69, 74, 93
Piney Winston (character) 34, 46, 67, 68, 69, 74, 75, 99
"Playing with Monsters" (episode) 115, 117
"Poor Little Lambs" (episode) 12, 113, 153
pornography: adult 43, 47, 87, 111, 155; child 151, 161, 163
"Potlatch" (episode) 68, 71
power: club 14, 21, 33, 59, 132–133; gendered 4, 16, 17, 29, 34, 40, 42, 51, 55, 57, 72, 81, 88, 101, 104, 108, 111, 112, 139–143, 145, 149, 158, 159, 162; higher 83, 87, 90–91; societal 3, 24, 26–28, 56, 66, 68, 120, 156
prayer 77, 80, 112
pregnancy 18, 52, 110, 125–126, 127
prison 6, 14, 24, 30, 31, 6, 58, 60, 68–72, 77, 88, 101–102, 110, 113, 114–115, 126–127, 130–144, 154

profane 78, 88
prophet 61, 82, 87
protection 2–5, 14, 22, 25, 32, 34, 35, 56, 60, 70, 73, 83, 109, 111, 112, 114, 115, 121, 132–135, 137, 138, 141, 151, 156, 163
"The Push" (episode) 155

queerness 146–149

race 5, 25, 30, 33, 39–49, 59, 102, 128
racism 20, 26, 27, 29–33, 36, 37, 41, 42–43, 44–47, 48, 102, 152, 155
rage 55, 87, 114, 142, 159, 162, 165
rape 14, 19, 21, 46, 99–100, 139–141, 161
Rane Quinn (character) 2
rebel 4, 54, 143, 145
"Red Rose" (episode) 113
redemption 6, 97, 145–156
Redwood charter 2, 24, 51, 66, 77 85, 90, 130, 138
religion 6, 77–92
representation 3, 6, 32, 54, 108, 119–129, 157–166
retaliation 12–15, 122, 130,134–135
retribution 123, 135, 137, 138
RICO 77, 134–135
*The Rifleman* 120–121
rite(s) 77–92, 131
ritual(s) 75, 78, 89–90
romantic relationships in *SOA* 11, 17, 20, 22, 56, 75, 113, 146, 153–155, 158, 160, 163
Romeo Parada (character) 31
Rule of Saint Benedict 84–90

sacred 32, 78, 81, 83, 88, 89, 91, 166
Sagal, Katey 102–104, 150, 159
Saint Bernard of Clairvaux 79, 87–89
"Salvage" (episode) 112, 150
SAMDINO 83
scapegoat 78, 87–90
*Scarface* 108
score, musical 6, 62, 93–105
*The Searchers* 119
"Seeds" (episode) 36, 69
September 11th 3
"Service" (episode) 31, 70, 71, 149
sex, sexual act 3, 9–23, 54, 58, 67–71, 78, 89, 91, 104, 108, 125, 126, 148
sex work(ers) 9–23, 87, 156, 160, 162–163, 165
sexual abuse, assault 14, 112, 151, 161, 165
Shakespeare, William 5, 42, 65–76
shame 86, 149, 159
*Shane* 120–121
sheriff 30, 35, 102
Siff, Maggie 40
"The Sleep of Babies" (episode) 70, 75
"Small Tears" (episode) 135
"Small World" (episode) 112
Smits, Jimmy 6, 57, 107, 108, 119, 123, 150, 160

"SO" (episode) 20
"Some Strange Eruption" (episode) 75
son(s) (family relationship) 19, 34, 41, 44–45, 51, 52, 60–61, 66, 68, 75, 99, 100, 107, 109–111, 113, 119–128, 150, 157, 159, 161–163, 165
*The Sopranos* 40, 44, 96
soundtrack, of *Sons of Anarchy* 93–105
"Sovereign" (episode) 113, 114, 155
spina bifida 60, 110, 125
stepchildren 52, 74, 116, 123, 160
stepparent(s) 41, 51, 53, 56, 66, 88
stereotype(s) 20, 43, 108, 113, 123–125, 140 158, 159, 161
"Stolen Huffy" (episode) 75, 111, 112
"Strange Fruit," Billie Holiday 102
"Straw" (episode) 114, 115, 127, 155
submission 67, 81
subservience 80
suicide 12–13, 30, 31, 32, 67, 72–73, 80, 83
Sutter, Kurt 1, 5, 6, 24, 50, 65, 77, 91, 96, 107, 138, 142–143, 145, 146, 148, 150, 157
"Sweet and Vaded" (episode) 110, 111, 150, 153, 160, 161, 162, 163
sweet butts 15
symbolism 4, 13, 28, 42, 72, 75, 78–79, 82–84, 90–92, 102

Tara Knowles Teller (character) 16–18, 25, 27, 33–35, 37, 40–41, 46, 48, 53, 55–57, 61, 67, 68, 73, 75, 77, 78, 87, 88, 90, 99, 102, 109, 111, 112, 114, 127, 128, 138, 155
tattoo(s) 4, 67, 108, 114, 123, 132, 142; *see also* ink
Thiele, Bob 97, 103
Thomas Teller (character, Jax's son) 61, 107, 109, 114, 117, 120, 123, 124, 127, 128
Tig Trager (character) 6, 14–18, 29, 31, 36, 61, 62, 73, 90, 100, 112, 145–156, 157–166
"To Thine Own Self" (episode) 115, 139
"Toad's Wild Ride" (episode) 110

"Toil and Till" (episode) 114, 116
torture 14, 47, 139–140
toxic masculinity *see* masculinity
tradition 3, 32–33, 78–80, 82
transgender 6, 112, 145–156, 157–166
transitioning (gender) 158, 161–162
transphobia 150, 160, 162, 163
transwoman 158, 159, 165
trope(s) 18–19, 30, 41, 74, 121, 125

*Ugly Betty* 157
uniforms 24, 28, 30, 35, 36, 55

Venus Van Dam (character) 6, 62, 112, 145–156, 157–166
Veronica Pope (character) 14
Vietnam War 55–56
violence, in *SOA* 1, 4–5, 9–23, 24–26, 42–43, 44, 46, 48–49, 52–54, 62, 66–68, 72–74, 78–92, 94, 97–99, 104, 107, 108, 113–117, 119–122, 127, 130–144, 145–154, 157–165

War Machine 21
Wayne, John 119
Wayne Unser (character) 36, 56, 99
Wendy (character) 16–18, 60, 61, 74, 75, 78, 90, 110, 116, 125, 127
*West Side Story* 74, 108
Westerns 6, 32–33, 62, 119–129
white supremacists 30–33, 55, 99, 152
whiteness: and masculinity 2, 56–57, 62, 104, 146, 151, 154–155, 157, 158–159, 166; and privilege 37, 39–49, 83, 93, 119–124
*The Wild One* 157
"With an X" (episode) 32
"Wolfsangel" (episode) 110, 142

"You Are My Sunshine" (episode) 114

Zito, Chuck 2

www.ingramcontent.com/pod-product-compliance
Lightning Source LLC
Chambersburg PA
CBHW032104300426
44116CB00007B/882